HIDE AND SEEK

HIDE AND SEEK

The Story of a Wartime Agent

Xan Fielding

Foreword by Robert Messenger

PAUL DRY BOOKS
Philadelphia 2013

First Paul Dry Books Edition, 2013

Paul Dry Books, Inc.
Philadelphia, Pennsylvania
www.pauldrybooks.com

Frontispiece: Xan Fielding in Cretan dress. Photograph by Daphne Bath.

Printed in the United States of America

Library of Congress Cataloging-in-Publication Data
Fielding, Xan.
  Hide and seek : the story of a wartime agent / Xan Fielding ;
foreword by Robert Messenger. — First Paul Dry Books edition.
    pages cm
  Originally published: London, Secker & Warburg, 1954.
  ISBN 978-1-58988-084-9 (alk. paper)
  1. World War, 1939–1945—Underground movements—Greece—Crete.
2. Fielding, Xan. 3. Intelligence service—Great Britain—History—20th
century. 4. Great Britain. Special Operations Executive. I. Title.
  D802.G82C7426 2013
  940.53'4959—dc23
                                                    2013003228

Contents

Illustrations

Xan Fielding: A Brief Life
(1918–1991)

by Robert Messenger

Xan Fielding was ever the supporting player. His first wife, Daphne, was a famous Bright Young Thing and even more famously married to the Marquess of Bath. His second wife, Magouche, was the painter Arshile Gorky's widow.

A member of the British Special Operations Executive during World War II, Fielding was the main on-the-ground organizer of the resistance movement on Crete, but it was his great friend Patrick Leigh Fermor who got the popular acclaim thanks to his kidnapping a German general and spiriting him away to Cairo in 1944. Fielding had been Fermor's first choice as a partner in the mission, but it was felt that his small stature and swarthy looks made him a poor candidate to impersonate a German officer. The job went to W. Stanley ("Billy") Moss, who wrote a best-selling book in 1950 about the exploit, *Ill Met by Moonlight*.

If Fielding is remembered today, it is likely because of Fermor's renowned accounts of walking across Europe in the 1930s, *A Time of Gifts* (1977) and *Between the Woods and the Water* (1986). These evocations of a vanished world begin with a letter to "Dear Xan." And with good reason. Fielding had walked the same roads, with the same picaresque urgings. "Like him, I had tramped across Europe to reach Greece," Fielding wrote in his wartime memoirs. "Like him, I had been almost penniless during that long arduous holiday—but there the similarity between our travels ended, for whereas I was often forced to sleep out of doors, in ditches, haystacks or on public benches, Paddy's charm and resourcefulness had made him a welcome guest wherever he went."

After Crete, Fielding served in occupied France. When he was arrested at a German checkpoint in southern France in August 1944, he was reprieved from death by the bold action of another SOE agent, Christine Granville. On the Italian border organizing the defection of a Polish unit pressed into Wehrmacht service, she heard that Fielding and two companions had been captured in Digne and were likely to be tortured and shot. She drove straight to the town and confronted the French policeman who had made the arrest. Identifying herself as a British agent (and so forfeiting her life if the gambit failed), Granville pointed out that the Allies had just landed on the Riviera, that the town would soon be liberated, and that he would surely die in reprisals for causing the deaths of three important agents. (She also claimed to be the niece of British General Bernard Montgomery for good measure.)

The Frenchman helped her bribe the guards, and when Fielding was taken out of his cell expecting to face a firing squad, he was instead led to a car where Granville sat behind the wheel. Yet even so extraordinary an adventure was merely one more accident of Fielding's life. Granville had acted to save another of the prisoners, Francis Cammaerts (codename "Roger"), one of the most important resistance organizers. "Had Roger not been arrested with us," Fielding wrote, "Christine would have been perfectly justified in taking no action if action meant jeopardizing herself. Indirectly, then, I owe my life to him as much as I do, directly, to her."

In the late 1960s, Fielding even learned that his "mother" was actually his grandmother. His real mother had died in childbirth. The newborn was adopted into the older generation, and his father, Major Alexander Wallace of the 52nd Sikh Frontier Force, was simply never mentioned again. His brothers and sisters turned out to be aunts and uncles. According to Fermor, he related this tale with "considerable humor and bewilderment."

Alexander Percival Feilman Wallace was born in 1918 in India—at Ootacamund, one of the summer capitals of the Raj, where the British hid from the relentless Indian heat. He was adopted by his grandparents and raised at the Chateau Fielding in Nice. He followed an education at Charterhouse with a peripatetic career at the universities in Bonn, Munich, and Freiburg in the late 1930s. These years added to his set of European languages and gave him a clear sense of the evil of Nazism. (He was so appalled by Chamberlain's appeasement policies that he contemplated becoming a communist and tried to enlist on the Republican side in Spain.) Fielding thought about a career as a painter, but was restless more than determined and set out across Europe on foot.

September 1939 found him in Cyprus. He'd been sacked from the local English newspaper and was running a bar. He said it took him "almost a year to decide what attitude to adopt towards the war." He wasn't "afraid of fighting," but he was "appalled by the prospect of the army." The news in the summer of 1940 that Greek-speaking Englishmen were wanted to help raise a Cypriot regiment finally brought him to volunteer, and three months shy of his twenty-second birthday he was commissioned a lieutenant.

Far from the fearful martinets he expected, the officers of the 1st Cyprus Battalion proved to be misfits. Life revolved around the commanding officer's desire to organize a regimental sports day to encourage his unenthusiastic soldiers. "The Cypriots have never had a military tradition, and it soon became clear that they were not going to break a habit formed before the first century by taking kindly to soldiering in the twentieth." Fielding found these among the most carefree months of his life: "The incidence of venereal disease among the men rose to a height which was only surpassed by the officers' drunkenness."

The fall of Crete in May 1941 changed everything. Cyprus was thought the next German target, and a defense had to be organized. Fielding was drawn into the creation of a fake "Seventh Division" whose presence on the island might deter the Germans. Numerous regimental headquarters were made to communicate with one another in ways that German agents in Turkey were expected to notice. "Since all these phantom units were represented only by myself, I spent most of every day travelling between them on a motor-bicycle in order to put in an appearance at each."

It was Fielding's first taste of intelligence work, and it appealed—both for its excitement and the relief from regimental chores. When the threat to Cyprus passed in the wake of the German invasion of Russia, he was offered a chance at real clandestine work on Crete. In December 1942, he reported to the Cairo headquarters of the SOE. The first question his new boss, Jack Smith-Hughes, asked was "Have you any personal objection to committing murder?"

Sent to Crete in January 1942, Fielding's first task was to make contact with the two British officers Smith-Hughes had left there with a wireless set, and then begin organizing the evacuation of the British and Commonwealth soldiers still on the island. He also started building an intelligence network. By the time Crete became the staging ground for the German Afrika Corps offensives in the spring of 1942, Fielding's network was providing almost daily reports back to Cairo of troop movements. The Germans certainly felt the weight of these activities—their new airfield at Tymbaki was bombed by the R.A.F. on "the very day the runways were completed." German troops poured into the hills searching for the agents, and Fielding played a tense cat-and-mouse game. In August, Fielding was taken off Crete and had a month's leave in Syria and two weeks of parachute training. Returning to the island at the end of November, he spent fourteen grueling months organizing the resistance to aid the hoped-for Allied landings to liberate Greece.

Back in Cairo in January 1944, he was discouraged by what he learned. He realized that "the Second Front would be opened in Western Europe. Crete was therefore doomed to remain in enemy hands until the end of the war, when the Germans stationed there would simply lay down their arms." With an increasing distaste for the internal politics of the Greek struggle—the communists and nationalists were already beginning their civil war—and feeling that his efforts in Crete had all been in vain, Fielding asked for transfer to SOE France, where he hoped his native knowledge might be an asset. "Since I had been brought up in the South of France and knew the language and the country from childhood, I had little hope of being accepted," he wrote, reflecting on the surreal habits of army bureaucracy. "To my surprise, however, I was."

There followed his misadventure in Digne and rescue by Christine Granville. In 1945, he spent two more months in Greece (seeing the liberation of Athens and revisiting Crete), all the while growing disenchanted with the postwar settling of scores and the failure of resistance heroes to be rewarded as opportunists gained power. (The new local leader appointed in Vaphes, where Fielding had long been headquartered on Crete, was a man so afraid of the Germans that he had threatened to inform them of Fielding's presence in the village.) Like many SOE veterans, Fielding then transferred east where the war against Japan continued, and he saw brief service in Indochina. Short stints in occupied Germany and as an observer at the postwar elections in Greece and the Balkans brought his military career to an end. He held the rank of major.

Demobbed, Fielding fit no better into metropolitan life than he had in the 1930s. A last attempt at university failed—at Oxford, where he chafed at English strictures. A job on the Express newspapers was even less congenial. These were years of wild parties in London. Fielding and Fermor shared an apartment above the Heywood Hill bookstore and could be found nightly drunk with the likes of Dylan Thomas and Stephen Spender, the painters Ben Nicholson and Lucien Freud, and the philosopher Freddie Ayer. Barbara Skelton, soon to marry Cyril Connolly, noted in her diary in 1950, "Xan dislikes any form of work more than most. What a pity he can't be kept by the state for doin' nothin'." He had appeared on her doorstep that morning to borrow a typewriter, as he had a job helping with an Egyptian's memoirs.

Fielding placed an ad in the *London Times* of July 31, 1950: "Tough but sensitive ex-classical scholar, ex-secret agent, ex-guerrilla leader, 31, recently reduced to penury through incompatibility with the post-war world: Mediterranean lover, gambler, and general dabbler: fluent French and Greek speaker, some German, inevitable Italian: would do anything unreasonable and unexpected if sufficiently rewarding and legitimate."

In 1951–52, he returned to Crete to revisit places he had known only furtively, and his wanderings resulted in a pioneering travel book, *The Stronghold: Four Seasons in the White Mountains of Crete* (1953). It's a documentary-like record of days among Cretan peasants blended with history and literature.

The book's photographs were taken by his future wife Daphne, who joined him for some weeks of his travels. In her memoirs, she remembered lengthy climbs up to remote villages and the shrugging replies she got to her queries about where they might be spending the night. "With my godbrother" was Fielding's standard reply. And everywhere they went, they received a warm welcome punctuated by endless rounds of drinks and the death sentence of a chicken or two. "For during the war, when he organized the resistance movement in this area, he . . . stood as godfather to countless baptisms—a position which in the Orthodox Church bound him and the parents of the child he christened closely together in a sacred and eternal union."

Fielding was particularly proud of the baby girl he and Fermor had jointly christened Anglia Eleutheria Nike—"England Freedom

Victory" in Greek. "For the rest of the occupation Stathis had shouted for his daughter as loudly as he could whenever any German was within ear-shot." *Hide and Seek* (1954) is his vibrant account of his SOE service and a classic of World War II literature.

The Fieldings married on July 11, 1953. They first lived in Cornwall before a long sojourn in Tangier. *Corsair Country* (1958) recounts a journey from Tangier to Tripoli in search of traces of the Barbary Pirates—"a year driving slowly," Fielding called it. It's another blend of history and encounters with a local culture, this time focused on the "unchanging and perhaps unchangeable qualities of North Africa." Fielding found immense interest in the meeting of Islam, colonialism, and modernity. The strict Islam of Djerba was welcome, for instance, for discouraging the riff-raff who attached themselves to all tourists. At the trip's end, Fielding admitted— "at the risk of appearing a chauvinistic Pharisee"—that "after these months spent in the shadow of Islam I've never before been so conscious and proud of my European and Christian background."

There followed six years in Portugal before the Fieldings finally settled in Uzès, in southern France, when they thought they would finally receive the proceeds of a protracted lawsuit. The Fielding family property in Nice had been misappropriated when the Corniche road was expanded, but the suit dragged on endlessly. The couple had to mortgage their house and work to keep afloat. He became a prolific translator of popular novels from the French, most famously Pierre Boulle's *Planet of the Apes* and *The Bridge on the River Kwai* and Jean Larteguy's *The Centurions* and *The Praetorians*; Daphne wrote her memoirs and a novel (the roman-à-clef-like *The Adonis Garden* featuring a very Xan-like hero and a particularly barbed portrait of Cyril Connolly). He also worked during this time on his history of the casino in Monte Carlo, *The Money Spinner* (1977)—a subject the inveterate gambler in Fielding greatly enjoyed.

In 1978, he and Daphne divorced, and he married Magouche the following year. They lived in Andalusia, and his last decade was spent on a biography of his wartime comrade Billy Maclean—whose SOE career in the Mideast and Albania was out of a John Buchan novel—an edition of the letters of Gerald Brenan and Ralph Partridge (two more friends and Bloomsbury stalwarts both), and a personal study of the winds in myth, *Aeolus Displayed*. (It appeared in German in 1988 and was privately printed in English in 1991.)

Fielding was stricken with cancer in 1991, but he was able to travel to Crete in May for the celebrations of the fiftieth anniversary of the battle. He spent ten days visiting wartime comrades and, with six other Allied officers, was awarded the Greek commemorative medal of the resistance. He died three months later on August 19. "Xan Fielding," Fermor wrote in a memorial, "was a gifted, many-sided, courageous and romantic figure, at the same time civilized and Bohemian, and his thoughtful cast of mind was leavened by humour, spontaneous gaiety and a dash of recklessness. Almost any stretch of his life might be described as a picaresque interlude." Magouche and Fermor carried his ashes to Crete.

The biographer Roger Jinkinson describes meeting Magouche in 2008: "I asked if anyone was writing her biography and she put me carefully in my place: 'No, I appear in other peoples'.'" The statement would be equally true of her husband, who has brilliant cameos in books about figures as diverse as Lawrence Durrell, Dirk Bogarde, and Bruce Chatwin.

Fielding met Bogarde in 1957 during the filming of the movie of *Ill Met by Moonlight.* The actor was cast as Fermor in the depiction of the wartime kidnapping of General Heinrich Kreipe in Crete, and Fielding had been hired as the technical adviser. Expecting a stern military hero, Bogarde at first avoided any meeting, but they became fast friends. Filming done, Bogarde and his partner and the Fieldings drove north for Paris together. They stopped for the night in Digne at a favorite hotel of Bogarde's. It was only at dinner that Fielding mentioned that the building next door to the hotel was the one where he had been held awaiting execution during the war. Bogarde was shocked and apologetic, but Fielding dismissed the concern: "I don't mind a bit. In fact I'm glad to be back here in such different circumstances. After all this time. Twelve years . . . Good heavens, it's twelve years exactly, to the very day!"

"This calls for a bottle of champagne," said Bogarde.

Foreword

by Robert Messenger

ON MAY 20, 1941, German paratroopers dropped from the sky over Crete. The ten-day battle for the isthmus-like island, the southernmost part of Greece, was a catastrophe for defender and attacker alike. It was the first airborne assault in military history, and the elite German soldiers were slaughtered in large numbers by the British and Commonwealth troops as they landed and attempted to form into viable fighting units.

Cryptographers had given the Allies advance warning of almost every aspect of the invasion, and they were prepared. The first landings, which targeted the airfields at Maleme, Herakleion, and Retimo, on the north coast of the 160-mile-long island, were contained. But mistakes and miscommunications on the second day allowed the Germans to find a foothold at Maleme, and they poured in reinforcements by plane. They gained air superiority, pounding the defenders and towns, and brought in artillery and heavier units to push in from the coast. On May 26, the Allied commander ordered a general retreat to Sphakia on the southern coast. The Battle of Crete was lost, and tens of thousands of soldiers began a confused trek over the island's spine of mountains.

The Royal Navy made heroic attempts to rescue these men over four nights (action during the day being impossible due to the German bombers). Some 16,000 British, Commonwealth, and Greek soldiers were taken off, at the cost of three cruisers and six destroyers sunk and serious damage to four other major ships of the Mediterranean fleet. On June 1, evacuation operations were halted with almost 12,000 troops still on the island.

Crete was in German hands and became the staging ground for the campaign in North Africa. The island, though, had a millennia-old history of resistance to outside powers. Cretan partisans who had aided the British during the battle took naturally to opposing the Nazi occupation. A story is told of one of the local leaders, Satanas, appearing at the British headquarters in Herakleion on the night of May 28 and declaring to the 14th Infantry Brigade's commander, "My son, we know you are going away tonight. Never mind! You will come back when the right time comes. But leave us as many of your guns as you can, to carry on the fight till then."

The initial phase of the occupation was one of reprisals against civilians, who the Germans thought had murdered wounded soldiers against the rules of war—more than 1,000 Cretans were executed over the course of the summer of 1941. This only hardened the determination to resist. One of the earliest forms was by aiding the Allied troops who were still on the island and desperately hoping to remain at large until a way could be found across the sea to Egypt. They were hidden and fed by villagers in the mountains, and in July, the Royal Navy sent Commander Francis Pool to try to organize an evacuation. He had planned on one quick trip, but discovered thousands of soldiers because of the generosity and courage of the Cretans.

One of those Pool evacuated was Jack Smith-Hughes, an officer in the Royal Service Corps who had made the long march to Sphakia only to be left on the beach. Captured, he had been forced to make an even more unpleasant journey back over the mountains as a prisoner of war. Held in Aghia, in the broad valley between Canea and the White Mountains, he escaped into the hills where he was sheltered at Vourvoure by an ex-Greek army colonel named Petrakas Papadakis. His nephew then took Smith-Hughes to the monastery of Preveli, where hundreds of soldiers were hiding until transit could be arranged. Back in Cairo, Smith-Hughes reported on what he had seen and found himself transferred to the Special Operations Executive.

The SOE had been founded after the fall of France in 1940 to aid the resistance movements of conquered Europe and to perform acts of sabotage and propaganda. Smith-Hughes was sent back to Crete to "feel out the country to see who had influence." He was accompanied by Ralph Stockbridge, a member of the Inter-Services Liaison Department (the cover name for the foreign intelligence service, what we now call MI6, in the Mideast during the war). The ISLD and SOE were often rivals, but they worked hand-in-hand in Crete. Smith-Hughes quickly made contact with Papadakis and set up a wireless station to relay coded messages to Cairo. In November, he returned to Egypt to begin organizing the support, supply, and funding of the Cretan resistance—what he would later call keeping the "gaberdine swine" of the regular army at bay.

His immediate job was to find Greek-speaking officers who could pass as Cretans. Xan Fielding was his first recruit and was landed on Crete on January 11, 1942. After a grueling march across the Marmara Plain to the hills, Fielding began establishing a network of agents in the White Mountains and in the Canea region, especially near the airfield at Maleme and the port at Souda Bay. Tom Dunbabin would arrive in April to organize the resistance in the Herakleion region. They traveled constantly to meet and recruit agents and stay ahead of the German pursuit. The epic hardiness of the Cretan shepherds allowed information to be passed quickly by runner—though Fielding particularly enjoyed visiting his networks in the towns and rubbing shoulders with the enemy.

By 1942, Crete had become a giant German transit camp supporting Rommel's offensives in North Africa. As Fielding remembered, "Reports kept pouring in about the daily concentrations of aircraft at Maleme. Transport planes loaded with troops, fresh water and even cooked meals were leaving the airport every few minutes to reinforce the Afrika Korps advancing on Alexandria. I only had to signal their timetable and line of flight for them to be met by an R.A.F. fighter squadron over the sea."

At this stage of the war, with control of Egypt at stake, the SOE agents were focused on the intelligence-gathering tasks of the ISLD. The historian Antony Beevor, author of the standard account of the war in Crete, noted, "In spite of the occasional unmilitary image in intelligence reports, such as 'mines cylindrically the size of a jeroboam of champagne,' the information collected and collated was most impressive in its detail. It covered: telephone systems; the state of every gun position, whether machine-gun nest, flak battery or heavy coastal artillery; satellite airfields; military roads; and the grid reference and defence details of each garrison and guard post with their strengths and armaments. Every aircraft in and out of the main airfields was logged with its direction of departure. Every ship or caique, loading and unloading in the harbours of Heraklion,

Rethymno and Canea, was noted with its cargo. Landing beaches and dropping zones were reconnoitered." All this information was collected by the courageous Cretans and passed up to the hills, where it was coded for transmission to Cairo.

For Fielding and Dunbabin, these were endless days of waiting, cold, and hunger, punctuated by sharp scares when the heavily armed German patrols appeared. Dunbabin once ran into a German officer whom he knew from archaeological digs before the war. His dirty disguise was enough to keep him from being recognized. Fielding picked up work as a laborer (the pay was 700 drachmas a day, less than the price of two eggs) in order to gather information on the new German fortifications. Patrick Leigh Fermor, who was landed on Crete in August, characterized these days in an official report in April 1943, "Merely the struggle for existence is a full-time job. On looking back, my six months seem to have been one long string of battery troubles [with the wireless sets for sending messages back to Cairo], faulty sets, transport difficulties, rain, arrests, hide and seek with the Huns, lack of cash, flights at a moment's notice, false alarms, wicked treks over the mountains, laden like a mule, fright among one's collaborators, treachery, and friends getting shot."

Yet for all the difficulties, what lingered in the officers' memories was the comradeship. In a letter to the Dowager Duchess of Devonshire in 2001, ten years after Fielding's death, Fermor recalled the Christmas of 1942: "If I'm ever asked again [referring to an annual Christmas house party, where they had sung carols], do you think they could manage 'The Holly and the Ivy'? It's such a strange one, and so seldom heard. I'm particularly fond of it because I remember Xan singing it—with all the words, which I don't know, in Crete at Christmas, 1942, in his strong basso profundo voice, while we huddled under the stalactites of a snug cave, roasting cheese on the ends of our Cretan daggers, delicious Cretan rarebits, washed down with tremendously strong wine out of a calabash."

The brotherhood wasn't just with fellow officers, but also with the Cretans whose food and way of life they shared. No figure loomed larger in Fielding's mission than George Psychoundakis, the shepherd who had guided Jack Smith-Hughes from Vourvoure to the Preveli monastery. He served as Fielding's runner, carrying messages and intelligence from officer to wireless operator. Known for his high spirits—nicknamed "Changeling" and "Changebug"—

Psychoundakis was a gifted natural poet and a master of the Cretan *mantinades*, the rhyming couplets improvised to any and every tune. The SOE men learned these songs and taught the Cretans their own. Fermor describes Psychoundakis on the march reciting a two-hour-long poem he had composed covering "the invasion of Poland, the Fall of France, the Albanian triumph and disaster, the German invasion of Greece and Crete and Rommel's final advance." It was June 1942, the nadir of Allied fortunes, yet the poem ended with a triumphant note, "which he emphasized by borrowing my pistol and firing it again and again into the sky with the remark that we would soon be eating the Cuckolds alive."

With the Allied victories at El Alamein and Stalingrad in late 1942, the tide of the war turned. The morale of the German garrison was crushed by these defeats, and they began preparing for an Allied invasion of Crete. The resistance campaign changed, too. The last of the stragglers from the Battle of Crete were finally evacuated on May 7, 1943, ending one part of the original mission. Fielding and Fermor began a propaganda campaign of leaflets and graffiti—insidious articles in German describing the war as lost and Hitler and the Luftwaffe as having abandoned the men on Crete. They were printed on the backs of official German maps or orders to make them seem like the work of disaffected soldiers. Then there were the dirty postcards—complete with a cartoon image of "an obviously Latin lover lying on a bed, stark naked and in a state of advanced eroticism, next to an equally obvious German lady, likewise naked and sexually excited"—explicitly suggesting how the soldiers' wives were being pleasured back home by the gallants of the Italian Labor Corps.

Over the summer, the decision was made at headquarters to step up the arming of the local guerilla bands—some were even supplied with makeshift uniforms including Australian bush hats. This was a part of the massive deception campaign the Allies ran to convince the Germans that the invasion of Sicily in July was simply a feint and the real landings were to occur in Sardinia and Greece. But domestic politics—the battles between the Greek nationalists and communists (with a royalist faction thrown in, too)—also affected such decisions. Fielding, Fermor, and Dunbabin were finding it harder and harder to keep the resistance united and focused. Arming the bands kept them in check and encouraged organized resistance, as expectation of an Allied landing ran high among the population.

The Italian capitulation in September 1943 only complicated matters in Crete. The eastern end of the island, Lasithi, had been held quite peaceably by a division of Italian troops since 1941. The British hoped the Italians might fight their erstwhile allies and were prepared to help with air support and arms—assuming it would lead to a general uprising on the island. But the Italians dithered, and the Germans moved in, imprisoning the Italian units or turning them into work brigades. Fermor, who had been negotiating with the Italian general, spirited him away to safety in Cairo.

The Quebec Conference the month before had settled the planning for the eventual invasion of France, and the eastern Mediterranean was being quickly relegated to a backwater in terms of military and financial support. The chance of an Allied landing in Greece was past, and the British mission's main trouble was now the growing violence between nationalist and communist. In November, Fielding managed to arrange a peace accord at Therisso, which held in great measure through the war's end and even after.

It was one of Fielding's last acts in Crete. Early in the new year, he was taken off the island and transferred to SOE France. His replacement was Dennis Ciclitira, who in May 1944 organized the evacuation of Fermor and his band after they kidnapped Heinrich Kreipe, the German general in charge of the airborne division occupying Crete. This celebrated exploit drove Cretan morale to new heights, but also led to brutal reprisals in the White Mountains, where numerous villages were razed as the Germans sought to restore order on the island. Yet the hills increasingly filled with new recruits for the guerilla bands as news of the Russian advances in eastern Europe and the D-Day invasion reached Crete.

Dunbabin found he had more agents on the island than he knew what to do with—eight SOE officers alone, along with OSS and various other intelligence services. The danger years had passed. On September 8, 1944, SOE Cairo ordered an end to all resistance activities that might bring a reprisal, hoping to spare the Cretan population with the end of the war so clearly in sight. The communist bands no longer obeyed such orders, but the Germans were beginning a steady drawing-in of their forces, and clashes grew less frequent. By mid-October, the occupiers were themselves holed up in Canea. The R.A.F. and Royal Navy were established on Crete and supplying all needs. The Germans—safe behind their walls and unwilling to surrender to Cretans—held out in Canea until spring. A battalion of the Royal Hampshires arrived on May 13, and the Germans surrendered to Brigadier Patrick Preston the next day. Jubilant Cretans freely poured into the city after four years of occupation.

Xan Fielding was not present at the liberation of Canea or war's end in Crete. He had been posted to the Far East. But his actions in encouraging an accord between the communist and nationalist resistance leaders was key to the SOE's legacy in Crete—for the island was spared most of the terrors of the civil war that engulfed Greece in 1946–49. George Psychoundakis wrote his own memoir of the war, *The Cretan Runner* (1955), which Fermor translated into English and Fielding helped annotate. He described the "demonstrations of joy everywhere" in the Spring of 1945, but also the division of the island into two armed camps and the expectation that "the two sides might come to blows" with the Germans defeated. But the exhilaration of freedom overwhelmed faction in the end. "Shouts and music and cheers" were all Psychoundakis recalled from liberation day.

Fielding saw that the civil war had been mild in Crete when he returned in the early 1950s to spend a year traveling in the White Mountains and writing *The Stronghold* (1953), a record of days spent visiting wartime comrades in peace. His memoir of his SOE days, *Hide and Seek*, appeared the following year. It is a classic of British war literature, an understated account of a man's coming-of-age thanks to the sudden shouldering of great responsibility. Fielding is deprecating about the dangers and his own achievements. Antony Beevor noted that Fielding "always played down his role in the non-aggression pact." Having set the meeting in motion and specified the terms, he claimed "to have drifted off to sleep from exhaustion after the march across the mountains." It is typical of the quiet and reticent man who preferred to live outside the limelight and wrote matter-of-factly about the war rather than with a gloss of adventure or heroism. There's a scene, late in 1943, when Fielding and a group of partisans study the German's list of "wanted" men. He notes "with regrettable but only human pride that the entry under my local pseudonym, which outlined in detail my physical characteristics, aliases and activities for a period of eighteen months, took no less than three-quarters of an octavo page in closely-set smallpoint type." The Germans had surely measured his worth.

Author's Note

A COMPLETE HISTORY of Cretan resistance during the German occupation still remains to be written. It would be a pleasant and honourable task to record in full the most recent example of that indestructible nation's heroism. Now that the hand of Military Censorship no longer turns to dross all that it touches, one or two volumes have indeed appeared which describe certain aspects of Cretan war-time activity. But these accounts, however admirable, are personal impressions, limited to one particular phase of the occupation or confined to one specific area of the island.

This narrative of mine can make no further claim. When I embarked on it, I had hopefully envisaged a work of wider scope, properly documented and supported by contemporary evidence—a work, in fact, which might have been worthy of its subject. The necessary material was, and still is, in existence: in the shape of reports which my brother-officers and I despatched while serving in Crete from 1941 to 1945. But these remain inaccessible—not, so I am assured, because of any outworn dictate of the Official Secrets Act, but simply through lack of personnel available to extract them from the files of the War Office.

Inevitably, therefore, my only authority has been my memory, and the book I planned has been reduced to the category of "war memoirs," to a volume admittedly incomplete and inadequate but intended, none the less, as a tribute to those comrades-in-arms whose worth was officially recognized only so long as the war lasted, and as a reminder of certain human qualities which went out of fashion with the advent of peace.

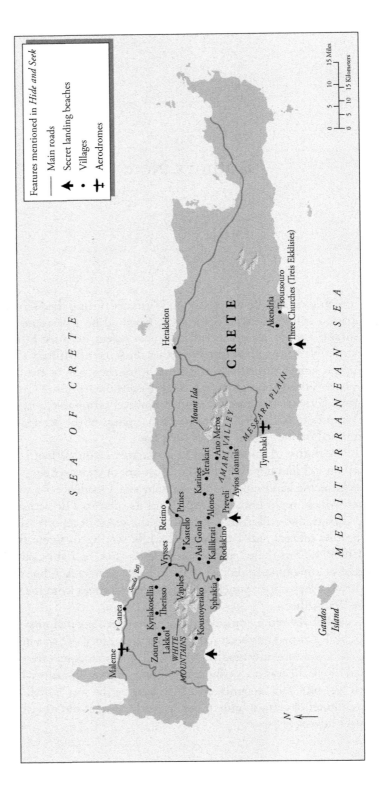

Features mentioned in *Hide and Seek*

— Main roads
→ Secret landing beaches
• Villages
✝ Aerodromes

SEA OF CRETE

Herakleion

CRETE

Mount Ida

Retimo
Prines
Karines
Yerakari
Vrysses
Kastello
Ano Meros
Asi Gonia
Kalliktati
Alones
AMARI VALLEY
Rodakino
Preveli
Ayios Ioannis
Koustoyerako
Sphakia
MESSARA PLAIN
Tymbaki

Canea
Kyriakosellia
Zourva
Therisso
Vaphes
Lakkoi
WHITE
MOUNTAINS

Maleme

Akendria
Tsoutsouro
Three Churches (Treis Ekklisies)

Souda Bay

MEDITERRANEAN SEA

Gavdos Island

N

0   5   10   15 Miles
0   5   10   15 Kilometers

HIDE AND SEEK

CHAPTER ONE

1939–41

THE FALL OF CRETE at the end of May 1941 meant more to me than the loss of a strategically important Allied base. Not that I had any association with the island; but I happened to be stationed in Cyprus at the time, and Cyprus was the next enemy target.

Or so we all thought. None of us then realized that the German attack, though planned, was first postponed and finally cancelled largely because of the delay caused by the fierce opposition in Crete. The island was expected to surrender in a day; the battle there had lasted ten. Meanwhile reports and rumours (confirmed, a little later, by a boat-load of survivors) began to reach us in Cyprus. From them I learnt for the first time the details of that ten-day action.

Perhaps the main reason for the deep and immediate impression the Battle of Crete made on me was that it brought the war imminently closer. But there were also other reasons. In the first place, the fighting had been restricted to a small enough area and to a sufficiently short period for me to comprehend it, as it were, at a glance. (Because of their vast extent in time and space, apart from their remoteness, I had never achieved as firm and as ready a grasp of the campaign in France, for instance, or of the tidal struggle over the sands of the Western Desert.) Secondly, Crete had been the scene of the first airborne invasion in history—a fact which could not fail to interest even an amateur militarist like myself.

Yet it was not so much the military as the human factor that impressed me. Until then the war had seemed an impersonal business

I

conducted by "troops" or "units"—anonymous bodies which for the sake of security could not always be identified even collectively by regimental name or divisional number. And for me a nameless platoon or company was hardly more anthropomorphic than a tank or armoured car. Now, for the first time, I heard accounts of men fighting men and even, in several cases, of one man fighting another. This form of contest I could understand, and although I personally knew no one who had been through the Battle of Crete, I felt I could almost recognize as a separate individual every man who had. Accurately or not, I could certainly visualize the various groups taking part: the Maoris counter-attacking at Maleme, clutching in their fists the bayonets they had had no time to fix on their rifles; the New Zealanders and Australians breaking into Galatas behind the screen of a single tank; the Commandos landing with full equipment further down the coast when the withdrawal from Canea was already under way; and—more clearly than all these, possibly because they wore no uniform and so seemed more like men than soldiers ever can—the Cretan civilians who, although to all intents and purposes unarmed, cropped up to fight the invader wherever he appeared.

This concerted rising of the technically non-combatant seemed to me the most reasonable and intelligible action in the war. Compared to this simple urge to defend home and property, the cause to which I was subscribing appeared preposterous and remote. My own position as a member of an organized army became increasingly galling, and I felt that if I had to fight, the least ignoble purpose and the most personally satisfying method would be the purpose and method of the Cretans.

Bearded men wielding breach-loading muskets or shotguns, barefoot children behind them carrying the outdated ammunition, hooded women in support with kitchen-knives and broomhandles—the image of these people kept recurring and (no doubt as a form of escape from regimental duties) I gave in to it more and more, so that my longing to be part of it gradually became almost a mental realization. I cannot pretend I then had the slightest foreknowledge of my subsequent connection with Crete; yet in a few weeks I had so identified myself with the island that when one morning an unknown naval officer strolled unannounced into my office and offered me the chance of going there, I was less surprised than pleased and accepted at once.

This unexpected offer came at a time when I was most in need of a change. The vision I had privately formed of Crete and the Cretans was not the only cause of my dissatisfaction with regimental life; I had felt uneasy as an army officer ever since becoming one. It was a role for which I knew myself to be unsuited, and in the absence of fear—for I had then seen no action—my principal emotions for over a year had been irritation and boredom.

The outbreak of war had surprised me in Cyprus, where I had been sub-editing the local newspaper and, after being dismissed from that post, unsuccessfully running a bar. For various reasons I was not popular with the Cyprus Government officials, chiefly, I imagine, because I would not refer to the Cypriots as "Cyps" (an absurdly pejorative term, considering these people were members of a civilized society when we were still painting ourselves with woad) and also, perhaps, because I could speak a little Greek and was anxious to learn more—a suspect ambition in the eyes of district commissioners ignorant of the language of the people they administered. Furthermore I had little money, and "poor whites" are never welcome in British colonies.

My first reaction, therefore, when I heard that war had been declared, was flight. I had no idea what form hostilities would take, and was haunted by the dreadful possibility of finding myself blockaded by my country's enemies in an island ruled by my own. I might have made a decent escape by rushing home at once and joining up; but even if I had felt a romantic inclination to do so, I could not afford the fare back to England. Unworthily, then, I resorted to a compromise and fled to Greece, a country I already knew and loved. By the end of September 1939 I had found asylum on St. Nicholas, a small island in the Bay of Chalkis which was owned by a friend of mine, the anthropologist Francis Turville-Petre.

It took me almost a year to decide what attitude to adopt towards the war. I objected to it, naturally, but not conscientiously. I had no compunction about taking human life, and my aversion to wearing uniform was not due to any religious scruple. My reluctance to join up could have been attributed to cowardice only if I had felt the slightest fear of death or anxiety over the possibility of being maimed for life. But I felt neither. My anti-social instinct was therefore probably the cause—I was not afraid of fighting, but I was appalled by the prospect of the army.

I did not, of course, reach this conclusion at once. I came to it gradually, after realizing that each time I tried to visualize the war, it was not a battlefield I saw in my mind's eye but something which to me was far more horrid: an Officers' Mess. After a long time spent in pleasant solitude wandering about Eastern Europe and the Levant, I could not bear the idea of an enforced and artificial relationship with a set of strangers chosen to be comrades not by myself but by chance. I dreaded the companionship of adjutants and quartermasters more than the threat of shells and bullets. My instinctive action, therefore, was to keep away from the former even at the risk of being despised for avoiding, in consequence, the latter.

Not that I ran such a risk on St. Nicholas. Apart from an occasional visitor from Athens and a staff of half a dozen peasant boys, Francis was the only person I saw for the whole of the first winter of the war and for most of the following summer; and he was the last man to censure me for following my natural inclination. Certainly he had followed his. At the age of thirty, after laying the foundations of a brilliant career with his discovery of the Galilee Skull, he had abandoned anthropology because he found the profession interfered too much with his private life, and had come to retire in Greece. His pretext for settling on a deserted island was to excavate a mound on the mainland directly opposite; but it was easier to think of his premature retirement as a gesture of defiance, for the site ten years later was still untouched.

Inevitably, I suppose, he had earned a reputation for eccentricity. His appearance was unconventional: long straight Red-Indian hair framed a sad sallow face so lined that it was impossible to guess its owner's age; below it an emaciated body, always clothed in bright colours, stretched six feet down to an almost freakishly small pair of sandalled feet. His habits, too, were out of the ordinary: he would get up every day at sunset and sit down to a luncheon which had been ordered for three o'clock in the afternoon—a mere formality in any case, for he never ate anything at meal times but lived on brandy and dry bread supplemented by a weekly cup of Bovril. Those who did not know him well might have thought he despised the world. They would have been wrong—it was only public opinion he scorned. Any misanthropic tendency he might have had was checked by a tolerance of human foibles that was almost Armenian in its integrity.

The companionship and conversation of a man like Francis[1] did much to dispel my increasing sense of guilt, so that the report of the evacuation from Dunkirk and the account of the Battle of Britain caused me no more than a passing twinge of conscience. Yet I could not anaesthetize myself completely against the stab inflicted by the B.B.C., which we listened to every day. Francis would try to salve the wound by appealing derisively to reason. Emphasizing and clinging on to each consonant, purposely exaggerating a distinctive manner of speech which was half-way between a stammer and a drawl, he would ask me again and again:

"But what good do you think *you* could possibly be?"

This question, of course, was no answer to my problem. But I could find no solution myself. Even if I had wanted to join up—and by the summer of 1940 I was almost regretting I hadn't—it was too late; Europe and the Mediterranean were closed to me. I was in a mood to welcome any alternative to this state of frustration and indecision, so that when, some time in August, I heard that the British Military Attaché in Athens was on the look out for Greek-speaking Englishmen to officer the newly-formed Cyprus Regiment, I rushed to the Embassy and applied for an interview.

To judge by the six other candidates appointed with me, the Cyprus Regiment must have been in desperate need of officers—I need only say that, in appearance at least, I was by no means the most unsuitable. A week after our interview with the Military Attaché we were sent to Port Said and thence to Jerusalem where, two days before the first anniversary of the outbreak of war and three months before my twenty-second birthday, we received our commissions.

After a short period of training in Sarafand and Haifa we crossed over to Cyprus and reported to the Regimental Depot in Limassol. Here I saw the last of my travelling companions, who joined their respective mule transport companies (which a few months later played a valiant and decisive part in the Greek campaign) while I, being the only member of the group to have passed through an

---

1. One of the most stimulating and rewarding companions I have ever known; his death in Egypt a year later was a personal loss for which nothing has since compensated.

O.T.C., was posted to an embryonic infantry battalion which was
then being organized more in the nature of an experiment, I believe,
than for any serious military purpose.[2]

The headquarters of the 1st (and only) Cyprus Battalion was at
Mavrovouni, a copper-mining settlement in some foothills overlooking the north coast. At first glance the camp appeared forbidding.
Denuded hillocks, scarred and livid, surrounded the parade-ground,
which rang like a sounding-board as our feet tramped over the hol-
low shafts and corridors underneath. But less than a mile away,
where the foothills met the plain, we could walk through orange-
groves that seemed endless; while across the sea the highlands of
Anatolia sparkled distantly in the autumn sun. Our living conditions were no less satisfactory than the scenery. The men were bil-
leted in the empty miners' quarters, a miniature village of mud huts;
while we lived in the abandoned staff bungalows of the Cyprus
Mines Corporation, an American firm which had clearly been atten-
tive to the comfort of its officials. Their one-time club-house became
our Mess.

My brother-officers were not so fearsome as I had anticipated.
They had all been seconded from various other regiments, and were
either novices like myself or recalcitrant regulars who had proved
undesirable in their parent battalions. Our unit, then, was understandably free from any sense of regimental pride.

The Cypriots have never had a military tradition, and it soon
became clear that they were not going to break a habit formed
before the first century by taking kindly to soldiering in the twentieth. They preferred the brothels of the nearest provincial town to
the unwonted masculinity of the camp; while us officers, despairing
of ever transforming them into disciplined automata, light-heartedly
abandoned the attempt and, following in our own way the example
set by the men, transferred our attentions to the night-clubs of Nicosia. Fortunately for us, the Colonel showed as little interest in training as we did. With a serene indifference to the war, he devoted all
his energies to organizing the Regimental Sports Day, a project he
did not abandon until the Battle of Crete was over and the threat to
Cyprus was imminent.

So while the Battalion was kept busy with the C.O.'s plans for
turning the parade-ground into a running-track, the incidence of

2. It was disbanded, I subsequently learnt, long before the end of the war.

venereal disease among the men rose to a height which was only surpassed by the officers' drunkenness. One company commander turned up so fuddled at a court martial over which he was to preside that he had to be arrested on the spot and was subsequently tried himself. Another—martyr to a daily hangover—after being sick into a waste-paper basket in the company office, would call for an orderly, point at the steaming mess and shout:

"What's the meaning of all this? Take it out of here at once!"

Those months in the Cyprus Battalion were so farcically different from what I had expected army life to be that, in retrospect at least, they appear as one of the most carefree periods of my life. I even became reconciled to the Mess. Its members—with one exception—were as immature as schoolboys and, though hardly adequate as life companions, perfectly friendly. The exception was Mark Ogilvie-Grant.

I had not met Mark before, but already knew of him through the number of friends we had in common. He was the only person in the Battalion with whom I had no need to adopt a false attitude of heartiness and military self-assurance. He shared with me a love of Greece that was older than my own, and something else besides: scorn for the Colonel—with whom we were brought into closer daily contact than any of our colleagues; Mark, because he was the Adjutant; myself, because I was the Regimental Intelligence Officer. In consequence, the Orderly Room, when either of us was in attendance, belied its name by an atmosphere of latent insubordination.

Coming straight to the Cyprus Regiment from the Scots Guards, Mark had at first tried to infuse the unit with a sense of discipline and Brigade swagger—a laudable attempt, considering both were foreign to a nature as liberal as his. His efforts were not appreciated, least of all by the Colonel, who no doubt saw in them a possible hindrance to his Sports Day plans. So bit by bit Mark discarded the trappings of efficiency, which had cost him in the first place so much effort to assume, and became as careless as the rest of us.

I was in his office one morning, when the air-raid warning sounded. Through the open window we saw the platoons which had been at work on the Colonel's running track down tools and dive into the slit-trenches.

"What on earth are they taking cover for?" Mark muttered. "It's only a practice warning to test the siren . . . but, oh, my God, I forgot to say so in Battalion Orders!"

Before the Colonel could bellow "Grant!" from the adjoining room, Mark had opened the intercommunicating door, put his head round the corner and, with an engaging smile but in a voice that betrayed not the faintest hint of apology, said:

"Terribly remiss of me, sir, I know."

The Colonel never forgave this lapse, which threatened to retard by so many man-hours the completion of his sports ground; Mark left us very shortly afterwards. Months later I heard he had been secretly infiltrated into enemy-occupied Greece.[3]

———

My duties as Intelligence Officer were mainly devoted to drawing large-scale plans of the Battalion area and surrounding countryside. We had not yet been issued with War Office maps of the island, so my amateur sketches were appreciated more than they would otherwise have been. They were even admired by the G.O.C., who apparently considered that my prowess as a draughtsman fitted me for more important intelligence commitments, for he ordered me to be transferred at once to his own staff in Nicosia.

My posting to H.Q. Cyprus coincided with the arrival of the official maps from G.H.Q. Middle East, so I had no further chance of displaying my talents. Instead I was condemned to months of boredom, during which I censored out-going mail, and to occasional periods of apprehension, when I was ordered to accompany the General on routine tours of inspection. But in the early summer I became involved, for the first time, in duties which absorbed my whole attention.

At that time Cyprus was, to all intents and purposes, defenceless. Apart from the disorganized rabble at Mavrovouni, there were a few regular units dotted about the island: in strength, perhaps, no more than one brigade. Since no further reinforcements were expected, our only hope of making the enemy hesitate to attack us was by means of deception. Plans were therefore made for the creation of a notional "Seventh Division," whose presence on the island would, we assumed, eventually be reported to the Germans via the intelli-

---

3. He was captured shortly after being put ashore by submarine in the Peloponnese—in uniform fortunately; otherwise he would have been shot as a spy—and spent the rest of the war in a prison camp.

gence network we suspected them of running, despite all our security precautions, through Turkey.

The mechanics of the subterfuge were simple and required a minimum of personnel. Overnight, empty houses in outlying districts (previously reconnoitred by me) were transformed into the headquarters of imaginary brigades, battalions and batteries. Soon there was a steady flow of despatch-riders delivering messages (composed in my H.Q. Office) from one headquarters to another. Since all these phantom units were represented only by myself, I spent most of every day travelling between them on a motor-bicycle in order to put in an appearance at each.

In time the danger of invasion passed, and I returned to normal duties without ever discovering if the scheme had been in any way instrumental in dissuading the enemy from launching the attack we had expected. But it had given me my first experience of clandestine activity; so that when, a few weeks later, I was offered the chance of operating in Crete, I knew what sort of work such an operation would entail and had no need to ask any questions. Even if I had not known, I would have accepted without hesitation; for I recognized in the offer a God-sent release, not only from the military dead-end I had reached, but from militarism itself.

CHAPTER TWO

1941–42

I reported to H.Q. Special Operations Executive[1] about the middle of December. I had no difficulty in finding the place—a large block of flats originally named "Rustom Building" and now known, it seemed, as "Secret House" to every taxi-driver in Cairo. As a newcomer to the organization, I was rather startled that its identity and whereabouts should be such common knowledge. Since volunteering for clandestine duties, I had become increasingly obsessed with the importance of security—and also, perhaps, with my own self-importance; for if a stranger in the street even asked me for a light, I at once suspected him of ulterior intent and put myself grotesquely on my guard.

But my introduction to S.O.E. quickly dispelled this exaggerated alarm and restored my sense of proportion. There was nothing mysterious or melodramatic about my reception. I was simply taken in to see the Colonel in charge, who after a few formal questions suggested:

"You'd better have a word with Jack Smith-Hughes. He's just got back from Crete."

I was then shown into another room and introduced to a large man in a ready-made tweed coat and grey flannel trousers. His ap-

---

1. For security reasons, however, the organization was never at that time mentioned by name, nor even by the initials S.O.E. Its members referred to it simply as "the firm"; to other departments of G.H.Q. Middle East it was known, under a succession of aliases, as M.O.1 (S.P.), M.O.4, and towards the end of the war, when its nature was less clandestine than paramilitary, as Force 133.

pearance was not exceptionally imposing; the fleshy unlined cheeks, the dishevelled strands of hair on skull and upper lip, could almost be described as commonplace. Nevertheless, I was suitably impressed by these features, since they belonged to the first secret agent I had ever met. I was impressed, too, by the calculated question with which he opened the conversation:

"Have you any personal objection to committing murder?"

As the conversation proceeded I realized I was listening to someone with an intelligence of a high order.[2] In half a dozen well-chosen verbal strokes Jack Smith-Hughes outlined the salient events and personalities contributing to the Cretan situation at that particular stage of the war, and incidentally told me something about himself. I learnt that although he looked much older (which had led me to assume he was also senior), he was in fact a subaltern like myself and was younger than me by one day. I understood then why he had been so amused each time I addressed him as "sir."

Serving in the R.A.S.C., he was in charge of the Field Bakery in the Canea sector at the time of the German invasion. He was subsequently captured and imprisoned in the camp at Galatas, but not for long. Following the example of many of his fellow-prisoners, he cut his way through the wire one night and took to the hills.

Of the islanders who befriended him during his escape, one was a retired colonel who told him that plans for a Cretan resistance movement were already under way. That its potential strength would be enormous was proved by the number of Cretans who, at great personal risk, had helped our men to break out of prison and who, with equal disregard for their own safety, offered them food and shelter once they were free.

There were then over a thousand Allied stragglers wandering about the island, most of whom had made for the south coast in the hope of finding a boat to take them to Africa. A few had succeeded in getting away—in stolen dinghies with home-made sails and no means of navigation—and had miraculously landed two or three days later on some British-held Libyan beach. They reported to G.H.Q. Middle East that hundreds of their comrades still at large in Crete were then being housed and fed by the Abbot of Preveli Monastery. These men

2. Lt. (later Major) Jack Smith-Hughes, O.B.E., had been trained as a lawyer. His phenomenal memory and other mental attainments are now at the disposal of the Judge Advocate General's Staff, which he joined a few years after the war.

formed by far the largest Allied concentration in the island, and since the monastery was on the sea, could be the most easily rescued. Plans were therefore made to take them off; and one night in August, ten weeks after our official evacuation from Sphakia, a submarine surfaced off the Preveli coast and put on board as many of the stragglers as she could hold. Among them was Jack Smith-Hughes.

On his arrival he notified the authorities of the plans he had discovered for a Cretan resistance movement, and volunteered to return to the island and help with its organization. Meanwhile two naval officers were detailed to prepare a clandestine line of communication between Alexandria and southern Crete by means of small boats; and a couple of months later, in October, Jack went back accompanied by a wireless-operator[3] from I.S.L.D.[4] His mission was to contact the Cretan colonel whom he had met on his flight from prison, establish the operator and the transmitting set in his house—an isolated cottage in the White Mountains—and co-ordinate the activities of the other potential resistance leaders in the west of the island. In the east two guerrilla bands had already been formed; and to supervise these a second officer[5] was sent into Crete in November.

Jack accomplished his mission in ten weeks and returned to Headquarters to report. He had reached Alexandria in one of the small S.O.E. boats only thirty-six hours before my interview with him; and since he was now to remain in Cairo to organize the staff work of an embryonic Cretan Section, I was expected to take his place in the field and to leave for Crete as soon as possible.

Next morning I met the other members of our section.

In charge of naval operations was Skipper Pool,[6] a middle-aged ex-Merchant Marine officer, who before the war had maintained the

3. Sergeant (later Captain) Ralph Stockbridge, M.C.; now a member of the Foreign Office.
4. "Inter-Services Liaison Department"—a cover name for the clandestine Intelligence Service which was independent of, but often operated in conjunction with, our own paramilitary organization.
5. Capt. (later Colonel) the Hon. C. M. Woodhouse, D.S.O., who later was in charge of all S.O.E. operations on the Greek mainland; author of *Apple of Discord*, etc.; at present a member of the Foreign Office.
6. Commander Francis Pool, D.S.O.; post-war British Consul in Canea; died in Athens in 1946.

Imperial Airways base in eastern Crete, and so was well acquainted with the island, its people and their language. It was he who had organized the submarine evacuation from Preveli during the summer; it was to him, therefore, that we owed our first clandestine contact with enemy-occupied Crete.

Under Skipper were the captains of the two small boats, Mike Cumberlege[7] and John Campbell.[8] Mike had been engaged on subversive activity in Crete before and during the battle, and probably knew the coast-line of the island more intimately than any man alive. He had a corsair's flair for discovering unknown beaches and hidden coves, a pirate's passion for taking individual action at sea, and had shown an almost Barbarossian skill and spirit of defiance when roving off German-held shores in his diminutive undecked *Escampador*. He even looked like a pirate—short and square and stubborn, with one ear pierced by a small gold ring which made an anachronism of his modem naval uniform.

John and Mike both had the same rather specialized interests— they had known each other for years, and before the war had sailed all over the world together, each in his own small yacht—but, as so often happens in a friendship as close as theirs, the two were vastly dissimilar in character and appearance. Mike's conversation was, to say the least, robust; John spoke through clenched teeth in monosyllables—except during rare outbursts of temper, when he showed an equally masterly command of invective. Tall and powerful, with a tenacity and singleness of purpose bordering on fanaticism, he was saved from what might otherwise have been an appearance of sinister ruthlessness by conventional good looks that were far above the average and by an elegance that asserted itself even in the impersonal accoutrements of war-time service dress.

John commanded *Hedgehog*, the larger of the two small boats, from which I was to be landed in Crete during the last week of December.

But what I was to do when I got there was not quite clear. At that time S.O.E. Middle East was still in an initial stage of development—as far as I could make out, Crete was then the only country

---

7. Lt.-Commander Michael Cumberlege, D.S.O., who was later captured during an attempt to blow up the Corinth Canal and, while still a prisoner of war, was murdered by the Germans just before the end of hostilities.

8. Lt.-Commander John Campbell, D.S.O., now living in Ireland.

in which we were operating regularly—and every one of its agents was an untrained, inexperienced amateur. I knew I should have to devote some of my time to rounding up the remaining stragglers and arranging for their evacuation (though these duties were normally undertaken by M.I.9, a department that had been specifically created for the purpose). I knew too that I should have to occupy myself with intelligence, since I.S.L.D. was represented in the island only by one signal-sergeant who had neither the position nor the leisure to organize an espionage network. Co-ordination of the native resistance movement, which I supposed to be my main task, was such an ambiguous directive that not even Jack could brief me adequately on the subject. But Mike inadvertently dropped a hint as to one possible direction my future activities might take, when he said:

"You speak German, do you? Good. Then you'll be able to grill the bastards while we bastinado them!"

It was hard to reconcile this statement with the assurance Jack had previously given me that I was unlikely even to see a German since the enemy never ventured into the mountains. The alarm I felt at the prospect must have shown on my face. Probably, then, in the hope of strengthening my moral fibre and inuring me to subversion and violence—for I could see no other reason—I was sent to the Middle East Commando Depot on a short sabotage course.

For three days I was initiated into the mysteries of plastic high explosive, slow-burning fuses, detonators and primer-cord, and was given detailed instruction in the most effective method of blowing up a railway line. The knowledge that no railway existed in Crete did not dampen my immediate ardour for demolition work, and each morning I happily destroyed an increasingly longer stretch of the metals laid for us to practise on in the desert round our camp. Those daily explosions in the sand represented all the training I received before being recalled to Cairo a few days after Christmas.

It took me only a few minutes to draw my gear from the S.O.E. stores. The staff, then in its infancy, was as ignorant as I was of what constituted an agent's basic personal requirements. It was assumed, very properly, that anyone embarking on a clandestine venture into enemy-occupied territory would not wish to be hampered by supplies that were not absolutely essential, so that my equipment was reduced to the barest necessities: an electric torch, a small automatic pistol, a map of Crete printed on linen for discreet portability but of so small a scale as to be virtually useless, and a sum of money in currency so inflated that I found my total assets on landing amounted to little more than £16.

My operational wardrobe consisted of a black suit, white sweater and ammunition-boots. To complete my Cretan disguise I had begun to grow a moustache, since I was told that few adult males in the island were clean-shaven; but this, with my outrageous clothes, only succeeded in making me look like an unemployed Soho waiter.

Thus equipped, but mercifully not yet thus attired, I left with Jack for Alexandria.

In a gloomy suburban house near Ramleh Station, rented for security reasons in the name of the British Consul-General but used for expeditions such as ours, I was introduced to my future fellow-passengers on *Hedgehog*: Corporal Reg Everson, Staff-Sergeant Guy Delaney, Captain Guy Turrell and four young Cretans. Although, again for security reasons, we had not been allowed to meet each other before, Jack had already told me something about them. What he had omitted from his description was the physical peculiarity they had in common: each looked far younger than his actual age.

I had expected Everson, for instance, to show at least some sign of his ten-years' pre-war service. I had pictured him as a crafty veteran who was sure to adopt towards me that attitude of insolent condescension which almost every regular N.C.O. reserves for officers holding emergency commissions. But here was an engaging fair-haired boy who might have just left school. He was a wireless operator, recently recruited to S.O.E. from the Royal Corps of Signals, and was going into Crete with a second transmitting set for the use of Monty Woodhouse.

Delaney, on his own admission, was over fifty, but in any statement of his an allowance had to be made for his manifest inability to speak the truth. Not that he was a liar, but he had a clownish instinct for exaggeration and gesture—a characteristic that accorded well with his appearance. His crimson face was encased in a helmet of jet-black hair growing to within a few inches of charcoal-coloured eyebrows so close that they appeared to be a single growth, with theatrical side-whiskers as thick and furry as ear-muffs cunningly trained to follow the line of each cheek-bone. No one could, or did, take him seriously; yet he had shown more spirit and competence than any of the other Australian stragglers who had been evacuated with him from Preveli a few months previously. He had volunteered to return to Crete in order to report, as an armoury expert, on the number and condition of the rifles and other weapons then in Cretan hands.

I could tell Guy Turrell's age only by his medals, all awarded in the 1914 war except the Military Cross which he had won as a platoon-commander in Abyssinia earlier that year. His small sinewy body was hard and knotted after a lifetime spent in the more remote parts of Central Africa and South America. So, in many respects, was his mind. Years of comparative solitude in the wilds had made him scornful of most forms of urban civilization, but had developed in him qualities essential for the mission which he was about to undertake: sabotage of enemy shipping in Souda harbour. In this he was to be assisted by the four young Cretans, all of whom had been trained for the purpose in the S.O.E. school in Haifa. The only drawback to his appointment was that he spoke not a word of Greek and they understood no English.

In an atmosphere of suppressed excitement and under conditions of strict security which isolated us from the world outside, we got to know each other more quickly than we should have done in normal circumstances. We were not encouraged to go into Alexandria— the Cretans indeed were categorically forbidden to do so—and the only time we left the "safe" but otherwise uncongenial villa was for a meeting with Mike Cumberlege and John Campbell in their sumptuous flat overlooking the Sporting Club, where we discussed the final plans for our departure.

Apart from our personal equipment and the sabotage stores, we were to take in more than a ton of arms and ammunition for the two guerrilla gangs in Monty Woodhouse's area. The loading of all this material was naturally John's responsibility; the arrangements were therefore in experienced hands. But Turrell, with well-intentioned but tactless insistence, kept offering advice that was more applicable to a peace-time safari than a clandestine naval operation, prefacing each suggestion with the redundant statement:

"You see, I've lived so long in the bush . . ."

With commendable restraint Mike retorted in a barely audible whisper:

"Well, don't let me catch you crawling about in mine!"

But Turrell remained true to character. When we embarked on *Hedgehog*, as arranged, early in the morning on New Year's Eve, I noticed be brought with him not only full camp equipment, including a tin basin in a canvas cover, but also that egregious and outmoded symbol of Empire, a solar topee. In view of this it was not surprising that he should still be wearing battledress, while the rest of us had changed into operational clothes.

He was quite right, of course, to retain his uniform; for were we to meet the enemy at sea or on landing, he at least could not legally be shot as a spy if captured. It was only through bravado, then, that I affected to despise him for it. Secretly I envied him, not only because he had no fear of appearing ridiculous in our eyes but also because, had I had the same moral courage to retain my own service dress, I could have enjoyed wearing for a day or two longer my new badges of rank and corps insignia. For by then, so that my position in Crete might carry more weight, I had been promoted to the rank of captain and, in order to make my break with regimental soldiering formal as well as actual, I had asked for and obtained an official transfer to the Intelligence Corps.

Of *Hedgehog*'s crew of four only one was a sailor, a rating seconded from submarines, who was, apparently, so unused to travelling on the surface of the sea that he started to be sick a few miles out of harbour. Nevertheless, he and his three companions—a British sergeant-major, a South African sergeant and a Greek lad of sixteen, all hand-picked and trained by John and Mike, were by temperament and inclination more suited to privateering than a crew of regular seamen would have been. Their quarters were cramped even when there were no passengers on board, and now there were thirteen of us overflowing out of the four-berth saloon in which we had to eat and sleep in uncomfortable restless shifts.

I had had a bet with John that I would not be sea-sick, a bet which I eventually won only because, in the heavy swell running out of the south, I felt too frightened to be conscious of any physical disturbance. The sea had been reasonably calm when we set sail in the early morning sunshine, but by the afternoon we were scudding northwards under a sky that looked like ink-stained blotting-paper. I had never before been so far from land in such a small boat, and so could not tell if the seas, which to me seemed mountainous, were endangering it or not. Nor did I dare ask; while most of my companions, green in the face and groaning, seemed beyond caring.

My unvoiced question was answered shortly after midnight, when John, who had been at the wheel ever since the wind started blowing at gale force, gave a shout for all hands on deck. I stumbled out of the saloon just as our prow struck the base of a towering wall of water, and for the split second before I was washed off my feet I had the weird sensation of standing upright and alone in the middle of the Mediterranean.

John's call had been for us to jettison the heavy deck cargo in order to keep *Hedgehog* afloat. The waves as they struck felt so solid that I could almost brace myself against them as I helped to bundle the heavy cases of rifles and ammunition boxes over the side. I took this opportunity to throw Turrell's solar topee overboard as well; he was in no state to regret its disappearance.

But even with the decks stripped for action against the seas, *Hedgehog* was unable to hold her own. Early in the morning John wisely decided to turn back. I was greatly relieved, for even had we managed to reach Crete we should have been in poor condition on landing and incapable of taking resolute action in any emergency that might have arisen. But as we sailed into Alexandria harbour late that night, I anxiously wondered how long we should have to remain there before being able to set out again.

We remained only a few days. Since we could not reach Crete in a small boat, and since no larger craft was prepared to take us over the sea, arrangements were made for us to travel under it. Less than a week after our return to Alexandria we embarked with all our stores on *Torbay*, a submarine commanded by Crapper Myers[9] who had offered to go a little way out of his routine patrol in order to put us ashore; and less than a week after this second departure we surfaced in the dark off the coast of Crete, again in a full gale.

---

9. Lt.-Commander Myers, who later that year, while still in command of *Torbay*, won the Victoria Cross for a daring raid in the Aegean.

RIGHT: *Father John Alevizakis,*
village priest of Alones

BELOW: *Paddy Leigh Fermor in the*
White Mountains, January 1943

LEFT: *George Psychoundakis of Asi Gonia, the author's first guide*

BELOW: *Petro Petrakas, guerrilla leader of Asi Gonia*

CHAPTER THREE

1942

W E W E R E T O land at a point on the southern seaboard known as Three Churches, where Monty Woodhouse would be waiting to receive us, I hoped, with a convoy of mules to carry the arms and equipment we were bringing in. But the wind prevented us from standing off that exposed coast, and since Monty's pre-arranged torch signals had not been sighted, Myers resolved to make for the shelter of Tsoutsouro Bay a few miles to the east. Here, he told us, he would be able to put us ashore—if we were prepared to land "blind" on an unreconnoitred and possibly German-held beach. It was up to us to decide.

Not courage, I think, but fear prompted the decision we took. Although I found the atmosphere of the submarine less claustrophobic than I had anticipated, I still had not reconciled myself to the close quarters, the lack of fresh air, the restriction on smoking, all of which we should have to put up with for three more weeks unless we landed now; for otherwise we should have to remain on board for the remainder of *Torbay*'s patrol, during which we might be depth-charged in action—a prospect which I envisaged with far more dread than the possibility of running into a handful of Germans on dry land. My companions, no doubt sharing my anxiety and impatience, unanimously supported the proposal that we should disembark at once.

Since none of us could tell what awaited us on the beach, Delaney, who already knew that stretch of coast, gallantly volunteered to go ashore first and have a look round. If he found on landing that

the shingle was unmined and that no Germans occupied the row of
fishermen's cottages lining the bay, he would signal for the rest of us
to join him. About midnight, then, with everyone at action stations,
he paddled off in a collapsible canoe. Half an hour later his torch
was seen flashing from the shore.

Meanwhile the seas had risen still more, and waiting below in the
wardroom we received a succession of unnerving reports on the situation above deck. The remaining canoes had been smashed one
after the other in repeated attempts to launch them, and so it was
out of the question to land all the rest of the personnel or any of the
stores that night. Myers, however, whose uncompromising decisive-
ness was happily combined with a mental resilience susceptible of
last-minute changes of plan, had agreed to devote another twenty-
four hours to the operation and was willing to surface again the following evening to complete the disembarkation if the canoes could
be repaired in time and if weather conditions were favourable.

But there was still a chance for two of us to get ashore at once,
provided we were prepared to use an unwieldy rubber dinghy, the
only available means of transport that was left intact. "It can't sink,"
we were assured, "though it's a brute to manoeuvre. But don't try to
sit inside it in a sea like this, you'd only overturn. Get astride the
thing and ride it like a horse." Guiltily, and no doubt also roman-
tically, Turrell and I pictured Delaney waiting alone and by now
bewildered on the enemy beach. We felt that the least we could
do was to make an attempt to join him. The dinghy was therefore
inflated, and a moment later we were called up on deck.

After almost a week of enforced immobility and confinement,
I instinctively braced myself against the imminent impact of fresh
unrestricted air. I knew my encounter with the gale outside would
for a few seconds take my breath away, but I was not prepared for
the blast that struck me full in the face as soon as my head emerged
from the conning-tower—a gust as sudden and as violent as though
I had just leant out of the window of a fast train travelling at full
speed. The shriek of the wind through stanchion and wire cable
drowned every other sound, so that the waves, alternately surging
over and receding from the sleek porpoise-like flanks of the submarine, were uncannily inaudible.

Standing forward of the bridge, three ratings with lines in their
hands grappled with what looked like a grey monster-fish cavorting

in and out of the surf on the starboard side. It came swirling towards
us at full tilt up a steep bank of water, and as it poised for a second
motionless on the irrupting crest before slithering down again into
the trough that formed in its wake, I recognized it as our rubber
boat. In that recurring second of immobility, before it scampered
once more out of reach, we were to mount it one after the other.

So holding my paddle like a tightrope-walker's balancing-pole, I
waited till the boat rushed in at thigh level, slung one leg over it as I
stepped off the submarine's deck and went careering smoothly down
the maculated slope beyond. A slight jerk on the lines pulled me up
just before I reached the bottom, then a second wave took control
and sent me hurtling back in a wide parabola which conveniently
reached its highest point at Turrell's knees. He hopped on behind so
nimbly that I should not have noticed his presence there but for the
sudden change in the boat's trim, which we instinctively readjusted
during the sweeping descent out to sea that immediately followed.
This time there was no jerk on the lines. We had been set adrift.

Now that we were clear of *Torbay*'s strident rigging the silence of
the night was almost oppressive. The waves, with nothing to break
against, noiselessly rose and fell, and all we could hear was an occasional slap and thud as the flat rubber surface beneath us moved over
the corrugated surface of surrounding sea. We could have spoken to
each other without raising our voices, but even whispering would
have demanded an effort, for we had to save our breath and devote
all our attention to paddling a straight course. The boat, which was
almost circular, spun like a buoyant saucer trapped in a whirlpool,
and it was only by using our legs as outriggers that we managed to
keep it under control.

From the submarine the castellated outline of Crete had looked
surprisingly close. It still looked close as we paddled towards it, but
not appreciably closer even after half an hour's struggle; it was only
when I heard the wind rattling down the cliff-side gullies and the
regular surging sound of breakers just ahead that I knew we were
almost there. This aural evidence was soon confirmed visually by
the appearance of a shifting band of foam as white as teeth, and as
we were abruptly sucked forward into the dark maw beyond I felt
the toe-caps of my boots scraping on the pebbly bottom.

Before either of us could dismount, however, we were both thrown
face down into the shallows; but getting to our feet at once, we clung

to the bucking boat by its ropes, and dragging it along behind us, managed to crawl ashore before the next wave could again send us sprawling.

———————

I had not resolved in advance what our first move would be on landing. I imagined it would be settled for us by what Delaney had to tell us when we met him. But Delaney wasn't there. Keeping as far from the houses as possible, Turrell and I tramped along the edge of the breakers from one end of the beach to the other and back again. There was still no sign of Delaney. To my shame I found myself shivering, then realized with relief that my convulsive and uncontrollable shudders were caused not by fear but by cold; until then I had been unconscious of my sodden clothes, which were beginning to freeze and stiffen in the icy wind. Delaney must have had the same experience and had no doubt sought by now the refuge of a friendly house.

But Turrell, because he would never have countenanced such behaviour, refused to believe even in its possibility. "Delaney wouldn't dream of letting us down like that," he insisted, "however cold and wet he felt. Something must have gone wrong."

"But he signalled O.K.," I objected.

"That doesn't mean a thing. The Germans may have intentionally let him make his signal before nabbing him, in the hope of nabbing us as well."

I had to admit the logic of this conclusion. Turrell's caution was perfectly justified, and his experience of war was infinitely greater than mine. But so, apparently, was his trust in Delaney's sense of duty; and although I did not say so I felt this trust to be misplaced. I had seen a strip of light in one of the fishermen's cottages—the only light visible in the whole bay—and I was sure Delaney was in that house, probably warming himself in front of a fire and almost certainly having, if wine was available, a long life-giving swig. I was sure because, had I been in his place, that is exactly what I should have been doing myself.

But Turrell was made of sterner stuff than either of us and, very properly I suppose, assumed that the worst had happened and began to take precautions. To humour him I too slipped forward the safety-catch of my pistol, and feeling slightly foolish—and, in spite of my conviction, also slightly scared—I started creeping up the beach towards the light, which as I approached revealed itself as a gap in a shuttered window.

I could not see into the room beyond, but as I listened to the voices inside I heard one which I recognized at once. Turrell, crouching next to me, had not yet identified it. Before he could I decided to take action, partly in revenge for the twinge of fear his common-sense attitude had caused me, but mostly to gratify with the least possible effort my own sense of the melodramatic. "Be ready to give me covering fire," I whispered, "I'm going in."

I banged with my fist at the entrance. Footsteps approached us from the other side, and as I heard the heavy wooden latch being drawn, I kicked open the door, at the same time flourishing my pistol and flashing on my torch, to reveal, outlined in the rectangle of light thrown by an oil lamp, the surprised face of a greybeard blinking into the electric beam I held, and beyond him, sitting by a twig fire in steaming long-legged underwear which made him look like an old-time pugilist, Delaney.

"You've been bloody slow getting here," he said.

———

Our host, once he had recovered from the shock, welcomed us enthusiastically. Perhaps he imagined the hour of liberation was at hand, for even when I explained that we were not the advance guard of an Allied expeditionary force, it was only with difficulty that we restrained him from calling the whole village to arms. He seemed a little disappointed when I told him all we needed for the time being was the shelter of his house and the warmth of his fire. "But there's a German here in Tsoutsouro!" he protested, and was again disappointed when we refused to treat the presence of this enemy as urgent after learning he was only a deserter. But we promised to have a look at him as soon as we were thawed out and dry.

At dawn, then, we went to the house where the German was sleeping and made him our prisoner. The young man, a junior N.C.O. in the Luftwaffe, welcomed us almost as jubilantly as our host of the night before and was eager to give us any information we required. Unfortunately, he had none to give. His brain seemed to have been slightly affected after the weeks he had spent on the run; so instead of retaining him, as I had vaguely planned to do, in the hope of exploiting him later to our own purposes, I decided to evacuate him when the submarine returned that night. Meanwhile—as a purely formal gesture of precaution, for clearly the last thing he contemplated was escape—I detailed Delaney to act as his guard.

By then the rest of the village had been roused, and since there seemed to be no point in trying to keep our presence there a secret, I took them all—about twenty-four men, a dozen women and a handful of children—into our confidence, explaining that the submarine would be approaching again that evening and asking them to man as many boats as possible to help with the unloading. I also sent one of them to Three Churches with a message for Monty, who I hoped would still be there, for otherwise we should find ourselves stranded on this beach with a ton of rifles and ammunition, no instructions as to their disposal and no guides to lead us into the interior.

Turrell and I spent the rest of the morning looking for some suitable spot in the immediate vicinity where the cargo could be stored once it was landed. High up on the cliff overlooking the western end of the beach, accessible only by a rough goat track, we found a large dry cave: exactly what we wanted. Sitting at its entrance under a sky washed clean by the recent gale, fanned by a breeze which smelled faintly of wild thyme and charcoal, I was able for the first time to view my surroundings objectively.

These were confined by the sea on my right and a horse-shoe ridge of foothills behind the bay, the crescent of shingle between them containing a community more isolated than any I had hitherto seen. The square stone buildings planted along the inner circumference of the beach looked not so much like houses designed to be used as family homes as like miniature fortresses hastily erected for defence against a sudden piratical raid. Uncompromisingly utilitarian, they were as comfortless as a mediaeval grange.

Inevitably, then, their occupants led a life which would have been primitive beyond endurance but for the outlet they had on to the sea. It was the sea which provided them not only with a broad horizon, without which the landscape would have been intolerably oppressive, but also with most of their food. Their diet was therefore largely dependent on the weather, for they could not go out fishing in a rough sea, and since it had been stormy for almost a week before our arrival, there was now not much to eat. But what they had they willingly shared with us; and our luncheon of rock-hard rusks which had to be soaked in water before they were fit to eat, accompanied by herbs and wild grasses cooked in slightly rancid olive oil, tasted all the better for being offered to us with such spontaneous generosity.

As soon as it was dark we started signalling out to sea. For a long time we could barely distinguish between sky and water, but gradually, as our eyes became accustomed to the moonless gloom, the horizon shifted into focus—a long frontier dividing two vast areas, each a slightly different shade of grey. I kept my eyes trained on this line of demarcation, expecting *Torbay*'s silhouette to appear at any moment at some point on it; but it was much lower down, and at least two hours later, that the black shape of the submarine at last revealed itself, so close that it seemed to be almost within hailing distance. Three boats which had been put at our disposal at once set out towards it, the first carrying our grateful young prisoner armed with a letter of introduction from me to Myers.

The shuttle service between shore and submarine was completed well before dawn, Everson and the four Cretan saboteurs landing with the first returning boats; but long after *Torbay* left, having unloaded its last consignment of weapons and explosives, we were kept busy on the beach shifting the growing piles of stores from the water's edge to the cave up above—a task which occupied us until almost midday, when a deputation arrived from Monty led by our favourite locally-recruited agent, Niko Souris.

I had already heard much of Niko from Jack Smith-Hughes and Mike Cumberlege. Although employed by us in Crete, he was not a native of the island but a Greek private soldier from Alexandria, a straggler who had been left behind after the battle like the countless Australians and New Zealanders whose escape he had assisted while volunteering to stay on himself to help with further evacuations and clandestine landings. He spoke perfect English in a gentle tone of voice issuing incongruously from a body of cask-like shape and durability. He also sang beautifully, but only when he felt depressed or anxious. I was glad to note that he was not singing as he scampered down the cliff-side to greet us.

He told me Monty was waiting to meet me at Akendria, a village further inland; so leaving Turrell and Everson behind to look after the stores, Delaney and I set off at once accompanied by a young Cretan lieutenant, Costa Paradeisianos, who was to act as our guide.

Compared to the rather stunted and ragged fishermen of Tsoutsouro, Costa was a flamboyantly dashing figure in black silk turban, black silk shirt, mountaineer's breeches and black riding-boots, the standard dress of the highlander. So close to the sea, he looked out of

place—even his carriage and gestures seemed ill-adapted to the flat
surface of the beach, over which he moved with a curiously stealthy
gait—but as soon as we reached the foothills and started climbing
he was in his element at once, bounding from stone to stone with
a speed and precision which defied our breathless attempts to emu-
late him. Alone, he would have reached Akendria well before sunset.
With Delaney and me clumsily in tow, the journey took far longer:
it was getting dark by the time we ambled into the village.

For a moment I felt as though we had entered an Anzac encampment. The chorus of *Waltzing Matilda* filled the dusk as loudly as a
wireless switched on at full blast against a background of yowling,
spluttering atmospherics composed of typically Antipodean sounds
of revelry; and through the open door of the village coffee-shop I
saw a horde of frenzied giants in tattered khaki and slouch hats. All
these men had hoped to be evacuated from Three Churches two
days before and were now, understandably enough, drowning their
disappointment—an easy feat in Crete, where wine and raki were
both more plentiful than food.

The sight of them reminded me of the last time I had had to deal
with drunken Australians: in Tel Aviv, a few weeks after I had been
commissioned. Six of them were celebrating the end of twenty-four
hours' leave by looting a Jewish house and beating up the inmates.
I happened to be passing down the street when a terrified woman
leant out of the window, screamed for help and begged me as an
officer to intervene. But the Australians were not so impressed as she
was by my obviously new Sam Browne belt and the single star on
my shoulders. As I went inside one of them simply picked me up by
the scruff of the neck and demanded:

"Whose side are you on, Galahad?"

I did not wish a similar scene to be enacted in the coffee-shop
of Akendria, so I discreetly quickened my pace until I reached the
house where Monty was waiting.

I recognized him as soon as I entered the room, in spite of the
mountaineer's clothes he wore under a superb shepherd's cloak. He
would have needed a far more subtle disguise to pass unnoticed in
a Cretan crowd, for he had not even grown a moustache and his
extraordinarily juvenile complexion betrayed him as much as his fair
hair. But although he looked as young as an undergraduate (as so
many of his fellow Wykehamists seem to do until well into middle
age) he showed to a marked degree that mental maturity and adult

gravity which likewise distinguish the Wykehamist, even at the age of thirteen, from any other schoolboy.

He quickly outlined my itinerary to our clandestine wireless station—the same route that his messengers always took when delivering signals for Stockbridge to transmit to Cairo—and explained that the more hazardous stage of the journey would be the initial march across the Messara Plain. This was the only part of the Cretan hinterland which the Germans regularly patrolled, since the main road to their important aerodrome at Tymbaki ran straight across it. In the mountains beyond we should be less likely to encounter enemy detachments and so would be able to travel in reasonable safety by day, but across the plain it was essential to move only under cover of darkness.

Since I felt no particular urge to remain in Akendria that night, I decided to set off at once taking Costa and Delaney with me.

CHAPTER FOUR

1942

THE BENIGN DISPOSITION of human memory, whereby only the pleasant events of the past are recalled with clarity while the less agreeable recede into the background of the mind, has long since reduced that first march across the Messara Plain to the tenuous web of a half-forgotten nightmare. The only deep impression that remains is of utter physical weariness, to which Delaney and I would willingly have succumbed but for Costa's example and exhortation. For even the threat of capture and its inevitable outcome, the firing squad, were not sufficient to induce us to keep walking after the will to move our legs had died. On the contrary, I found myself longing for the sudden appearance of a German patrol to put an end to our increasingly unbearable muscular fatigue and sleeplessness.

Had we known what was to come, we should never have started out immediately after two consecutive days with little rest or food. But no one could have foretold how the ground we were to traverse would be affected by the storm that broke in the night. For over fifteen hours we struggled through a steady downpour, stumbling along paths which on the flat were transformed into morasses, on a slope into torrent-beds, until, when the dawn at last broke with but a bare improvement in visibility, we reached the southern foothills of Mount Ida and the entrance to the Amari Valley.

But even there, in the relative security of mountain-dyke and dell, we had to contend with an additional abnormal hazard. A German search party had chosen that day of all days to start combing the area for Petrakogeorghis, leader of one of the two guerrilla bands which were then operating in the east of the island; it was therefore impossible for us to approach his village, where we had planned to have something to eat and to rest for twenty-four hours before pushing on the next morning. Instead, we were forced to scuttle up into some inland cliffs, and take cover under a deep overhang of bush-encircled rock, where some of the villagers whom Costa had contacted eventually welcomed us with loaves of bread, goatskins of wine and a vast copper cauldron of cold oily beans. But I was too tired to eat or drink and fell asleep at once.

When I woke again in the late afternoon the situation had improved. The Germans had withdrawn to the nearest garrison town and the path to the west was now clear. More encouraging still, a man had come in from Platanos, a village up the valley, with the news that Ralph Stockbridge had spent the previous night there and was at this moment on his way to meet us, having heard of our presence in the neighbourhood by the same means as we now learnt of his: local gossip.

This report illogically made the journey before us seem much shorter, for even though I knew we should eventually have to complete the whole of our itinerary, I had associated the end of the march with our arrival at the wireless station and my meeting with Stockbridge—and here I was already about to meet him, four days sooner, and therefore eighty miles or so more close, than I had originally hoped. But I still had not the faintest idea what had brought him so far from his established base.

Of all the British agents in the island, Ralph Stockbridge was the most subtly disguised. The rest of us—with the possible exception of Turrell, whom I could not judge since I had not yet seen him out of uniform—had adopted a distinctive style of dressing in the hope of being taken for highland peasants. Monty relied on a shepherd's cloak to hide his smooth pink cheeks and camouflage his nordic height. Delaney accentuated his Mediterranean shock of hair by letting his side-whiskers grow, as though these comic hirsute appendages would compensate for his all but total ignorance of the language. As for myself, with my short stature and tolerable command of the local dialect, combined with the black turban I had now been given and with a moustache which no longer looked as though I had simply forgotten to shave that day, I was reasonably confident of being able to pass for a native, even at close quarters—little realizing that my wastefully energetic manner of moving over uneven ground would give me away at a distance of a mile.

But Ralph disdained such elementary measures. He washed and shaved carefully at least once a week. He wore shoes, not boots, and instead of a cloak, an overcoat. His jet black hair he kept uncovered. He stumbled over the countryside as though he was too short-sighted to avoid the obstructive stones in his path, confirming his myopia by what in Crete no rustic of his age would ever own: a pair of horn-rimmed spectacles. In no way, then, did he look like a peasant; yet more readily than any of us would he have been taken for a local inhabitant. For his appearance, his movements and his mannerisms were exactly those of what he was pretending to be: a village schoolmaster. His disguise, in fact, was so unobtrusively perfect that when I first met him I should not have been able to single him out from the group of men with whom he arrived, had he not introduced himself by first rummaging for something in his pocket, then holding out his hand and saying casually in English:

"Have a raisin . . ."

The main reason, he told me, for his unexpected presence in this part of the island was the mounting irritation he had felt after several months of isolation in the sole company of Andrea Papadakis, the Cretan colonel from whose house he had been operating our transmitting-set ever since Jack Smith-Hughes's mission. In order not to hurt the Colonel's feelings, however, he had told him he was going to the Amari so that the wireless station should be nearer Monty Woodhouse. But since his arrival in the valley he had been plagued by a series of technical hitches—it was almost impossible to "beam" the set on to Cairo with the great mass of Mount Kedros in between—and, to crown all his difficulties, there had been this latest German raid. He had had no alternative but to slink back once more to his original base, and he was reluctantly planning his return when he learnt by chance of our recent arrival—a stroke of luck; for now that Everson was in this district with a second wireless exclusively for Monty's use, there was no longer any excuse for Ralph to remain. He could therefore rejoin Papadakis without losing face by admitting the real reason for his return.

Since he had been off the air for several days, he was anxious to get back as soon as possible to resume contact, and suggested that Delaney and I accompany him at once.

Our path up the Amari Valley, a district so bountiful that among us it earned the code-name of "Lotus Land," led through villages which later formed one of the most important vertebrae of the backbone of Cretan resistance. During the early weeks of the occupation stragglers in greater numbers than anywhere else had found here refuge and sustenance. Since then Jack Smith-Hughes had laid the foundations for a courier line which passed straight through this area, so that the messengers now running between Monty Woodhouse and the wireless station were spontaneously housed and fed. Later still this mountain track—the only provincial thoroughfare between east and west that was not pullulating with Germans— was used so constantly by Allied agents that it came to be known as "The High Spy Route." And already, when I first arrived, transport arrangements were so well organized from one village to the next that at each successive stage we were automatically provided with a guide and with a mule for carrying the wireless set and batteries.

Delaney, even more than myself, was delighted with the slow progress we made since it was the heavily-laden mule which set our pace. For during his escape a few months before, he had made friends in almost every house we now passed, and their owners one after the other insisted that we stop and drink a glass of raki with them—we could always catch the mule up later. By ten o'clock in the morning of our first day's march he was happily blaspheming in a mixture of Greek and English and slapping everyone we met on the back.

Our first organized halt was at Ayios Ioannis, where Jack had advised me to call on Manoli Papadoyiannis, an influential local leader who in peace time had been Governor of Crete. In view of this distinguished gentleman's position I asked Delaney if he would try to act in a slightly less unreserved manner when he met him. Delaney did his best. He was ominously well-behaved throughout the excellent luncheon of eight roast partridges between the four of us, during which Ralph and I discussed resistance plans with our host; but as we drank the last of many glasses of wine before leaving, his self-control snapped. Lurching to his feet, he seized our elegant benefactor by the shoulders, kissed him on both spruce cheeks and broke the silence he had kept so long with this unusual expression of admiration and gratitude:

"You bug-whiskered old bastard, your blood's worth bottling!"

Soon afterwards we were deprived of Delaney's exuberant company. At our next halting place, Ano Meros, he announced his intention to go no further. Encouraged no doubt by the favourable augury of yet another copious meal and abundance of wine, this time provided by a Falstaffian village priest, he abruptly decided to make the Amari his base for future operations. "I've got to start work somewhere," he ingenuously explained, "and this seems as good a place as any." So Ralph and I pushed on alone to Yerakari, the large village at the head of the valley, where we spent the night with Alexander Kokonas, a saint by nature and a schoolmaster by profession.

Although everyone in all these villages was equally cooperative and whole-heartedly eager to help us, I found myself associating each community—probably because it was easier to remember no more than one name in each place—with one of its inhabitants alone, usually the one who had acted as our temporary host. Thus Karines, which we reached the following evening, was in my mind represented by Eleni Zourbaki and her pretty daughter Popi, both exceptionally emancipated for Cretan peasant women, most of whom, I had noticed, remained silent and hooded in the background while their menfolk entertained us.

Here, since we had left the Amari behind us, we were in poorer territory: stony uplands fit only for goats, punctuated at rare intervals by the olive-groves and vineyards which marked the existence of human habitation and industry; and by the time we reached the little hamlet of Alones on the last night of our journey, the food and accommodation we were offered were of almost neolithic simplicity. There was not even a bed in the priest's house there, and we lay down to sleep under hand-woven blankets spread on the bare boards of a loft. But for this lack of comfort we were amply compensated by the company of our host, Father John Alevizakis, a patriarchal figure with a grey forked beard, who practised in every detail what he preached.

From here it was less than four hours' march to Vouvoure, where Colonel Papadakis lived. We reached his house in the early afternoon—an ugly little building isolated on top of an exposed treeless hill, over which the winds from the snow-covered White Mountains swept without respite—and I was able to form an immediate impression of the Colonel's character from the opening words with which he greeted Ralph Stockbridge:

"Ah, so you're back again. I knew you'd soon realize you couldn't do without me. Another time don't forget that I'm the only man in Crete who can offer you true service."

———————

I tried hard not to judge Papadakis from his appearance alone. His swept-back grey hair and iron-grey clipped moustache were typical of any senior Greek Army officer; but his hard black eyes glittered with peasant cunning and his general expression could best be described by the American term of "sour-puss." His voice oscillated between arrogance and plaintiveness; at a moment's notice he would switch it from the didactic tone he used when exploiting his rank, of which he was exaggeratedly proud, to the wheedling notes of a pauper begging for alms.

But I did my best to overlook these unattractive qualities, remembering that he was the first man in the island to have established contact with the Allies and to have put himself at the disposal of our clandestine service. He alone had maintained Stockbridge and the wireless station ever since we started operations in Crete, and he had thereby reduced his own standard of living, which on his small pension would in any case not have been high, to a bare subsistence level—at Vouvoure there was nothing to eat but seed potatoes.

But his gestures of selfless patriotism, his quixotic plans for the freedom of Crete, were largely prompted by a personal ambition so vainglorious that he scarcely bothered to conceal it. He had set himself up as the head of a "Supreme Liberation Committee," unrecognized by anyone except its four members, all of whom had been elected by himself. This would have been an admirable venture had it lived up to its rather grandiloquent name—for in Crete bombast and bluster were not necessarily divorced from courage and efficiency—but from the first conversations I had with Papadakis it became increasingly clear that, like himself, his fellow members were less interested in organizing immediate resistance than in securing post-war political positions.

Even this ulterior activity could have been put to good purpose had the committee been prepared to co-operate with the other local leaders whose names I had been given in Cairo; but Papadakis was reluctant to enlist their assistance in case, I suppose, he should have to surrender to them a vestige of his self-arrogated authority or, worse still, in case they should recognize that authority for what it was: a purely notional attribute. So during the first week I spent in Vouvoure, while I vainly enquired after the potential strength of his organization, its dispositions and eventual requirements, Papadakis not very craftily avoided the issue by claiming that nothing could be done until he received official recognition from G.H.Q. Middle East. Since I was not prepared to commit myself on this point, nothing practical was done.

If the Colonel's attitude was frustrating to me, who could at least converse with him in Greek, it must have been infinitely more so for Turrell whose only means of communication was French, a language which he himself spoke little and which Papadakis understood even less. Turrell had turned up a few days after my arrival and was anxious to start blowing up ships in Souda harbour as quickly as possible. Papadakis, instead of offering advice and assistance, refused even to discuss the matter with what he called "this madman who wants to destroy us all." His main reason for suspecting Turrell's sanity was the latter's insistence on brewing "tea" made of orange peel (the only available ingredient) regularly once every hour; and he was also understandably nonplussed by his laborious, constantly reiterated complaint:

"Mais, mon colonel, vous ne m'avez pas mis dans le tableau!"

In these circumstances Vouvoure was an uncongenial spot. With the snow-laden wind whistling outside, we sat for what seemed weeks on end crouching distractedly over a small smoky stove with nothing to look forward to all day but two messes each of seed potatoes and a dozen mugs of orange-peel tea. The Colonel whiled away the time drafting lengthy memoranda in connection with his committee; Turrell nursed his grievances; and Ralph and I played endless games of rummy.

Our only reading matter, a volume of Shakespeare's sonnets, on which our double-transposition cypher was based, had to be shared between the three of us, and except for the routine wireless transmission to Cairo the boredom of our days was unrelieved. The arrival of a runner with a message from Monty Woodhouse was all too rare an occurrence to afford us even an illusion of activity, and this period of inaction, deliberately enforced by Papadakis, seemed likely to be prolonged indefinitely. I could see no immediate way out of the impasse we had reached.

But although the Colonel's scheme was questionable, the men whom he exploited in the hope of furthering it were without exception admirable. His young nephew, Levteri Kaltsounakis, did all the housework. This lad of eighteen had got into some trouble in his own village and had had to leave home. His uncle had subsequently offered him asylum, for which Levteri paid a high price—no less than the complete renunciation of his personal liberty and independence. Taking advantage of his youthful indiscretion, which had put the boy in his power, Papadakis used him as a serf and treated him like one, sending him, whatever the weather, on daily errands to Kallikrati, a village two or three miles away, where Mrs. Papadakis and the Colonel's two small children were then installed. But nothing could disturb Levteri's cheerful equanimity; his smiling peasant face and jovial Sphakian accents were the only features of our otherwise unbearably sullen household that I can recall with unqualified pleasure.

The other members of the Colonel's staff were less permanently established. His chief runner, Yianni Tzangarakis, came from a village several hours' march away—a silent sad-eyed man of about forty, tireless on the road and an expert at rolling cigarettes. His loyalty to the cause was no less unshakable for being based in effect on personal loyalty to Papadakis; for at that time he had no reason to suspect the intentions of the self-styled leader.

Nor, until he realized a few weeks later what those intentions would entail, did Petro Petrakas have the slightest suspicion. Petro had acted as best man at the Colonel's wedding—a sacred duty, according to the rites of the Orthodox Church, and one which binds the two men together in a brotherhood as strong as any relationship due to common parentage. It was natural, then, that he should support his relative. And Papadakis derived considerable profit from this support, for Petro was universally recognized as an influential local leader. The whole of Asi Gonia, the village nearest Vouvoure, was at his orders; and its inhabitants, acting as sentries and look-out men on the surrounding mountain peaks, were an invaluable adjunct to the security of our headquarters. But it was not Petro who told me of these priceless precautions. This unassuming heavily-built man with the spirit and complexion of a Viking spoke hardly at all and never about himself. It was his modesty, perhaps, that contributed more than any other characteristic to the feeling of quiet confidence he engendered.

Contact between Petro and Papadakis was maintained mostly through a young shepherd called George Psychoundakis, who was therefore a regular visitor to Vouvoure. When I first knew him George was just old enough to have grown a moustache. His flock of sheep had been stolen during the first weeks of the occupation, since when he had been penniless and without employment, but thanks to "Uncle Petro" (as Petrakas was known to every villager in Asi Gonia irrespective of his age), he had been recruited into the organization as messenger and guide and had already undertaken several important missions to Preveli and elsewhere.

Although he had not even completed his elementary education at the village school, George was the most naturally wise and instinctively knowledgeable Cretan I ever met. Not that he was a ponderously serious young man—on the contrary, his fellow villagers acknowledged his sense of humour by nick-naming him "Jester"— but he had a flair for exploiting the experience he gained at each fresh encounter with people from other districts whom, but for the war, he would probably never have met. And his innocent appearance—the youthful mane of black silky hair, the dark appealing eyes—was a never-failing passport through the German lines.

It was George, then, whom I chose as my guide when, in a more than usually violent fit of irritation at the Colonel's ambivalent attitude, I decided to call in person on Major Christo Tziphakis, the officer Jack Smith-Hughes had nominated as resistance leader of the county of Retimo, but whom Papadakis had refused to recognize as such and had therefore prevented me from meeting.

––––––––

It was a whole day's march to Prines, the village on the main Canea–Retimo road where Christo Tziphakis lived, but in George's company the time passed quickly and the hardships of the mountain track seemed negligible. I had not yet developed the habit of studying the countryside for purposes other than tactical, and so the only feature of the landscape that I still retain in mind with any clarity is the Moudros Gorge through which we passed, wading several times across the river running at the bottom of it, in order to reach the pleasantly flat country of the northern littoral. Prines was then a German garrison, and I felt childishly excited as I walked down

its streets brushing shoulders with members of the Wehrmacht—
the first Germans, apart from our deserter in Tsoutsouro, that I had
seen since the beginning of the war.

I met Tziphakis in the house of Mr. George Rombolas, a wealthy
provincial factory-owner with a large family of sons, all of whom
were engaged on practical espionage and organization. Within a
few minutes of meeting them I learnt more about German dispositions and Cretan potentials than I had learnt from Papadakis in as
many weeks.

Tziphakis was not a colourful character—his short rotund body
and circular face beaming behind rimless spectacles gave him the
appearance of a benign Teddy Bear—but he was obviously and hon-
estly in command of every village in the district assigned to him.
Nor was Rombolas particularly flamboyant—he dispensed his information gently between leisurely puffs at a bubbling narghile, his
only form of self-indulgence—but the information he gave was fac-
tual and accurate, and after a splendid dinner followed by a ten-
hour sleep in a comfortable bed—the first proper meal and rest I
had had for weeks—I left these two new comrades-in-arms, knowing that the county of Retimo at least was in friendly and capable hands.

CHAPTER FIVE

1942

As MONTY WOODHOUSE put it in a message we received from him towards the end of February, the whereabouts of our wireless station had become known "to everyone between Heaven and Charing Cross." Papadakis had also been warned through his private network of informants that a raid on our headquarters was imminent. For if the Germans did not previously realize that British agents were at work in Crete, they must at least have suspected our presence and activity now that their splendid new aerodrome at Tymbaki, on which we had been keeping a watchful eye, reporting back to Cairo each stage in its construction, had been successfully bombed by the R.A.F. on the very day the runways were completed.

We therefore thought it advisable to evacuate Vouvoure; and so as to offer less of a target for local chatterboxes and enemy marksmen, we also decided to reduce the personnel of the station. Everson had recently arrived to swell our numbers, for since the second transmitting set he had brought in with him had proved unserviceable, there had been no point in his staying with Monty, who had consequently sent him on to us. He was to remain with us and act as Ralph's assistant in whatever cave Papadakis had chosen to establish the new station.

Meanwhile, the rest of us were to move further afield. Turrell had for some time been trying to get in touch with General Mandakas, a Communist leader, who he hoped would be more open to suggestions of sabotage than Papadakis had been. But since Papadakis refused to co-operate with anyone outside his own committee, contact with the General had never been achieved. So Turrell now decided to approach him in person.

With a guide provided by the Colonel's organization he set off for Lakkoi, the General's village, which was two days' march away. During those two days he succeeded, despite his inability to converse in anything but sign language, in antagonizing his companion so unforgivably that the latter left him half a mile short of his destination. Whereupon Turrell, with typical foolhardy courage, walked into Lakkoi unknown, unannounced and unaccompanied, and also unable to explain either his presence or purpose since the only word of Greek he knew was the General's surname.

He complained to me afterwards that no one in the village had even tried to understand him—"not even when I spoke to them in French," he indignantly declared—but on the contrary everyone had looked on him with suspicion. Little wonder! By then too many people in these remote districts had been caught out by individual Germans posing as stray Englishmen or Australians, and had immediately paid with their lives for the indiscreet charity they had mistakenly shown towards them. Turrell had been lucky to escape unscathed, for it subsequently became the local practice to hand these bogus stragglers over to the nearest German garrison—ostensibly as an act of eager subservience, which not only enabled the captors to vent their feelings on the enemy with impunity but also obliged the authorities to thank them for doing so.

But Turrell did not count his blessings. He was so appalled by his experience that he did not stop to ask himself who was to blame. He simply abandoned his mission and forthwith set off on the return journey to Tsoutsouro with the intention of leaving Crete by the first available means of evacuation.

———————

I was more fortunate. For some time I had been thinking of establishing a base nearer Canea, the capital; for in these southern mountains I was isolated from current events and potential sources of information. Unlike the wireless station, for which security was naturally the first consideration, the intelligence network and guerrilla organization that I had in mind would depend on speed of communication, and this could only be achieved by a certain sacrifice of personal safety. I therefore planned to make my headquarters somewhere near the main north-coast road, where, although I should be more accessible to the Germans, they in turn would be more accessible to me.

A perfect spot was found for me by Andrea Polentas, the secretary of Papadakis's committee. Like many of the Colonel's subordinate associates, this young lawyer was a far better man than his self-styled superior, whom he easily surpassed in natural intelligence, conventional education and patriotic fervour. His most attractive quality was a sincerity so deep that it precluded any outward show of charm. His smooth, rather fleshy face was hardly ever creased in a smile, but the solemnity of his expression was not assumed: it reflected a genuine gravity of purpose which was immediately apparent in his conversation.

Although he loyally recognized the Colonel as the source of the committee's inspiration, it was quite clear to me that he alone, and not Papadakis, was responsible for its practical planning. His home was in a strategically important position—Vrysses, a small German garrison at the junction of the Retimo and Sphakia main roads—and he arranged for me to live in the neighbouring village of Vaphes, about a mile further inland.

The house that was to be my headquarters for several months stood at the top of a small rocky eminence overlooking the motor road which linked the main part of the village to Vrysses. This little hill was populated almost exclusively by two branches of one family, the Vandoulas, who had already sheltered so many of our stragglers and escaped prisoners that old Niko Vandoulas, who now offered to be my permanent host, had come to be universally known as the "British Consul."

He and his wife lived alone with an unmarried daughter called Elpida; their only son, Vangeli, a young lieutenant in the Greek army, having left Crete with Jack Smith-Hughes in order to be trained at our sabotage school in Haifa with a view to returning later as an expert on irregular warfare. His parents and sister obviously knew of his whereabouts and activities, and must have known that I too knew of them; but although they were simple peasant folk, their sense of security—a rare virtue in Crete where careless talk was the rule rather than the exception—was so deeply ingrained that for several weeks they never mentioned him even to me; nor did they give the slightest indication that they suspected my own activities, but behaved as though I was simply one of the many hundred Allied soldiers still at large in the island.

Uncle Niko's brother, Antoni, lived in the house next door. The two old men outwardly resembled each other in every feature except the shape of their thick white moustaches—individual growths which I often thought conditioned their owners' respective characters. For Uncle Niko's was a drooping crescent which seemed to epitomize his resigned, almost despondent outlook on life; while his brother's, curving upwards like twin scimitars above his lips, was a living symbol of his choleric impatience.

Uncle Antoni differed from his brother in one other respect: he had a large family of sons. One of these, Pericles, who acted as my guide and runner, soon became a close and trusted friend. He, based on my headquarters, and George Psychoundakis, operating from the direction of Asi Gonia, together maintained the line of communication between me and Ralph Stockbridge who was now installed with the Colonel and the wireless set in a cave above Kallikrati.

It was a happy geographical accident that isolated the Vandoulas neighbourhood from the centre of the village; for the people of Vaphes, although no doubt well-disposed to the Allied cause, were not all equally co-operative. Unlike the inhabitants of the smaller and more remote mountain hamlets, these plain-dwellers formed a less homogeneous community and were divided among themselves by differences of political opinion and personal interest. Also, I suppose, the proximity of an enemy garrison did not encourage them to parade their eagerness to help the Allied cause, even had that eagerness been universal. As it was, not everyone in Vaphes would have welcomed my presence had I appeared there as openly as I had elsewhere.

In the circumstances, therefore, I admired my individual hosts and protectors all the more. For whereas in Alones, Asi Gonia or the Amari, only a very brave man would have dared *not* to help a British agent, here in Vaphes it required rare courage and self-sacrifice for a relatively poor family like the Vandoulas to support me indefinitely in face of the anxious disapproval of some of the wealthier and more influential inhabitants. To avoid antagonizing the latter, I seldom ventured into the village except at night. I was therefore grateful for the isolated patch of ground round Uncle Niko's house, which allowed me more freedom of movement than if I had been forced, as I otherwise should have been, to keep indoors all day.

Since Uncle Niko was usually at work in his fields, my only regular companions were his wife and his daughter Elpida, a jovial industrious girl whose faith in England was as firm as her own well-developed muscles. Pericles would also visit me from time to time, bringing a fresh consignment of books—an exceptional boon in such surroundings, where the few who could read limited their reading to the perusal of half a dozen daily newspapers. But Pericles was an exception to his fellow-villagers. He had not only read but had enjoyed and could discuss the Greek translations of the French and Russian classics he lent me. These books of his and the packets of signals from Cairo which George Psychoundakis delivered once or twice a week, accompanied by a covering letter—often in brilliantly facetious verse—from Ralph, helped to while away the empty hours that remained after my daily conference with Polentas.

———

The plans that Polentas and I had been evolving together were two-fold: first, to appoint in each province of the two western counties for which I was responsible a local guerrilla leader who would notify me of his potential strength and eventual requirements; secondly—a more immediate task—to organize sources of information throughout the same area, who would report on German movements and dispositions, and to arrange for a system of runners and code-words between them and me. In the districts where Polentas and Papadakis had friends and acquaintances these plans were already in force; but in the far west, despite the Colonel's boast that his committee was represented throughout the island, we had no contacts at all.

I determined to remedy this deficiency myself not because I was unwilling to entrust the task to Polentas—on the contrary, he would have performed it inevitably more efficiently than a stranger could ever hope to do—but because I wanted to visit the west coast in any case to reconnoitre possible landing beaches there. But since I was the first British agent to have come even as far west as Vaphes, the limit of the area over which our organization then stretched could be reached in less than a day's march, so that when Pericles and I set out one gusty morning in early spring, we knew we should be sleeping that night in virtually unknown territory.

Our only introduction was to one of Polentas's acquaintances in a village a few hours away, who, we hoped, would put us in touch with another trustworthy contact further on, and so on until we had covered the whole area. It seemed a ponderously amateur way of setting about the task, but a start had to be made somewhere.

Arthur Reade with the author
shortly after the November landing

Arthur Reade (smoking pipe) and Niko Souris (holding rifle),
with villagers from Koustoyerako, just after
landing in November 1942

Paddy Leigh Fermor (left) with Alec Tarves

The author disguised as a Cretan shepherd

Meanwhile, for the benefit of anyone we passed on the road or with whom we chanced to spend the night, we resorted to the sub-terfuge—innocent enough, and to my mind slightly comic, though absolutely essential since two apparently purposeless strangers from another province would be objects of curiosity if not suspicion—of passing ourselves off as a couple of shepherds in quest of a stolen flock. And as a final precaution, so that my accent might not betray me, I pretended to be deaf, dumb and slightly demented. Pericles therefore did all the talking, prefacing his conversation with an apologetic remark, repeated so often that I came to hate the sound of the words:

"You must forgive my poor cousin: he hasn't been quite the same since the bombing of Canea."

Without wishing to flatter myself, I have to admit that posing as a deaf-mute imbecile did not come naturally to me. It was the hard-est performance I have ever undertaken, and I had to keep it up for over a fortnight. But when, on reaching the west coast, I tore off my clothes and plunged into the still icy water—my first bath since my arrival in Crete almost three months before—Pericles, who, like most of his compatriots, had never so much as dipped his big toe in the sea, simply asked me not to behave like a lunatic when it was no longer absolutely necessary.

As I started to dress again, he must have thought I was still play-ing my assumed role, for I was stupidly unable to identify the vermin which I noticed for the first time pullulating in my underclothes. Through him I learnt that these legions, which I ignorantly mistook for a peculiarly torpid breed of albino flea, were lice. I lost count after freeing two hundred of them from my vest alone.

But this was not the only knowledge I gained during our jour-ney. I discovered that throughout the west everyone was eager for an opportunity to strike back at the forces of occupation. The few local leaders to whom I admitted my mission were enthusiastic to co-operate and, though I swore them to secrecy, I knew they would infect their areas with their own enthusiasm by declaring that offi-cial contact had at last been made with the Allies—a statement so beneficial to public morale that it was worth whatever security lapse it inevitably entailed. That the ordinary peasants were prepared to help us practically as well as in theory, was immediately apparent from the number of Australians and New Zealanders who were still being housed and fed in those villages.

Each time I encountered these cheerful tattered men roaming about the countryside, usually singly or in pairs, I felt conscience-stricken; for I could offer them no immediate hope or assistance. Until arrangements could be made to take them off from one of the nearby beaches I had just reconnoitred, the only advice I could give them was to stay where they were. For now that enemy patrols were more active in the mountains thanks to the better weather and the improvement in German counter-espionage, it was impossible to assemble them, as we had done in the early stages of the occupation, and send them down in a body to the evacuation points on Monty's part of the coast.

Most of them, considering their condition, were in surprisingly high spirits, and would have taken any pity I might have shown them as an insult. But there was one whom I could not help regarding with feelings of the deepest compassion. I was told about him on the last day of our return march, as we were passing through the tiny hamlet of Kyriakosellia whose inhabitants had taken it in turns to look after him; for he did not live with one particular family but in a cave above the village. It was here that I first saw him—lying on a bed of twigs, from where he greeted us and apologized for not getting up and shaking hands. He then explained why he could not move: from the neck down he was completely paralysed.

Rheumatic fever had reduced him to this state. The villagers told me they remembered him as a giant of a man, immensely strong. Now he was incapable even of feeding himself. I did not know which to admire more—the fortitude with which he bore the discomfort and humiliation of total immobility, or the steadfast courage with which his protectors attended to his needs. Had he been even now willing to give himself up, he would have had a chance of recovering in a German military hospital. Had they even at this stage handed him over to the enemy, they might have incurred no penalty—for surely no one, not even a German, could have looked on active sympathy for him as a crime. But since he was unwilling to surrender, they had respected his wishes—even at the risk of being eventually shot for it.

Once more, and still more forcibly, I was reminded of my inability to help. I could offer him no more assistance than I had to the rest of his compatriots; all I could do was note down his name and particulars, as I had theirs, and include them in my next signal to Cairo.

The intelligence network and organization we had now introduced throughout the provinces would have been incomplete if it did not include the capital town as well; so shortly after returning to Vaphes I started making plans with Andrea Polentas for a visit to Canea. This venture was bound to involve a greater risk and entail more detailed arrangements than my recent jaunt with Pericles through the country, where the listless sentries in the sleepy provincial garrisons had scarcely bothered to notice, let alone question, us. But Andrea, with typical courage and care, at once prepared catering for the hazards we might possibly have to encounter.

He proposed that we travel by bus, since pedestrians entering the town were stopped and questioned individually and were often searched by the sentries manning the road-blocks, whereas a whole car-load of people usually got no more than a cursory glance after having their identity cards examined. The counterfeit card that I had was forged sufficiently ably to pass such a hasty inspection, and unless we were unlucky enough to be held up by a snap Gestapo or Sicherheitsdienst check, we should have little to fear—provided I kept my mouth shut in the hearing of our fellow-passengers. So on All Fools' Day—an appropriate coincidence, not a date intentionally chosen—we set off by the early morning bus from Vrysses.

My main impression during the journey was of physical relief and childish excitement at being able to travel at last on wheels after so many weeks of marching everywhere on foot—a sensation so pleasantly potent that my nerves were anaesthetized against the shock and apprehension I might otherwise have felt at the sight and proximity of enemy soldiers in every main road village.

This soporific indifference to my surroundings, induced less by confidence than resignation, continued when we reached Canea, where I was less conscious of the latent danger in the thousands of Germans pressing round us than of my delight at being once more in an urban atmosphere. For the capital, though shabby to the point of dereliction and no larger than the humblest English market-town, seemed a brilliant cosmopolitan metropolis compared to the dim and draughty villages I had been living in, all devoid of even the most elementary comfort.

While we were there I was entirely in Andrea's hands, a constant responsibility to him since he had to guide and discreetly direct every

movement I made in these strange houses and unknown streets where
one false step on my part would have sealed his fate as well as my
own. During the meals we took together in restaurants, and in the
hotel where we spent the night, I had to reduce my conversation to a
more or less incoherent murmur; only twice was I able to admit my
identity and speak out openly without the inhibitions forced upon me
by my disguise.

The first occasion was an interview with the Mayor of Canea,
Mr. Nicholas Skoulas, who had already been in touch with Andrea,
though he hardly expected to meet a British agent in his own office
in the Town Hall in the middle of the morning. As we walked in,
passing three German officers on their way out, he looked aghast;
but once the room was cleared, he began to appreciate this rather
crude joke that Andrea had played on him by arriving with me
unannounced.

Nicholas Skoulas had no military pretensions. He was a seden-
tary, burly townsman of over sixty, whose age, occupation and phy-
sique would have been disadvantages in a potential guerrilla leader.
But these drawbacks could be discounted since armed organization,
far from being necessary at this stage, was dangerously premature.
The immediate need was the formation of a strong nucleus of resistance, trained and prepared to come under paramilitary command
when the situation demanded drastic action, but not before; and in
this the Mayor would be of immense value, both as a figurehead and
rallying-point, for by virtue of his position and personal qualifica-
tions he wielded more influence than any other man in the western
half of the island.

We therefore proposed that he be nominated head of the movement in the county of Canea, on the same basis as Christo Tziphakis
was recognized in Retimo, and we further agreed to give this clandestine activity a name: The National Organization of Crete, which
sooner or later was bound to be known by its Greek initials, E.O.K.
This last proposal was more than a mere formality; for although I
was in general opposed to superfluous terminology of this kind, it
could here be put to valuable use in counteracting the underground
propaganda and recruiting drive of E.A.M., the Communist-con-
trolled National Liberation Front which had recently begun to operate in Crete as well as on the Greek mainland.

My second official interview that day was with Marko Spanouda-
kis, a dark good-looking army captain and engineer, who was then

employed as a civilian adviser on German defence works. He was therefore in a better position than most to give us information on enemy installations. He was also even more eager than most to do so. After having listened for so long to the shrill protestations of Papadakis, I was all the more impressed by Marko's thoughtful approach to the problem and by the sensible questions he put in a deep measured voice. He was one of the very few Cretans I met who readily confessed his ignorance of subjects he did not understand and was always prepared to ask for enlightenment.

This national inability to admit being in the wrong—a weakness I had noticed even in Polentas—had already caused me some inconvenience. A few weeks before, I had been informed that more than half the troops then stationed in Canea were parachutists, and further reinforcements were arriving almost daily. With some reservations—for though the numbers seemed improbable, I could not discount the possibility of another airborne invasion elsewhere in the Mediterranean—I had passed the information on to Cairo. Headquarters were understandably dubious of my signal and had asked me to check the source of my intelligence. So once again I tackled Polentas on the figures he had provided. He insisted they were correct. And now, as though to prove them so, he drew my attention to at least one in every two Germans we passed in the street, nudging me and whispering:

"You can see for yourself, I was right all the time."

But the men he pointed out were all wearing Luftwaffe insignia, which he had mistaken for the badge of the parachute corps. For this revelation alone I felt my visit to Canea had been worth while.

CHAPTER SIX

1942

Nₑws about Papadakis and the wireless station was brought to me on my return to Vaphes, not by my usual messenger, George Psychoundakis, but by Petro Petrakas, who had come all the way from Asi Gonia to tell me himself of the latest developments. The most urgent item, as far as he was concerned, was the outcome of a row he had recently had with the Colonel.

"He now tells me," Petro began, "that I'm no longer allowed to work with you English. Is that true?"

The poor fellow was desperately upset. But he had no need to be. Whatever had happened between him and Papadakis, I should instinctively have supported the cause of this man with the guileless blue eyes against any argument put forward by the querulous Colonel. I therefore assured him that as long as I was in Crete he would continue, if he wanted, to work with me, whatever Papadakis told him—an assurance which I repeated with even greater vehemence as soon as I heard what he had to say.

"I've been slow to see through that godbrother of mine," he explained, "but now my eyes have been opened. You remember when we were expecting the raid on Vouvoure? Well, it wasn't only Papadakis they were after—I was also on the German list. One of the Colonel's men, the police inspector of Myriokephala—he had been detailed to act as guide to the raiding-party—suggested that if I gave myself up and took all the blame, suspicion would be averted from Papadakis. What do you suppose the Colonel's reaction was to that? Believe it or not, he said it was a good idea—me, his own god-

48

brother, a married man with seven children! Of course, I refused. So we parted company, and here I am."

He then went on to describe the parachute drop that Ralph Stockbridge had recently organized on a small plateau close to the station. Supplies had been running short—now that the Colonel's house was evacuated, there was not even a seed potato to eat—so Ralph had asked for a consignment of flour and tinned food to be sent in by aeroplane, also footwear and clothing for our messengers and runners, and, as a special gift for the Colonel, a wireless receiving set, which could be worked on the transmitter's batteries, to enable him to listen-in to the B.B.C.

A parachute drop in an island as mountainous as Crete was always an arduous and hazardous business. Suitable sites were hard to find, and the slightest breeze would send the containers drifting off the dropping-zone on to inaccessible crags or into neighbouring valleys, where they would then be pillaged by the local inhabitants, or land, as once happened, right in the middle of a camp of Germans who, though surprised, were mercifully also too delighted—for they were on almost as short rations as ourselves—to pursue the matter any further.

On the night of this particular drop a strong wind had been blowing. Papadakis had arranged for some of his men to collect brushwood—a difficult task in that all but treeless limestone wilderness—for the bonfires which would be spaced out in a prearranged pattern and then set ablaze as a signal to the approaching aircraft. Other men were posted on the surrounding heights to give warning of any German activity in the neighbourhood and to try to spot the containers as they came floating down.

The aeroplane had turned up on time and launched its load, but only a small percentage of the expected stores fell within the dropping-zone. Sacks of flour were seen to burst like bombs on distant rocks; cataracts of boots and boot-soles poured over sheer precipices and into scarcely negotiable crevices; and in the morning, when the little that was retrieved had all been collected together, Papadakis discovered it amounted to no more than flour sufficient for a few loaves of bread, enough boot-soles to provide for half a dozen of his own sentries—and, miraculously intact and in working order, the wireless set he had asked for, its polished wood unscratched, its chromium fittings gleaming and unblemished. Everything else, he claimed, was lost.

This was not the only news that Ralph Stockbridge sent me. I now learnt for the first time that a new officer, Tom Dunbabin,[1] had been infiltrated into Crete to take the place of Monty Woodhouse, who had just been evacuated. Turrell had left at the same time. So had Everson, for there had been no point in his remaining now that Tom had brought with him a transmitting-set and operator of his own. And so had Guy Delaney who, after spending these last few months being happily entertained by his friends in the Amari, had sent word to Headquarters that since he had examined and repaired all the arms that were to be found in the length and breadth of Crete, his mission had been completed.

There was still further news. Ralph himself was due to be evacuated in a month's time, and had decided to take with him the Colonel's most frequently employed runner, Yianni Tzangarakis, who was in urgent need of a rest. Corresponding with Ralph, as I often did, in verse, I added to the letter I now sent back to him a postscript in the form of a rather fulsome sonnet, sentimentally dedicated *To Those Going Away From Those Staying Behind*, which began with the lines:

> Remember, now you're leaving us, to take
> The thread of Ariadne in your hand . . .

Ralph's reply to this, which I received a week or two later, was a sonnet of his own, brilliantly debunking mine, entitled *To Those Staying Behind From Those Going Away, or Stuff That Thread, Ariadne!*

This was the last communication I had from him.

Meanwhile I sent George off with a message for Tom suggesting that we meet in the near future somewhere halfway between his area and mine, and we finally decided on the Zourbakis house in Karines as the most convenient place for our conference.

Tom was already there when I arrived in the late May sunshine of the first really warm day that year. The weather had increased my enjoyment of the forty-eight hours' march from Vaphes, for despite the slight risk of running into a German patrol and the weariness of walking for mile after mile over solid rock and loose stones, I

---

1. Capt. (Later Lt.-Col.) T. J. Dunbabin, D.S.O., who after the war reoccupied his original position as a Fellow of All Souls College, Oxford.

was glad of this pretext for escaping for a few days from the confinement of Uncle Niko's house. I was also looking forward to talking to someone whose recent horizons had not been limited to these
Cretan mountains. This conference with Tom, then, was little more
than an excuse for the pleasure I anticipated in his company.

I was not disappointed. Although it was well before siesta time
when I reached the Zourbakis house, I found Tom stretched out
on a polythrone in the big room upstairs—not that he was tired; he
was simply following the system, which I now realized I had been
unconsciously practising myself, of sleeping whenever the chance
occurred, in the same way that the Cretans ate at every opportunity, whether they were hungry or not, as a safeguard against a possible lack of opportunity later. Lying there asleep in ragged breeches
and black fringed turban, with his overgrown corkscrew moustache
coiling and uncoiling in the breeze of his own breath, he looked like
a successful local sheep-thief at rest. It was only when he got to his
feet that his great height and muscular bulk betrayed his Anglo-
Saxon ancestry, even though he greeted me in faultless local dialect,
not knowing to begin with who I was.

Those few words of welcome in a foreign language told me more
about Tom than anything he ever said about himself in English,
for he was an almost unnaturally modest man considering his professional achievements and personal qualities. I thought I spoke
Greek reasonably well, simply because I spoke with an accent that
was not immediately noticeable, but Tom's demotic fluency—he
even managed to introduce a characteristic note of hysteria into his
high-pitched voice that was comically out of keeping with his serious demeanour and external appearance of rock-like solidity—made
me feel ashamed of my facile and incomplete command of the language. And I stopped priding myself on my knowledge of Crete and
the Cretans, when I realized he had already lived here months longer than I had, as an archaeologist before the war. I therefore had far
more to learn from him, although he had only recently arrived, than
he could learn from me during our so-called conference, and I willingly fell in with his suggestion that I accompany him as far as the
Amari and spend a few days there with him and the local leaders.

Early summer was the best time of year for a visit to this Lotus
Land. The cherry trees lining both sides of the valley had shed their
blossom and now carried the heavier burden of their fruit. In the
groves round Yerakari, where I stayed with the saintly schoolmaster

Alexander Kokonas, we spent all day drinking and feasting, while the village girls—bareheaded and in every other respect less conventional and inhibited than the young household drudges who were their counterparts in the dour and frowning County of Canea—sang traditional patriotic songs to the accompaniment of lyre, lute and Cretan mandolin. Every day seemed to be treated as a saint's day, an excuse for celebration which put the war and enemy occupation temporarily out of mind. This delightfully inappropriate Arcadian existence was what I most needed after the months of austerity I had spent, often in solitary confinement, living on bread made from carob beans, herbs, snails and raisins—an almost universal diet that winter in the poverty-stricken Vaphes area, though Uncle Niko occasionally managed to find an egg or two which, with typical generosity, he would reserve for me.

By the time I got back to his house from the Amari, summer had really set in, and with the good weather I decided to start sleeping out of doors, both as a security measure and to enable me to enjoy more sunlight. I therefore moved into the Vandoulas vineyard in the foothills a mile or so away from the village.

My presence there was kept as secret as possible, but even so it reached the ears of the owner of the land next door—a well-to-do retired army officer, whose fear and resentment at having me camping, as it were, on his doorstep led him to threaten Uncle Niko with exposure. Nevertheless, I promised myself that if ever I was cornered here by an enemy raiding-party, I would at once slip over the intervening wall so that, if I was caught or shot while trying to get away, it would not be on Uncle Niko's land but on the property of his cowardly neighbour, who would consequently find it hard to explain my presence there to the Germans. If he was subsequently executed himself, he would at least have the consolation of dying a patriot's death even though he had not deserved such an honour.

I felt comfortable and contented in the vineyard. All day long I could sit half-naked in the sun, reading or writing my reports and messages, or wander about the parched acre watching the progressive miracle of tight yellow clusters and sinuous tendrils turning into heavy bunches of blue-black grapes under their broad green canopy leaves protected by a sea-blue dust of copper sulphate. At night I would creep into the little stone shed in a corner of the dry-wall surrounds, where, with my legs from the knees down protruding from the tiny entrance, I was just able to stretch out on my bed of twigs and scarlet blankets. In the morning Pericles would bring me food for the day and a large calabash of wine since there was no water close at hand.

Uncle Niko also used to drop in from time to time, groaning as he climbed over the high wall, sighing less because of the effort than on account of the war situation. The news was bad that summer—the Allies were being pushed back in the Western Desert—and Uncle Niko regarded the set-back almost as a family disaster. These depressing reports from Africa affected his brother just as much, but Uncle Antoni, who likewise visited me occasionally, showed his feelings in a more violent manner. Leaping nimbly down from the piled-up stones and landing with scarcely a thud at my feet, he would at once start to storm and ask me what the devil we thought we were doing, as though I was in personal command of the whole of the Eighth Army. His passionate love of Great Britain made him so angry with her temporary lack of success on all fronts that I understood and even welcomed his illogical criticism of me, the only British representative he knew.

This criticism became downright abusive, however, when he found me in the vineyard one afternoon with Pericles and the two village school-mistresses.

"Women!" he screamed. "You're turning this place into a whore-house!"

He did not then know that these two girls were two of our most valuable agents. Since they lived in the northern half of the village which overlooked the main road and the road linking Vrysses, they were able to notice any German movement from that direction far sooner than the Vandoulas in their house tucked away on the southern hill. Pericles had therefore made arrangements for them to warn any member of his family on the approach of an enemy patrol. It was thanks to them that I managed to avoid what might have been an embarrassing encounter.

For, one afternoon a little later, some Germans suddenly arrived in Vaphes and, without staying more than a minute in the village, set off through the fields in the direction of my hut. No one in the Vandoulas neighbourhood would have learnt of their expedition, had not one of the school-teachers warned Elpida, who at once took a short cut straight up the hill, reaching me less than a hundred yards ahead of the leading enemy soldiers. Seeing those uniformed figures approaching through the olive groves, I could not tell if they were simply a group of men intent on spending a few hours off duty looting the nearest vineyards or whether they were part of an organized raid on my headquarters. I did not stop to ask but took to my heels—making sure that my line of withdrawal ran straight through the property of Uncle Niko's nervous neighbour.

One day shortly afterwards, George Psychoundakis's face appeared over the top of the vineyard wall. His grin of greeting was even wider than usual. "This time I've brought you some really good news," he said, and climbing over, handed me a heavy flat parcel. I opened it to find a set of large-scale maps covering the whole of my area, a bundle of drachmae-notes equivalent to several hundred pounds, and a packet of correspondence: my first tangible contact with the outside world, apart from our routine signals, since my arrival in Crete almost six months before. All this had been brought in on the boat which had evacuated Ralph Stockbridge.

Presumably, then, a replacement for him had been sent in at the same time, although George had not yet definitely said so—to live up to his nickname of "Jester," he liked to keep one guessing till the last moment. But he finally admitted that a new operator had indeed arrived—a Greek called Manoli—and was already installed with Papadakis in the mountains above Alones.

This was the best news of all. To be out of wireless communication, as I had been for the last fortnight and more, always produced a certain sense of panic and loss, as though God had ceased to exist. For the invisible and distant Headquarters which were responsible for my fate had assumed in my eyes a quasi-divine power. For practical reasons also it had been frustrating to be out of touch at this particular stage of the war. Crete was then being used as the largest German transit camp in the Mediterranean. Reports kept pouring in about the daily concentrations of aircraft at Maleme. Transport planes loaded with troops, fresh water and even cooked meals were leaving the airport every few minutes to reinforce the Afrika Korps advancing on Alexandria. I only had to signal their timetable and line of flight for them to be met by a R.A.F. fighter squadron over the sea; and I was subsequently delighted to learn that the re-estab-lishment of my wireless contact with Cairo coincided with a palpable increase in the number of Luftwaffe transports shot down in flames almost within sight of the Cretan coast.

But Manoli's arrival was not the end of the good news George had brought in from the east. Someone else had arrived with him, though it was only after half an hour's persistent banter and cross-questioning that George finally admitted who it was: "Uncle Niko's son, Vangeli. He's down in the village at this moment."

Ten minutes later George and I were also in Uncle Niko's house.

Vangeli Vandoulas, at first glance, was not an exceptionally impressive figure. He was barely five foot tall, and his features betrayed a disquieting mixture of peasant cunning and townee slickness. The candid brown eyes inherited from his parents were scarcely noticeable above an obtrusive pencil-thin moustache which accentuated his slightly rodent appearance. But what I first mistook for an expression of baleful shiftiness soon proved to be nothing more than the outward manifestation of quick wits coupled with a natural inclination towards caution and suspicion—a healthy sign, I felt, since this quality, rare in Crete but unmistakably evident in Vangeli, would in his case temper with a measure of security and forethought the dash and urge for action common to all Cretans.

What appealed to me most about him was the speed with which he had seen through Papadakis. On the way to Vaphes he had stopped with the Colonel in his mountain hide-out just long enough to introduce the new operator, but in that short time he had recognized him as an obstructive megalomaniac. "That man's dangerous," he now assured me. "I hadn't been with him more than five minutes before he started ranting about his committee and telling me I was under his orders. I told him I was under orders from Cairo, and be didn't like that at all. Frankly, I don't see how we're going to work in with his mad ideas . . ."

I told Vangeli what I had told Petro Petrakas in similar circumstances: that we had no need to worry about Papadakis so long as we had the whole-hearted co-operation of Polentas, who was the mainspring of the entire organization. Yet I should have taken this warning more seriously, for a few weeks later the crazy Colonel succeeded in antagonizing yet another valuable member of our network: our indispensable runner George Psychoundakis.

George appeared at the vineyard one morning looking utterly unlike his normal self—glum, anxious, angry and depressed. I thought at first that his mood might be due to the appalling war news—

Tobruk, our last outpost in the Western Desert, had just fallen and there now seemed nothing to stop the German tanks from rolling forward as far as the Suez Canal. To make matters worse, our contact with Cairo had broken down—for some days the home station had been mystifyingly silent—and since we could get no reply from G.H.Q., there was no means of knowing whether the current German boast, that Hitler had already ordered a banquet at the Mena House Hotel to celebrate the complete collapse of our Middle East command, was true or false.

But these disasters, though uppermost in George's mind, were understandably not as urgent for him as his more personal worries. "Papadakis has just thrown me out," he declared, "and told me never to come back."

He was as upset as poor Petro had been. But, again as with Petro, he had no need to be. For I had adopted him as my personal guide, and nothing that Papadakis could say or do would alter my friendship with this young shepherd or my faith in his loyalty and ability. I reassured him at once on that score, and asked him to tell me what had provoked this latest outburst from the Colonel.

"All I did," George explained, "was to ask him for a pair of soles so that I could mend my boots—as you see, they're completely worn out. I knew there was quite a lot left from that parachute drop—Levteri, the Colonel's nephew, told me he had helped to collect masses of the stuff, both food and clothing, and had stored it away with Mrs. Papadakis in Kallikrati, as the Colonel had told him to do. I saw some of the stuff there myself. Well, as soon as I told him I was almost barefoot, he started raving and insulted me as though I was a criminal. But I still don't see what I've done wrong."

George was understandably mystified. He did not know the Colonel had told me that nothing had remained from the drop apart from his own wireless set, a few pounds of flour and half a dozen boot soles, which he claimed to have distributed on the spot. I was more than mystified, I was furious. Without causing a premature breach with Papadakis, I could hardly accuse him of falsehood and dishonesty in front of his subordinates. But after what George had just told me, I was determined to create a breach with him which would be more diplomatic and permanent. I therefore set off at once for his hide-out to confront him, not with an accusation, but with a proposal which, even though it would put an end to his activities for good, I felt certain he would not refuse.

CHAPTER SEVEN

1942

My scheme for the disposal of Papadakis was prompted by Vangeli's recent return. This young lieutenant had at once shown immense drive and resource, enthusiastically falling in with the plans which Polentas and I had drawn up for the organization of Canea and suggesting useful innovations of his own. My only concern was that I had so far been unable to provide him with a specific appointment in which this energy of his could be properly canalized. Furthermore, in spite of the repeated requests of Polentas, who still remained loyal to Papadakis, Vangeli was steadfast in his refusal to co-operate with the Colonel. As far as I could see, the only way of settling these two problems at one stroke would be for him to assume the Colonel's position himself and take on the responsibility for the security and accommodation of our wireless station. This plan was feasible only if Papadakis could be persuaded to leave Crete forever.

As soon as I reached the Colonel's hide-out in the hills above Alones, I knew that little persuasion would be needed. Since it was the German practice to seize the relatives of a "wanted" man as hostages, the Colonel's family had taken the precaution of leaving their home in Kallikatri to join him in the mountains, and were now living as he was, like hunted refugees out in the open.

At first glance, their little encampment among the rocks might have been taken for the site of a happy holiday picnic. Couches of blanket-covered twigs were built into convenient crevices; cutlery and kitchen equipment were tidily stored by the side of an oven made of flat stones; and above these a sheet stretched on an eccentric assembly of four rough poles gave protection from the sun. Here, while the Colonel sat writing his interminable memoranda, his wife—a lovely woman half his age, with jet black hair and grey-green eyes—played with her children, a little girl of six and a boy a year or two younger. It was an idyllic scene but for the incongruous background of denuded scree and boulders lining both sides of the narrow shadeless cleft, from which they dared not move into the open for fear of betraying their whereabouts. For the Colonel had very properly enforced strict security measures, and the site of his camp still remained unknown to all except the runners from Alones, through whom he had kept in contact with me, and the shepherds from a nearby fold who brought him food and water every day.

Food was already beginning to be a problem. The shepherds could provide barely sufficient milk and cheese—a diet which they generously supplemented with meat by sacrificing once a week part of their tiny flock. If they continued to do this they would hardly have a sheep left by the end of the summer, when in any case they would be forced to leave these heights for winter pasture in the valleys. Long before that happened a solution would have to be found, and the best solution, as I explained to the Colonel, would be for him and his whole family to be evacuated as soon as possible.

He agreed without a murmur.

Since his wife and children could not be expected to undertake the long march to the beaches at the east end of the island, I devoted the next few days to a reconnaissance of the coast below us, and with the help of the local shepherds found the ideal spot for a clandestine departure—a small deep-water cove half-hidden in a cataract of rocks, almost invisible from the cliff above and at least half a mile from the nearest German coastguards. Twenty-four people or more could safely lie up here without attracting attention, provided they first took the precaution of approaching over the bare rocky littoral under cover of darkness. All that now remained was to wait until wireless contact with Cairo was re-established, when we would be able to notify our plans and position.

Luckily, we did not have long to wait. The silence from our home station must have been even more frustrating for Manoli, the operator, than for me. Every day he tuned in and for half an hour tapped out his call signal—all to no effect. It was as if Headquarters had simply packed up and left. We did not know at the time that that, exactly, was what had happened. It was only days later, when our signal was at last picked up, that we learnt that the Cretan office had indeed closed down while being transferred to Palestine during what came to be known later as The Great Flap—the evacuation of all clandestine services staff from Cairo in view of the German threat to Middle East G.H.Q.

For the first time since the much-vaunted advance of the Afrika Korps had begun, I received news that was reassuring. The enemy had been brought to a halt outside Alexandria; there was no danger of collapse in Egypt; our submarine base had been shifted to Beirut so that a clandestine sea line to Crete was still being maintained. It was therefore possible to evacuate Papadakis and his family during the next moonless period, about the middle of August.

I had decided to stay where I was until Papadakis left, but an unexpected visitor to our cliff-top encampment caused me to alter my plans. I was sitting talking to Manoli one morning when I saw, behind the shepherd who brought us our daily rations, a man whose face was familiar but whom I did not immediately recognize simply because I could not believe he was here in Crete. Yet from the nimble way he approached us over the jagged rocks I should have known, even at a distance, that this was Yianni Tzangarakis, the runner who had been evacuated with Ralph Stockbridge only a few weeks before. He came up to us now, his sad face momentarily relieved by a grin which was due as much to the pleasure he derived from our bewilderment as to the joy of seeing us again.

We had been out of touch with Cairo so long that Yianni's arrival was our first indication that in the meantime yet another landing had been made in Tom's area, and a third British officer with an operator and wireless set was now safely infiltrated. Yianni had volunteered to return to Crete as his guide. He had been sent to fetch me from the Colonel's hideout with a message from Tom asking me to come to Yerakari as soon as possible to meet this new colleague of ours. Characteristically Tom did not mention him by name, but Yianni told me it was an old friend of mine called, as far as I could make out, "Leverman." Even allowing for Yianni's outlandish pronunciation of English, I could not think of anyone I knew with a name remotely resembling these three syllables; so it was with deep

curiosity that I set out once again for the Amari to establish this unknown friend's identity.

The cherry season there was over, the orchards deserted. Now
that the grapes were ripening, the life of Yerakari centred round the
vineyards, and it was in a vintner's hut that I was introduced to
Yianni's "Mr. Leverman"—Paddy Leigh Fermor.[1]

To say that we were old friends was an exaggeration, though I had
already met him once, for five minutes in a Bloomsbury café years
before the war. Since then I had heard about him in various parts
of the world, for his career had in many ways run parallel to mine.
Like him, I had tramped across Europe to reach Greece; like him,
I had been almost penniless during that long arduous holiday—but
there the similarity between our travels ended, for whereas I was
often forced to sleep out of doors, in ditches, haystacks or on public
benches, Paddy's charm and resourcefulness had made him a welcome guest wherever he went and his itinerary was dotted with the
châteaux, palazzi and Schlösser in which he had been put up before
moving on to his next chance host.

This charm of his was still apparent beneath his shabby disguise.
Though we all wore patched breeches, tattered coats and down-at-
heel boots, on him these looked as frivolous as fancy dress. His fair
hair, eyebrows and moustache were dyed black, which only added
to his carnivalesque appearance, and his conversation was appropriately as gay and as witty as though we had just met each other, not
in a sordid little Cretan shack, but at some splendid ball in Paris or
London. His frivolity was a salutary contrast to Tom's natural gravity and to my own temper, which had lately grown progressively
shorter. It was also a deceptive quality, for although it enhanced
his patent imaginative powers, it concealed a mind as conscientious
and thorough as it was fanciful. His pre-war experience of Greece
combined with an instinctive philhellenism gave him an immediate grasp of local problems even though he had only just arrived in
Crete and had not yet been afforded an opportunity to apply his talents for administration which less than two years later he exploited
so brilliantly when kidnapping the German General Kreipe.

Meanwhile we discussed how best to allocate our duties in the two
halves of the island now that there were three of us to share them.

1. Capt. (later Major) P. M. Leigh Fermor, D.S.O., O.B.E., author of *The Travel-
ler's Tree, A Time to Keep Silence, The Violins of Saint Jacques*, etc.

Tom was then in no greater need of a second officer in his area than I was in mine, but since I was already overdue for leave—Jack Smith-Hughes had originally told me I would not be expected to remain in enemy-occupied territory longer than six months in succession—I welcomed the suggestion that I be evacuated at the same time as Papadakis and thus leave a temporary vacancy for Paddy to fill.

I returned at once to the station above Alones, notified Headquarters of the proposal, received a reply consenting to it, and a few days later Paddy joined me. He stayed with us only one night, for he was anxious to push on to Vaphes as soon as possible. But his short visit was memorable. He had brought with him a litre of raki—an unheard of luxury for the regular inhabitants of the Colonel's austere hide-out—and after we had all drunk each other's health, wishing success to the mission of the new arrival and fair winds for those about to depart, Paddy and I finished off what was left while the rest of the encampment slept.

We sat there alone on the bare stones talking of Cairo, Crete and the friends we had in common, while the moon shone down to provide us with sufficient light to fill and refill the empty cigarette tins which served us as glasses. As each shadow it cast slowly swept over us, we would shift our seat to the nearest rock that still glittered brightly under the midnight beams, until it too was first bisected, then completely submerged, by the incoming tide of darkness. By the time the raki was finished we had moved by successive stages almost the entire length of the shelving cleft, and as I fell asleep on my narrow ledge of twigs I could not be sure whether it was the strong spirit, Paddy's company or the prospect of Egyptian flesh-pots that was responsible for the happiest night I had so far spent in Crete.

The week or so that remained between Paddy's departure for Vaphes and the day appointed for our evacuation seemed to pass as slowly as a decade. The long hours of daylight went by with the monotonous regularity of the sun which, burning overhead and reflected from the rocks on every side, transformed our hide-out into a radiant oven. Long after that dazzling light was extinguished by nightfall, the surrounding stone retained a heat which imperceptibly diminished during the short hours of darkness, only to be revived again by the dawn. The twenty-four-hour period that followed, punctuated by two identically meagre meals, would differ from its predecessor only in the time of our routine wireless schedule which, for security reasons, took place at a different hour every day.

Manoli, the operator, being the only one among us to have even these few minutes of distracting occupation, accordingly supported more cheerfully than we did this burden of successive empty days which stifled us, mind and body, and weighed us down as heavily as an ill-advised prolonged siesta. In the circumstances his company was all the more refreshing. This heavily built, rather hairy young man with dark fanatic eyes which, when they flashed, gave his face the expression of a professional revolutionary, had been a schoolmaster in the Dodecanese before the war. Though only a private soldier now, he was superior in intellect and mundane ambition to most of the Greek officers I had met; but even had he not been I should have found him more rewarding to be with than the Colonel, whose affection for me was less ardent than ever now that he saw that George Psychoundakis was still in my service and likely to remain so. Papadakis made no comment on this point, however, and I in my turn was careful not to refer to what George had told me, so that usually an uneasy silence reigned between us, as though there was no other topic of conversation than this one subject which we had both instinctively declared taboo.

Yet there was something which could be discussed without embarrassment or inhibition, and that was the detailed plan for our departure which we drew up in accordance with the information received from Headquarters. The number of passengers travelling with us would have to be limited since it was a submarine, not a surface craft, that was due to take us off; and since Jack Smith-Hughes was also going to be on board, much of the cramped quarters would already be occupied by his excessive bulk.

Apart from the Papadakis family and myself; there were a few others who for various reasons had to leave Crete. One of these was Niko Lambathakis, a young lieutenant who had done some useful work for us in Canea but whose activities had since reached the ears of the Germans and had consequently forced him to go into hiding. Another was George Alevizakis, the youngest son of the village priest of Alones, an exceptionally intelligent boy whom I wanted to have trained as a wireless operator. At the last moment these numbers were further increased by the sudden appearance of Jack Smith-Hughes's former guide, Pavlo Bernardakis, who had hitherto been known to me only by name since he, too, had long ago fallen out with the Colonel and had therefore until then steered clear of our hide-out. And the passenger-list was finally completed with the arrival of Alec Tarves,[2] Tom's operator, who had left his station in the hands of the colleague who had landed in Crete with Paddy, and had come now to my area to instruct Manoli in the use of the new "one-time pad" system of coding which was to replace the "double transposition" cypher we were still using although it was known to have been "broken" by the Germans in the early stages of the war.

Our encampment, then, was crowded out; for besides these additional temporary members who joined us on the morning of evacuation day, Andrea Polentas and Vangeli Vandoulas had also come to see us off. Moving this little company down to the beach in the dark would in any case have presented a problem, but the difficulties of the manoeuvre were doubled by half a dozen of the Colonel's friends and relations who unexpectedly turned up in the evening, just as we were about to set off. Without consulting me Papadakis had invited them to accompany us, but had purposely told them to remain out of sight until the last moment, for fear that I should refuse to include them on the passenger-list. Not one of them had any reason for leaving Crete—they had not been in our employment, nor were they in any danger on their own account—but for security reasons I was reluctantly forced to let them come with us now that the Colonel had betrayed to them the date of our departure and the location of the beach.

Papadakis and I had already exchanged angry words over the arrangements I had made. Commodities of every kind were in such short supply in Crete that it was then the normal practice for those being evacuated to go on board barefoot and almost naked, abandoning their boots and suits to their comrades staying behind, for whom any form of footwear and clothing in whatever state of disrepair and dereliction was still of some value. The Colonel, however, who prided himself on his patriotism, had provisionally arranged to take with him not only all his clothes but also the wireless set which he had conveniently acquired in the recent parachute drop. I reminded him that there were people in Crete who were risking their lives for the rare opportunity of listening in to the B.B.C., and

2. Sergeant Alexander Tarves, M.M., whom, much to my regret and loss, I have not heard of since the end of the war.

I quietly threatened to cancel the whole evacuation unless he left
his set behind. He was finally shamed into agreement and had indeed abandoned his precious toy—not, however, for others to use in
his absence but, as I heard long afterwards, with instructions that
it should be safely buried in some hole in the mountains until his
eventual return.

Not unnaturally, then, I was angrier than ever with the breach
of faith he had committed in summoning his friends and relations,
and I rashly repeated my threat that if he refused to abide by the
arrangements I had made, I in my turn would refuse to give the
required signals out to sea. Knowing him as I did, I had intentionally omitted to tell him what those signals were to be.

Our descent to the beach took longer than I had anticipated, for
I had not allowed for the complete blackness of the night or for
the delays caused by carrying the Colonel's two children over the
more dangerous cliff-side drops. But mercifully without mishap we
reached the water's edge a little before midnight and I started flashing the message in Morse which was to guide the submarine in to
shore. It was so dark that even the horizon was invisible, and I soon
gave up trying to guess at which point in the deep black area ahead
the shape of the vessel was likely to loom into view. Staring out to
sea I lost all sense of the passage of time, until I realized that the
dividing line between sky and water had gradually become discernible, not because my eyes had got used to the dark but because the
light had improved—dawn was about to break. There was therefore
no chance of the submarine appearing until night fell once again.

It was always disappointing when an evacuation boat, as frequently happened, failed to turn up on the night it was expected; but
this was no cause for immediate alarm since we usually allowed for
a margin of at least three days in case of unavoidable postponements
or last-minute changes of plan at the vessel's port of departure. Papadakis knew this as well as I did, so that I divined an ulterior meaning in his ill-natured enquiry:

"Are you quite certain you gave the right signals?"

I assured him there was no reason for him to believe otherwise,
but I noticed on the following evening, when I started flashing out
to sea again, that two of the Colonel's friends had been posted a few

feet behind me, each with a tommy-gun trained on the small of my back. That night seemed to pass more uncomfortably slowly than its predecessor, and when a second dawn broke still with no sign of the submarine, I was careful not to fall asleep as I had done the day before.

My precaution proved to be justified, for later that morning Vangeli came to join me in the most secluded spot I could find: a crevice in the rocks accessible from one direction only.

"I've just been talking to the Colonel," he said. "The man's absolutely out of his mind. He's just promised to see I get promoted—on condition I shoot you dead!"

So the presence of those two armed men behind me during the whole of the previous night was not, after all, accidental, as I had been trying to persuade myself. Papadakis evidently had the unshakable idea that I was paying him back for his own betrayal by treacherously giving false signals. Since he did not know the right ones, however, there seemed little point in his scheme for getting rid of me, apart from some misguided notion of revenge, but Vangeli assured me that in so far as a madman could be said to be serious, Papadakis was in deadly earnest. No doubt this final disappointment over the submarine, added to the rigours and anxieties he had recently undergone in the mountains, had completely unhinged his mind which in any case had never, since I at least had known him, appeared to be in a perfect state of balance. Even Polentas's faith in his chief's sanity was now beginning to waver.

"We'll just have to sit quiet and watch our step," Vangeli went on. "In his present condition it's no use trying to make him see reason, and if we tackle him or make any drastic move ourselves, there'll be trouble from those two henchmen of his. They'd probably start shooting, and then the whole lot of us would be in for it. I don't like the look of them at all. Still, they can't do much to us at the moment. But I'll keep them covered with my revolver as soon as it gets dark—and for God's sake be on your guard yourself all the time you're signalling. Have eyes in the back of your head—and let's hope the submarine turns up all right tonight."

That day appeared to me the longest I had ever spent. It was a hardship not to be able to sleep in safety, for there was no other means of passing the time. Everyone's movements were restricted since we were obliged to keep under what cover the rocks and boulders afforded, and in addition to the boredom and immobility we had to contend with hunger and thirst as well, since the food and water we had brought with us were now both exhausted. Pavlo Bernardakis succeeded in stripping a wild fig tree which he found growing miraculously from the bare cliff-side, but the little fruit it yielded, when distributed among so many of us, seemed to stimulate rather than assuage our appetite and sharpened our longing for a drink.

The man I was most sorry for, and at the same time most admired, was Alec Tarves. The rest of us could at least find some relaxation by talking to each other. Alec, not knowing a word of Greek, sat silent and aloof—and completely unperturbed—as he gazed out to sea from dawn till dusk without shifting his position except to turn to me from time to time with a cheerful grin and say in a Perthshire accent so thick that the words were at first almost unintelligible:

"I still see no ships!"

I was beginning to despair of ever seeing any myself—even when night fell and, torch in hand, I resumed my position at the water's edge. Behind me, the two men with the tommy-guns silently took up theirs, and I noticed that Vangeli sat facing them a few feet away with his pistol unobtrusively cradled in his lap. Then once again I started flashing Morse at regular intervals into the curtain of darkness in front of us.

By now I had grown so accustomed to the emptiness stretching ahead that I hardly expected anything would ever emerge from it. I therefore thought my eyes were playing me false when, after hours of anxious peering into the void, I noticed the presence of a small rowing-boat, so close that I could have almost stepped into it from where I stood; and the voice of one of the two men manning it, though raised scarcely above a whisper, was perfectly audible as he said:

"Quick! Jump in!"

But there was no sign of a vessel out to sea. Furthermore the man who had addressed me (but who was almost invisible in the dark) had spoken in Greek, while I was expecting to hear, if I expected anything at all, the unmistakable accents of a British sailor. In my confusion at this abrupt turn of events I instinctively suspected a trap which I vaguely, and in the circumstances perhaps not unreasonably, connected in my mind with the raving machinations of the

CHAPTER SEVEN: 1942   67

Colonel. But in this I was doing Papadakis an injustice. The man in the boat, seeing me hesitate, impatiently explained:

"It's all right, I tell you. Quick, get in! It's the *Papanicholis*, but there's an English army officer on board. We've only just picked up your signal."

Headquarters had not told me to expect a Greek submarine, and I could still see no submarine of any nationality at all; so even the reference to the Englishman on board did not completely allay my suspicions. To make sure, I asked what he looked like.

"Rather fat and untidy," was the answer.

Reassured by such accurate information, I ordered the embarkation to begin at once, and in small groups we were ferried one after the other out to the vessel, which was so hemmed in by the dark that as I approached it I could hear Jack's ribald greeting from the bridge at least a minute before the bridge itself loomed into sight.

In half an hour we were all on board, and exactly a week later we stepped ashore in Beirut harbour.

CHAPTER EIGHT

1942

By this time our Headquarters, after its recent transfer to Jerusalem during the Great Flap caused by the German midsummer advance, had returned once again to Cairo; but the offices, though reinstalled as before in the block of flats called Rustom Building, were to me completely unrecognizable. The handful of experts who had welcomed me when I first joined the organization were now heavily outnumbered by a whole regiment of strangers, most of whom had recently arrived from England. The Colonel in charge had been replaced by a civilian director with authority equivalent to that of a general; and in close support was a formidable array of officers wearing red tabs, each responsible for departments, sections and sub-sections which previously had never existed. In this incessant gale of professional activity the building seemed to rock like a top-heavy transatlantic liner, and I regretted the milder climate of enthusiastic amateurism in which I had originally known it.

Through this confusing labyrinth, studded at every turn with code-names and cabalistic signs, Jack skillfully steered me, so that in a week or two I was able to find my way about the separate administrative and operational offices scattered throughout the building like the islands of a tropical archipelago. So much for the new constitution of our unit, to which Jack introduced me. For its internal politics—the departmental bickering, sectional jealousies and personal strife—my unofficial guide was Arthur Reade.[1]

Arthur was probably better equipped than anyone else in the organization to provide an objective unbiased picture of its personalities and their functions. As head of a top-secret section responsible for the accommodation, employment and welfare of the agents and refugees from the various countries in which we were then operating, he was concerned less with the routine and mechanics of the firm than with its human aspect.

Though junior in rank he was equal in years to the senior staff officer, a brigadier, but their age was the only thing they had in common. For the Brigadier, a globe-shaped choleric little militarist, did his best to conceal his natural and professional shortcomings by a show of blood-thirsty activity and total disregard for the agents in the field, whom he treated like so many expendable commodities. Arthur, on the other hand, whose duties and personal inclinations involved him in close companionship with the operational personnel, set out to prove that efficiency and decent behaviour were not necessarily incompatible.

Had he shared the Brigadier's mentality, he too, I suppose, might have allowed his physical eccentricity to affect his moral outlook and social conduct—for he was almost freakishly tall, with bright red hair falling over his forehead like a schoolboy's and a fulminatingly virile moustache which only stressed his excessively gentle expression. This sweetness of disposition immediately noticeable in his features and in every action of his daily life was to a certain extent mitigated by a razor-sharp critical faculty which made him fiercely opposed to any form of official negligence, malice or plain stupidity. In Rustom Building there was much for him to criticize.

The Brigadier's senior assistant was a middle-aged colonel with lemon-coloured hair and eyebrows so fair as to be well-nigh invisible. He looked like a native of Estonia and had, in fact, spent much of his life in that country. He was an expert on the Baltic States and so, in view of officialdom's geographical ignorance and passion for inappropriate postings, it was scarcely surprising that he should have been put in charge of the Balkan department. Nor was it, in con-

---

1. Capt. (later Major) A. E. E. Reade; a barrister who later took part in prosecuting war criminals at Nuremberg; now living in Cyprus.

sequence, surprising that our Greek and Jugolav sections suffered
from muddled policy and lack of direction. One frustrated agent
accurately summed up the situation in these words, designed to be
sung—but sung, of course, in secret—to the strains of a popular
dance tune:

> We've the Partisan itch,
> But there's Mihailovic,
> And the Foreign Office doesn't seem to know which is which . . .
> We'd better close down,
> We're the talk of the town,
> For nobody's using us now.

> We've got lots of mugs,
> Whom we've trained as thugs,
> But now they're at the mercy of the Greeks and the Jugs . . .

The Colonel did not hold his unsuitable post for long. One morning, quite unexpectedly, he died at his desk. The news spread quickly
through the building, and for the rest of the day the Brigadier was
pestered on the internal telephone system by a succession of anonymous messages of sardonic congratulation. For it was known that
with his usual interest in sudden death—other people's, not his
own—he had been longing to determine the efficacy, by practical
experiment, of a certain poison destined for operational use in enemy-occupied territory.

Such malignant insubordination could not, of course, be overlooked. The Brigadier at once undertook to discover the source of
the libelous calls and ordered the Security Officer to unearth at least
one culprit. But an investigation on these lines was not to the taste,
even had it been in the power, of the elderly major who was affec-
tionately known to all of us as "Slyboots." After several days devoted
to padding up and down corridors, listening at keyholes and div-
ing in and out of offices, he gave up the unrewarding search and,
reduced by now almost to tears, sorrowfully confessed:

"I'm not a security officer at all; I'm just a very tired old man."

My initiation into these domestic scandals was gradual, for after
writing my report and being debriefed, I had little to do with Head-

quarters for several weeks. Arthur's was the only office that I visited regularly—usually about six in the evening, when whisky and soda was automatically produced from the canteen next door. Each time I tried to pay for the drink, the corporal who brought it in refused my money with the mysterious explanation:

"It's all right, sir. This comes out of our lemonade fund!"

Arthur's personal staff had clearly been trained to attain his own high standards of hospitality. The other offices I found less congenial, and since I was supposed to be on leave I steered clear of them. All the same, I was given the chance of devoting some of my leisure to outside work directly connected with Crete.

The report I had written on my return included some rash and scathing comments on the navigating ability of the aircrews responsible for parachuting the stores we had ordered; each time, I claimed, they had either failed to find the dropping-zone or else had launched the containers from such a height that they drifted away and were lost. Since supplies were shortly going to be dropped in to Paddy on a plateau high up in the White Mountains, I was invited to join the sortie as an unofficial member of the aircraft appointed for the task, so that I might judge for myself the technical difficulties of the enterprise.

At dusk, then, on a stifling evening of early September, I found myself in the front gun-turret of a Wellington bomber about to take off from a desert airfield. Sweating under a helmet wired in to the inter-communication system and automatic oxygen supply, I was at first grateful for the draught which blew in through the gap left in the nose of the machine by the absence of the front gun which had been dismantled for this particular mission. But as we gained height I started shivering in my thin bush-shirt, and by the time we were over the Cretan coast I was so miserable with the cold and with the whiffs coming through my oxygen mask over which I had no control that I was incapable of guiding the navigator, as I had hoped to do, straight to the dropping-zone which I had imagined I should recognize at once.

In the blackness below us I could distinguish the northern coast, but was unable to tell which part of it we were approaching until some gun-flashes appeared from a point directly under the starboard wing, which I identified as the battery on the ridge behind Souda Bay. From then on I was too preoccupied with the shells bursting round us to give much thought to our target. Balls of fire kept reaching up to us, surprisingly slowly, but to my mind horribly close, and listening to the rear-gunner over the intercom, I was torn between relief at the unconcerned tone of his voice and fright at the words of his report: "Flak getting nearer and nearer . . ."

To get out of range of the guns we swooped low beyond the nearest protective ridge, and to me it seemed the surrounding peaks now towered above us. But even at this height I could not distinguish between the separate blazes—shepherd's fires, no doubt—that dotted each slope. It was the captain of the aircraft who picked out on the horizon a glare brighter than the others. We steered towards it, and in less than a minute I could clearly see the bonfires arranged in the pattern which we had been notified to expect.

During our preliminary run-in over these we dropped still lower, until each separate figure below could be seen moving and gesticulating in the light of the blazing brushwood. Maintaining this precarious height, we turned, and flying in again with bomb doors open, launched the containers.

From my position in the aircraft I could not follow the parachutes' descent, but I felt that if they had not all landed well within the dropping-zone, it would not have been for want of care. The crew had taken what seemed to me appalling risks to ensure their safe arrival, and as we turned for home I promised myself never again to criticize any of them or their colleagues.

A few days after this revealing flight I was sent on a two-weeks' recruiting-drive to Cyprus to see if I could find other Greek-speaking officers who were prepared to join our section. This proved likely to be nothing more than a pleasant holiday, for scarcely anyone, least of all myself, expected to encounter suitable volunteers at such short notice. I therefore looked forward to spending a fruitless and enjoyable fortnight motoring about the island from unit to unit.

My interviews, however, unearthed two candidates who impressed me as soon as I saw them. But although I forwarded their names to Headquarters with the strongest possible recommendation, they were never engaged. Had they been Lithuanian or Latvian scholars, perhaps, they might have been posted forthwith as assistants to our Colonel in charge of the Greeks and Jugoslavs. Since, in spite of this disappointment, they still wished to join the firm, I advised them they were more likely to be taken on as Greek-speakers if they applied for a vacancy in our Norwegian country section. After all, it was not for them to question the methods of the British Intelligence

Service which, by its baffling irrationality, had so far succeeded in outwitting the enemy at every step.

From Cyprus I flew over to Beirut, where I had arranged to meet Arthur for a week's leave, and it was then that I heard for the first time the plans that had been made for my return to Crete in the very near future.

For reasons which, to me at least, still remain unexplained, Arthur had been ordered to close clown the section he ran in Cairo within one month. He was therefore likely to find himself unemployed, for in view of his relations with the Brigadier he could hardly expect another post in our Headquarters and so would probably be returned to the Intelligence Corps Base Depot. He had consequently applied for service in enemy-occupied territory, volunteering, though scarcely hoping for permission, to be infiltrated into Crete—on the strength that he had visited the island twenty years before and still remembered a little modem Greek.

With an alacrity that should have aroused our suspicions at once, the Brigadier had told him that, provided I was willing, he could return to Crete with me. But we were both so delighted with the prospect of working together in the field that we were blind to any possible ulterior motive behind the ready acquiescence, and joyfully returned to Cairo to prepare for our expedition.

It was not until I embarked on these preparations that I realized what an agent had to suffer at the hands of the staff officers of the new S.O.E. regime. Holding the highest rank under the Director was another civilian, the Director of Finance and Administration, known locally as the D.F.A. His main function, it seemed to me, was to frustrate all attempts to mount an operation in accordance with the wishes of the man who was to undertake it. Since I had already spent several months in occupied territory, I was well aware of my requirements and felt justified in demanding them. But the one man who could not possibly have known them, the D.F.A., was the very man who, by virtue of his senior position, was entitled to deny them to me.

I was anxious to avoid the setbacks that had been caused in my previous mission by lack of proper stores and funds. Although no one in Crete was on an official pay-roll, money was still needed to feed and clothe whole families who had abandoned their normal

livelihood to work for us; messengers' shoe-leather and bus-fares also
had to be paid for; and a reserve of funds was always needed to meet
any occasion that occurred for judicious bribery and corruption. For
these purposes devalued drachmae were virtually valueless, and I
had asked instead for a supply of Egyptian pound notes, American
dollars and English sovereigns, the only really welcome currencies at
that stage of the war. I encountered such official opposition to these
demands that I was tempted to supplement the series of scurrilous
songs still current in Rustom Building with a composition of my
own, which began:

> Remember the Director and the D.F.A.,
> The only two in Rustom who have any say,
> These are the men who make this fighting business pay,
> Remember them . . .

However, there was no need to worry about the stores we planned
to take in with us, for Arthur had undertaken to equip the expedition himself. Now that his section was being forcibly closed down
and its funds could no longer be devoted to agents' welfare, he very
properly decided that what remained should be spent on the gear
of the last two agents for whom he was responsible—ourselves. In
addition, then, to the pistol and torch which had been the only
equipment I carried on my first landing earlier that year, I took my
pick from a wonderful assortment of knives, coshes, brandy-flasks,
binoculars, cameras, compasses and Borgia-like poison-rings; and
instead of a Soho waiter's suit, I had some splendid breeches and
boots made by an *émigré* Cretan craftsman.

In part of a sonnet sequence he subsequently wrote, Arthur described those responsible for our mission in the following lines:

> The Brigadier loved blood, the Colonel cared
> For rank, red tabs, his liquor and his chair
> Of idle office where in high arrear
> Mounted unread reports from those who dared
> Attempt the projects their superiors aired.
> For victory? No; planned, I rather fear,
> To earn promotion for the Brigadier,
> With his complaisant Colonel smugly paired
> In Cairo where intrigue is the road to glory;
> To lick the lolling buttocks of the great,

Snub all initiative, pass down the blame
For their own faults (the old, the dirty story).
Such were the chiefs we left to undertake
A mission which might magnify their fame.

These bitter lines were later proved to be justified, and even before leaving Cairo I was given some indication of the Brigadier's intentions. I had imagined that Arthur's duties in Crete would be limited to intelligence work, and I looked forward to his assistance in collecting and collating the information of our local agents. But during our final briefing I heard, for the first time, the task for which he had been selected.

Reports had been received that the Germans were preparing to refloat the battleship *York*, then lying damaged in Souda harbour. If these attempts were successful the vessel would become the first capital ship in the history of the British Navy to be manned by an enemy crew. Rather than allow such an indignity, the authorities had decided that *H.M.S. York* should be put permanently out of commission, and plans for sabotaging her were entrusted to S.O.E.

A subversive action of this magnitude would require a team of highly trained experts, and these would need to be specially favoured by fortune to accomplish such a hazardous mission. Yet it was Arthur, a forty year-old staff officer, a poor swimmer and ignorant of the technicalities of marine sabotage, who was now appointed for the task.

The Brigadier must have known that the suicidal enterprise was doomed in advance to failure, so I could only conclude that he was less interested in destroying a top-priority target than in getting rid of a junior officer with whom he was on bad terms. But I was not particularly anxious for Arthur's sake. Once we were in the field, I could easily notify Headquarters that the task could not possibly be tackled by an untrained amateur but should be undertaken either by a commando company or a squadron of bombers, thus releasing Arthur for the intelligence duties on which I originally hoped he would be engaged. My only concern, then, was to get him into Crete as soon as possible, even if it meant humouring the Brigadier's whims to the extent of first allowing ourselves to be posted to our Haifa school to undergo a week's emergency course in marine sabotage.

That autumn in Palestine was fortunately warm and sunny, and we spent the last days of October swimming every day in Haifa harbour weighed down with dummy explosives which we practised fixing on to the hulks lying half-submerged in the water. These bowler-hat-shaped limpets, filled with plastic and studded with magnets, were so heavy that even with one strapped to our chest neither Arthur nor I could struggle more than fifty yards without beginning to sink. To sabotage *H.M.S. York*, we should have to swim at least a mile and attach a minimum of half a dozen of these charges. We could therefore hardly be expected to take our daily exercise seriously, though we were both grateful for this period of training. It was the last seaside holiday we were to have for years, so we made the best of it before moving up to Beirut where we were due to embark on a submarine for Crete.

There we were joined by the other members of our team: Alec Tarves, who was coming in again as my wireless operator; and Niko Souris, who had been evacuated for a well-earned rest a few months before and had since been through the Haifa course so as to return fully trained to continue his useful work in Tom Dunbabin's area.

H.M.S. Medway, the original submarine depot ship, had been sunk after leaving Alexandria during the Great Flap, since when our underwater craft had been operating from a shore installation on the hills above Beirut. Here Arthur and I called almost every day to discover what arrangements had been made for our departure, which was being unaccountably postponed. The delay was no hardship, however, since we were living comfortably in a luxury hotel at the firm's expense—or so we thought.

It was customary for S.O.E. Headquarters to defray the costs of all agents waiting to embark on an operation, and Arthur and I rather foolishly vowed we would get our money's worth from the D.F.A. We therefore raised our standard of living to exaggerated heights, and our bill was correspondingly large. Made out, as it was, in Syrian pounds, it looked so astronomical that we were requested, quite reasonably, to pay half of it out of our own pocket. Our only means of providing such a vast sum was to allow our pay to be docketed for the next three months, so we were both relieved when we sailed off at last, towards the end of November, again in the *Papanicholis*.

CHAPTER NINE

1942

ONCE AGAIN we were to land "blind" without a reception committee, this time on a beach in the south-west corner of the island, an area which had not yet been reconnoitred. This decision was taken simply to suit the leader of an I.S.L.D. mission whose members had embarked with us and were likewise due to be infiltrated into Crete. He was a young Greek army officer called Stelio Papaderos, whose home village lay in the foothills a few miles behind the selected landing-spot. His colleagues were another Cretan, who was to act as his civilian assistant, and an English-speaking Cypriot, who had been a wireless operator in the Merchant Navy.

But since this team belonged to our "rival" organization, which was concerned exclusively with intelligence and had nothing to do with subversive activity, I was quite seriously advised, in the interests of security, not to let my own team fraternize with them during the journey—even though we were to travel together cheek-by-jowl for over a week in the close confinement of a submarine, and despite the fact that Stelio, being the only member of our joint expedition to be acquainted with the coast, would naturally be acting as guide to both teams during the landing!

A week after embarking we surfaced in midnight weather scarcely less appalling than the full gale that had blown during my first landing at the beginning of the year. Rain in diagonal streaks curtained off the dark crenellations of the mountains I had expected to make out on our northern horizon, so that it was impossible to judge the distance of our invisible landfall.

Though the seas were heavy, the deck of the *Papanicholis* was
barely awash, the waves on either side appearing to tunnel deep underneath her hull rather than break over the bridge, so that loading
our stores would have been a relatively simple matter had the task
been performed with the same efficiency as the crew of *Torbay* had
shown under conditions infinitely worse than these. But with typical insouciance the cheerful sailors of the *Papanicholis* had given no
thought to the systematic disposal of our various bits of equipment,
and Arthur and I were left to bundle them into the ship's dinghy
with our own hands before jumping in ourselves to seize the oars,
leaving a place in the stern for Stelio who was to steer us.

We rowed a few strokes away from the submarine's side to make
room for the two rubber boats in which the rest of the party were
to disembark, expecting them to follow us immediately; but in that
short time we were swallowed up in the dark and lost contact. There
was no alternative but to start pulling for shore on our own, hoping
that by some freak of chance we should all eventually fetch up on
the same beach.

Travelling backwards out of darkness into darkness deeper still,
Arthur and I could not tell what leeway we were making as we
splashed through the heaving water, and since turning round to peer
into the black void behind us only added to the efforts of such inex-
pert oarsmen as we were, we soon abandoned the navigation entirely
to Stelio.

I did not want to show that I doubted his ability, so I continued
to pull on my oar with every sign of confidence. But my alarm progressively increased, for Stelio, instead of giving us directions, kept
crossing himself in silence. Though I had no idea of the time, the
blisters coming up on my hands gave me some indication of the distance we must have covered, and as though my eyes had been suddenly transferred to the back of my head, I was conscious of the
cliffs pressing down close behind. My spirits soared when this presence was confirmed by Stelio's report—"I can see the shore quite
clearly now"—only to fall at once as he crossed himself yet again
and added: "But I haven't the faintest idea where we are!"

I felt like cursing him for his faint-hearted inefficiency, until I
looked over my shoulder and found myself facing a blank black
sheet consisting of almost equal areas of land and water which were
distinguishable from each other only by a white line of surf as jagged as the markings on a seismograph. On such a confusing chart

no one, however well acquainted he might be with the landscape, could be expected to pin-point a single feature.

The situation could not possibly improve if we were to remain where we were tossing dangerously about in the breakers, so we decided to creep in still closer and then row parallel to the shore on the off-chance that Stelio might pick out some familiar natural signpost. But as soon as we turned broadside-on, a wave swept over us and our waterlogged boat became almost impossible to manage.

Further reconnaissance was out of the question; our main concern now was to keep afloat and get ashore as quickly as we could. We therefore made for the nearest point where the foam seemed to splash less fiercely. Out of control, and with our speed alarmingly increasing, we were caught in the breakers and driven straight towards a solid block of cliff; and as I tensed my muscles in anticipation of the head-on crash, we were brought prematurely and unexpectedly to a standstill as the boat abruptly fell to pieces round us, spilling us out on to the rock we had struck. We clung to it as another wave dashed over us, bombarding us with bits of wreckage and bundles of equipment, which a second later were swept away and vanished out to sea.

We were wet through, bruised and rather shaken. We had lost all our gear but for the bits and pieces in the pockets of the sodden khaki drill we were wearing (for this time I had insisted we land in uniform). We were in enemy country, and beyond that we had no idea of our whereabouts. But for fully two minutes we could not stop laughing. This mood of hysteria was only dispelled by the cold, which reminded us of the need for immediate action.

Our torches, wrapped in waterproof cloth, were in working order, and masking as carefully as possible the stabbing beams they shed, we investigated strip by strip our surroundings. As far as I could make out, we had landed in a shallow gorge linking the coast to the foothills by a steep incline through the littoral cliffs. The rocks on which we had been wrecked stretched fifty yards or more to either side, as sharp and uneven as a partly demolished quay, but a few steps inland brought us to a shelving semi-circle loosely covered with poor earth and shingle and scattered with scrub and brushwood. The slopes all round were honeycombed with deep indentations, too exposed to be described as caves but affording at least temporary protection from wind and rain. I made for the largest of these, hoping to find some shelter for the night, but as I approached it I was brought to a breathless standstill by the sound of movements inside.

Whoever was there must have heard my footsteps, yet no one challenged me. Feeling slightly foolish, as I always do when I feel afraid, I fought against my instinctive urge to beat an immediate retreat, for I was now so close that scuttling away would not lessen the chances of my being attacked but would only put me in a worse position, with my back to an unknown assailant. I therefore took out my pistol and steadily, though far from boldy, advanced, directing the beam of my torch into the shadows. Scared by the sudden glare, half a dozen sheep stood there motionless for a second, as though posing for a flash-bulb photograph, before scampering into the furthest corner, bumping against the rocks and into each other in their panic.

I expected this stampede to be silenced by a shepherd's reassuring whistle, but there was no further sound. These beasts must surely be either part of a flock in winter pasture or else the hidden loot of a sheep-thief, and I could not help wondering why, in either case, they had been left unguarded. But while their presence here was a puzzle, it was also a proof that no enemy was near us, for neither rightful nor unlawful owner would have sheltered this small herd where hungry Germans were likely to seize it.

It was therefore safe for us to light a fire, and in a few minutes we managed to coax a reluctant blaze from the damp brushwood we had gathered, by sacrificing some of the ether pads we carried with us. These were intended for anaesthetizing any German sentry we might wish to dispose of silently and harmlessly. They now served a more immediate purpose by virtue of their instantaneous combustibility.

Not until we were reasonably warm and dry could we realize the implications of the position we were in. Until then we had been too preoccupied with our own discomfort to give much thought to the fate of our companions in the two rubber boats. There was no sign of any of them. And as we sat in silence round the fire, moving only to add another piece of scrub to the blaze, I knew, though none of us voiced the thought, that Arthur and Stelio were envisaging, as I was, two simultaneous shipwrecks more disastrous even than our own.

Our melancholy was increased by the strangeness of our surrounding, populated only by an abandoned flock yet full of rustling sounds which seemed too close and stealthy to emanate from half a dozen panic-stricken sheep. It was too dark to investigate the source of these movements, which were barely audible yet sufficiently distinct to prevent us from disregarding them completely, so that we spent the whole night with our senses more alerted than the situation in any case demanded. But at dawn the problem resolved itself, when we rose to our feet in the half-light to survey the landscape.

As Stelio got up he yawned, luxuriously stretching wide his arms and closing tight his eyes, which he opened with a start to find himself embracing a bearded figure that had silently emerged from a clump of lentisk just behind him. Before he could utter a word several other men had appeared, crawling from underneath bushes, abandoning the intermittent cover of rocks and boulders, and we found ourselves in a tumult of laughter and excited greeting. Stelio had been recognized by a group of his fellow-villagers.

Only then did we learn that we had been kept under observation all night, while this company of armed men had silently surrounded us and waited for the light of day to reveal our identity. "At first we thought you were Germans," they explained, "it's just the kind of trick those cuckolds would play, turning up out of nowhere in the dark in the hope of catching someone with a rifle. We almost shot you dead as you sat round your fire, but we wanted to make sure, so put it off till this morning. Lucky we saw Stelio with you, wasn't it?"

We had had an equally lucky escape, apparently, from an even more unpleasant fate. A few hundred yards to the west was an enemy coastguard station, and even though we might have landed there without at once attracting the sentries' attention, we should certainly have been killed a few seconds afterwards for the beach was thickly sown with mines. This news increased our alarm at the continued absence of the rest of the team, and a search party set out at once to make a cautious reconnaissance of the neighbouring bays.

Meanwhile our spirits were slightly raised by the arrival of three Australian stragglers, who had been living with these shepherds ever since the German invasion. If only they had been down on the coast last night, they would have heard Arthur's voice and mine and would have understood at once that we were English; but they had slept in a cave further inland and had not learnt of our landing until this morning.

The setback we had suffered from shipwreck seemed insignificant compared to the conditions in which the three of them had

been living for the last eighteen months. Though we had lost practically everything except the clothes we stood up in, our shirts were
at least unpatched and our boots intact; while these men were barefoot and in rags. Even so their morale was high, which said as much
for their own natural resilience as for the friendliness of their village
hosts, and their cheerful banter soon dispelled our sense of gloom
and foreboding. Like most of their compatriots, they were all three
expert swimmers, and when they heard of the loss of our kit they at
once volunteered to see how much of it they could recover.

Though the wind had dropped the sea was choppy, and the water
immediately below the rocks looked bottomless. It was hard to imagine this foam-flecked pool yielding any part of its treasure; yet after
their first dive, all three Australians reported they had seen a number
of bundles scattered in a narrow arc over the seabed close inshore,
and when they went down for a second time two of them struggled
to the surface grappling between them a waterlogged rucksack.

They spent the rest of the morning plunging in and out, and
only rarely came up empty-handed; until almost all the kit, which
I thought we had lost forever, was miraculously landed high and,
though not dry, at least undamaged since the more fragile items had
mercifully been wrapped in waterproof material. The recovery of
the last dripping parcel to be found happily coincided with a report
that the rest of the team had also been discovered further down the
coast; and, presently, we saw them approaching round the nearest
promontory, fortunately from the opposite direction to where the
German coastguards were established.

Like us, they had lost their bearings in the dark and had been
swept up on to some rocks, but the rubber boats had stood the shock
better than our dinghy and they had landed almost without getting
their feet wet. Since none of them knew the coast, they had not been
able to tell where the nearest village or enemy outpost might be.
But they had luckily resisted the temptation to reconnoitre further
inland and had kept the boats and themselves hidden on the beach
until they hailed the shepherds who had gone out to look for them.

The disaster of our arrival had at first seemed to augur ill for the
ultimate success of our mission, but now that it had been overcome I
regarded it as a favourable omen. For since misfortune had been defied, and every chance attempt on our lives and property thwarted,
I felt all the more confident of dealing with any subsequent unforeseen calamity.

Now that all the equipment and personnel were assembled, however, there was no point in tempting providence still further by remaining on this exposed strip of coast where we could easily have been cut off by an enemy patrol. So with the shepherds acting both as guides and porters, we trudged inland with our kit, climbing for an hour through the foothills till we reached an enormous isolated cleft in the mountains known locally as the Cave of the Cyclops.

In it there was ample room for several hundred people, which was just as well, for in the course of the afternoon most of the male population of the neighbouring village of Koustoyerako came in to welcome us with gifts of bread, cold meat, cheese and wine. A fire was lit, and soon half a dozen whole tree-trunks were ablaze, while we unpacked our sodden civilian clothes, cleaned our tarnished side-arms and put the contents of our money-belts out to dry. In the firelight the cave looked like the inside of a counterfeiter's den as the stacks of congealed bank-notes slowly uncoiled in the heat and, finally separating, fell in a crisp cascade on to the mud and stones of the floor.

Once we had donned our Cretan disguises and broken our equipment down into more easily portable loads, we were ready to move off. I was anxious to contact Paddy as soon as possible, and it was three days' march at least to his headquarters in Vaphes. The I.S.L.D. party were more fortunate. They were to set up their station in the hills above Stelio's village, which was less than an hour away.

So the fraternization between our two teams, against which we had been warned before leaving Beirut, was to come to an end at last. But before we parted company Stelio was good enough to flout this edict by yet another gesture of friendly co-operation. He appointed guides to accompany us all the way on our journey; so that it was thanks to him, and in spite of the decrees of our respective staff officers in Cairo, that our mission was successfully launched.

At dusk, then, with all our gear intact and in safe hands, we were led into Koustoyerako. There we enjoyed a blissful twelve hours' rest, for our hosts volunteered to stay up all night on sentry-go, so that each of us was guaranteed not only a bed to sleep in but also safety during that sleep; and early next morning we started the long climb over the back of the main White Mountain range.

CHAPTER TEN

1942

THE PATH WE TOOK was normally blocked by snow well before the first week of December, and even though this year's protracted autumn had kept it open and unobstructed, the cypress forests and upland slopes we passed were all deserted, the shepherds' annual descent to winter pasture depending apparently less on the weather than on the calendar. The ground, though steep, was fairly firm underfoot and gave promise of a reasonably easy passage, but the heavy load we each carried reduced our speed to a crawl. We took all day to climb as far as the Omalo Plain, an unexpected saucer of fertile land floating high in the surrounding sea of bare and jagged limestone.

Its circumference was dotted with small stone shacks, used in the summer by cheese-makers but abandoned at this season—or so we thought, until we noticed a group of men at the entrance to one of them. They could only be there for a purpose as illicit as our own, for no law-abiding peasant approached these heights so late in the year; and since they must be, like ourselves, outlaws, they would no doubt reciprocate the sympathy I instinctively felt towards them. Even so I hesitated to disclose our presence until we knew exactly who they were, so while the rest of us remained under cover, one of our guides went forward to find out.

In a few minutes, he came back with the news that the strangers were followers of Mandakas, the Communist general whom Turrell had in vain tried to contact earlier that year, and that the General himself was with them and anxious to meet me. I was equally anxious to meet him, for I wanted to know more about E.A.M., the National Liberation Front, of which he was the Cretan representative, and to see whether its activities could be synchronized with those of E.O.K., the National Organization of Crete, which I had sponsored under the leadership of the Mayor of Canea. So we joined forces for the night.

By the flame of the brushwood fire inside the hut it was hard to distinguish the General from his bodyguard of armed and bearded mountaineers. In his hooded cloak and baggy breeches he looked like a successful peasant proprietor, well-fed and massive, but far from flabby, for he had been on the run ever since the occupation started. Yet he did not give the impression of being a hunted victim, perhaps because he was attended by a retinue so overawed by military rank as to be reduced to a state of servility bordering on adulation. Clearly, in these conditions, he enjoyed being a fugitive from justice. The role suited him, and the characteristic lawless swagger with which he greeted me diverted my attention from his shifty manner and suspicious glances that I should otherwise have noted instantly.

The subject I had intended to bring up during this impromptu conference was never discussed, for he opened the conversation by reporting a disaster which drove every other thought from my mind: Manoli, our wireless operator, had been captured during a recent German raid on Vaphes, and Andrea Polentas had been arrested at the same time in Vrysses.

These bare facts were bad enough, but worse still was the absence of further detail. The simultaneous arrest of these two agents could only be attributed to treachery and must have seriously implicated the Vandoulas family, for Vaphes implied Uncle Niko's house—and it was there that I was expecting to meet Paddy in two days' time. Since there was no means of fixing an alternative rendezvous I would have to keep that appointment, even though I could no longer be sure of finding the house intact or any of its occupants alive.

This fear for the safety of our friends, though admittedly melodramatic, was none the less real and persistent. It occupied the thoughts of all of us during our two-day descent from the Omalo to the northern foothills, and not until we reached Kyriakosellia, the hamlet which had made itself responsible for looking after the Australian cripple, did we hear to our relief that although Manoli and

Andrea were in solitary confinement in Ayia jail, Uncle Niko's house had been spared and he and his family were safe.

So leaving Arthur and Alec Tarves behind in a temporary base outside this little village, while our guides started back for Koustoyerako and Niko Souris began his long trek to the east, I set off at once for Vaphes.

———————

To be on the safe side, I waited till it was quite dark before creeping into Uncle Niko's house. Any other household that had suffered the Vandoulas' recent experience might have been scared to receive me, and I should have felt no resentment had I been asked not to stay. But as soon as I stepped inside I was welcomed as though I were a safeguard against further risk instead of the additional source of danger I undoubtedly represented. Uncle Niko's pessimism was still evident, yet it did not prevent him from ordering a chicken to be killed for supper and from bringing out an enormous ewer of his best wine. Vangeli and Pericles joined him in toasting my arrival, while Paddy was summoned from his hide-out in a ravine just behind the village, and as we sat there drinking and eating till long after midnight I learnt the full story of the German raid and Manoli's capture.

The Germans had surrounded not the whole village, as was their usual method, but only the isolated hill where the Vandoulas lived, avoiding the main road as they encircled it so as to prevent any warning being given by the rest of the inhabitants. This seemed to confirm the suspicion, based on the simultaneous arrest of Polentas, that there was treachery involved. The Germans must have been forewarned to concentrate on Uncle Niko's house, though it was doubtful they knew they would find Manoli inside. For the wireless station had only just started operating from there—a risk that had had to be taken since Manoli's rheumatism had forced him to find somewhere indoors to work. Luckily, he had not been at work at the time, and his set and aerial were hidden away.

In the courtyard outside Vangeli had seen the Germans approaching, but could not avoid them for they had already seen him. He therefore went brazenly up to the nearest group of soldiers and asked them what they wanted.

"We're looking for Vangeli Vandoulas," they said.

"He's just this moment gone down to the village," Vangeli told them, "look, there he goes!"

And as the Germans raced after a figure he had pointed out, which happened at that moment to be ambling down the hill, Vangeli scuttled over the nearest wall and disappeared out of sight.

Meanwhile, the rest of the enemy patrol entered the house and found, fortunately, not Uncle Niko who was at work in the fields but Manoli, whom they promptly arrested. As he was being taken off he had the presence of mind to ask Elpida, who was also in the room, to give him one of the coats that were hanging on a peg by the door. She understood at once, took it down and helped him to put it on—after relieving him of the coat he had been wearing, the pockets of which were stuffed with his cypher pads and messages in code.

With the Germans still watching her, she carried it unconcernedly into the room next door, where the wireless and batteries were hidden. These heavy pieces of equipment she immediately shifted one after the other into a neighbouring field, where she buried them, so that the Germans found not a scrap of incriminating evidence during the search they had meanwhile begun.

Thanks to her, the entire station was saved. Thanks to an air raid a few days later, an operator was found to take Manoli's place. One of our bomber crews had been forced to bale out from their damaged aircraft and had been picked up on landing by a loyal shepherd who had at once contacted our organization. The airmen were now safely established in Tom's area, awaiting evacuation—all but one, a flight sergeant, who had gallantly volunteered to stay behind to operate our set. He was now in a hut outside Alones, to which Paddy had subsequently moved the station, and to him entirely we owed our continued wireless contact with Cairo, which would otherwise have broken down with Manoli's arrest.

Before Alec Tarves could go to Alones and relieve him, however, it was essential to organize suitable headquarters for Arthur. So the following morning, after spending the night in a cave outside Vaphes, Paddy and I set off for Kyriakosellia, accompanied by Vangeli and Pericles.

An ideal spot was found at the head of a long sloping valley, which normally would have been above the snow-line. Here, in a beehive-shaped hut connected to the village by a single path, Arthur would be able to lie up in comparative safety and still be within striking distance of what was supposed to be his ultimate target, Souda Bay, which lay due north less than a day's march away. Levteri Kourakis, who had accompanied me from Kyriakosellia to Vaphes the night before, arranged to provide him with a weekly supply of food and wine, and a village boy was appointed to attend to his daily needs, such as collecting firewood, for at this height the nights were appallingly cold.

The main disadvantage to the place was the size of the hut. Shaped like an igloo, it had an entrance like one, and the only way anyone of Arthur's build could get in was on hands and knees. But inside the chimneyless vault, even with half a tree-trunk burning, six people could be accommodated quite comfortably as long as they remained stretched out at full length on the mud and stone floor and did not raise their heads above the smoke which, for practical purposes, decreased the highest point of the low domed ceiling by a further two feet.

The night we spent there all together even seven of us managed to squeeze in, for George Psychoundakis had joined us to guide Alec and me on the following morning to Alones, where in two days time we were to meet Paddy, who meanwhile had to go down to a village on the main road for a conference with members of the Canea network.

———

Compared to Arthur's headquarters, the hut in the wood outside Alones where our wireless station was installed seemed almost luxurious. There was no furniture, of course, but brushwood covered the stone slabs which served as seats and beds, and there was a hole in the roof through which the smoke from the fire could escape. Alec, George and I reached it after dark and were only admitted after giving the password—"Victory"—and receiving the answer—"Freedom"—a system which Paddy had devised less for security purposes than for the amusement of the two occupants: Siphi, Father John's eldest son, who acted as our local messenger; and his English namesake Joe, Flight Sergeant Bradley, who was now operating our set.

Joe was a fair-haired Welshman in his early twenties who, like most of his compatriots, had a naturally fine singing voice, so that when Paddy, whose source of songs was apparently inexhaustible, joined us the evening after our arrival, we held an impromptu recital

to which George subscribed not only Cretan *mantinades*, the local
equivalent of the Caribbean *calypso*, but also this topical little ditty
in English which we had recently taught him:

Hitler has only got one ball,
Goering's got two, but very small,
Himmler's got something sim'lar,
But Dr. Goebbels got no balls at all!

This small-scale community singing was puerile and pathetic perhaps, and reminiscent of a glee-club short of members, but it was
one way of passing the time—an important consideration for a
group of men cooped up together in confined quarters for interminable hours, and sometimes days, of inactivity. There were no
books to read as a relaxation from conversation, which was normally
limited, as it would be for most men in similar circumstances, to
obscene and gluttonous discussions of the things we most lacked—
good food, hot baths, clean clothes and pretty girls, in that order
of desirability.

Circumscribed as it was, then, conversation became even more
of an art when practised in an obscure corner of a remote mountain
than it is usually considered to be in a sophisticated milieu where
it is infinitely easier to achieve. It therefore said much for the pro-
ficiency of my companions in Crete that I was not for a moment
bored or irritated in their company. Once I had learnt to understand
Alec's Highland vernacular, I willingly listened for hours to his pre-
war adventures as a salmon-poacher and to the accounts of his more
recent achievements in the stews of Beirut, while chapters out of
Paddy's life-saga sounded more engrossing than a Ruritanian novel
and were related with a spontaneous brilliance well beyond the powers of anyone but a naturally gifted story-teller.

As delightful as his conversation was the romantic attitude he
adopted to his mission in Crete. Each of us, I suppose—with the
possible exception of Tom, who was above such vanities—saw himself playing a role created only by his own imagination. I, for example, affected to regard myself as the Master Spy, the sinister figure
behind the scenes controlling a vast network of minor agents who
did all the dirty work. Paddy, obviously, scorned such an unobtru-
sive and unattractive part. He was the Man of Action, the gallant
swashbuckler and giant-slayer, a figure who would be immortalized
in innumerable marble busts and photogravure plates.

As though conscious of this notional fate, he was careful to keep up appearances. His moustache always had a dashing twist in it; his boots, which he wore out at the rate of one pair a month, were beautifully kept until they fell to pieces on his feet; to knot his black turban at the most becoming angle, he took infinite pains; and to complete his operational wardrobe he had just ordered a Cretan waistcoat of royal-blue broadcloth lined with scarlet shot-silk and embroidered with arabesques of black braid. This he wore, much to my envy, on our journey to the Amari, where we had arranged to meet Tom for Christmas.

Yerakari was in the same festive mood that I had noticed there on my two previous visits, in the cherry season and during the grape harvest. Though now it was too cold to sing and dance out of doors, the revelry was still of a peripatetic nature and we reeled happily from house to house eating and drinking with hosts who seemed as carefree as though no German had ever been heard of in Crete. We found the same conditions in every village we passed during our slow three-day procession down the valley, and the only evident effect of enemy occupation was the number of men who had been proscribed since I was last in this area.

Manoli Papadoyiannis, for instance, no longer lived in the lovely house in Ayios Ioannis where Delaney and I had lunched shortly after our landing almost a year before. Like many others who had helped us, he was on the German list of "wanted" men and found it safer not to sleep at home. In consequence, Delaney's irreverent description of him as "bug-whiskered" had proved to be prophetic, for his smooth cheeks were now covered in a shaggy grey beard, and to see him in Tom's hide-out just outside the village, squatting on the floor round a communal bowl of beans, no one would ever have taken him for a former Governor of Crete.

In such a friendly area, where every single shepherd was well known to us, a guide was scarcely necessary. So for the return journey Paddy and I decided to dispense with the services of ours and travel alone. Walking slightly drunk and unescorted gave us both an illogical sense of security, which turned out, however, to be without foundation a few hours after we set off.

A hundred yards or so outside Ano Meros Paddy felt he would have to make more room for the food and wine we knew we should be given there, so taking down his trousers he squatted behind a large rock a few yards to one side of the path. I was about to move on, when two Germans, one riding a donkey, the other on foot, came out of the village and made straight towards us. Since I was in full view of them there was no question of avoiding an encounter, so I slowly continued on my way, hoping to get past them with a conventional Christmas greeting and a cheerful nod of the head.

Clearly, they had just been well entertained. The one on foot staggered at every step he took over the loose slippery stones, while his companion sat slumped over the donkey's neck. But far from making them, as I had hoped, more insensible to anyone they might happen to pass, the wine had instilled in them an unwonted feeling of camaraderie, and as I approached they greeted me in broken Greek with exaggerated good-fellowship.

"Where you come from?" they asked.

"Ayios Ioannis."

"Where you go now?"

"Yerakari."

"No, no. You come with us—to Tymbaki."

This explained their unexpected presence in Ano Meros: they had obviously been recruiting the inhabitants for forced labour on the aerodrome, and now wanted to rope me in as well. But their method was pleasantly half-hearted, as though they themselves realized they were too drunk to enforce it. Yet with drunken persistence and broad grins they went on:

"You come with us—schnell, schnell, Tymbaki. You no come, you kaput."

But further grins accompanied this threat, which they clearly had no intention of carrying out—unless they turned suddenly nasty, as drunkards sometimes do. For the moment they were simply making sport of me, so, to keep them in countenance, I humoured them and answered with ponderous banter:

"No, no. You come with me—schnell, schnell, Yerakari." It was easy for me to return their grin as I spoke, for I was genuinely amused by their harmless behaviour, and my merriment increased at the thought of Paddy listening to this conversation as he squatted behind his rock, and at the sight of an old woman outside the nearest house repeatedly crossing herself as she witnessed the scene.

Still, I was anxious not to get too close to them, for I was conscious of the bulge made by the heavy Colt pistol I carried under my cloak, which would probably sober them up at once if they noticed it. And so, while we exchanged these pleasantries I kept edging away up the path, until they started hurling not threats but stones to chase me off all the more quickly. With a final unconvincing cry of "You kaput!" they proceeded on their way chortling with satisfaction, leaving me, also chortling, to continue on mine.

This encounter only increased the false sense of security that Paddy and I had started out with; and as we walked towards the garrison village of Prines, where we had been invited to spend New Year's Eve with Christo Tziphakis and the Rombolas family, we almost looked forward to meeting more Germans. We were sure of meeting one or two, for old George Rombolas encouraged them to visit him—his ostensible friendship with them facilitated his actual work for us—and he seemed all the more delighted when he had an opportunity of introducing us—"my young friends from Sphakia"—to them.

As we expected, then, when we entered his house we found it full of German officers and N.C.O.s who had dropped in to wish him the compliments of the season. In the convivial atmosphere of a room better furnished than that of any other village house, with our host sitting back contentedly puffing at a narghile, and his pretty daughter handing round drinks to the uniformed guests with whom she conversed with ease in their own language, it was almost impossible to have any feeling of apprehension or hostility towards these figures in Feldgrau all around us. They seemed to us so gullible and incapable of doing any harm, that we were almost tempted to drop our inhibitous disguise and enjoy the party openly under our own proper identity.

But our sentiments altered next day, when Paddy's runner, Yianni Tzangarakis, arrived with the news that in our absence an enemy patrol had surrounded Alones, captured the priest's son Siphi with an incriminating message in English on him, and raided the hut where our wireless station was installed. The set and batteries had fortunately been hidden away in the nick of time; and although Joe and Alec had managed to break through the German cordon and escape into the higher mountains, they were both still missing.

ABOVE: *The author delousing; candid snapshot by George Psychoundakis*

RIGHT: *Pavlo Bernardakis of Kastello (right) with two fellow-villagers*

LEFT: *Dick Barnes shortly after his arrival in Crete, October 1943*

BELOW: *Members of the Selino guerrilla gang*

CHAPTER ELEVEN

1943

We DECIDED to get back as quickly as possible to join the search for the two missing men that Petro Petrakas had started as soon as he heard of their disappearance; but with the Germans still combing the mountains in between, our march from Prines to Asi Gonia had to be undertaken in a succession of cautious stages which occupied the best part of two days. By the time we got to Petro's house, soaking wet after being out in the rain for the past forty-eight hours, Alec and Joe had been found—drenched like us, and hungry, but otherwise none the worse for their adventure.

After breaking though the cordon round Alones, they had made for the uninhabited trackless heights behind the village. Neither of them had been there before, but Alec, with a natural feeling for country that had not deserted him since his pre-war poaching activities in his own native highlands, had successfully led his companion in a wide loop round the western flank of the large-scale enemy patrol and found his way to Asi Gonia although he had only once before passed through it, and then only in the dark. Both of them were in high spirits and seemed to look on their uncomfortable flight as a welcome diversion. "It made a change from sitting all day in that mouldy hut," they explained.

I could see their point. Our wireless operators in Crete led a far more unpleasant life than we did. Much of our time was spent on forced marches and frustrating conferences, but we did at least enjoy a variety of friends, food and surroundings. But Joe and Alec were condemned to confined quarters, a dreary diet and the same daily companions whose language they could barely understand. Apart from the routine schedules to Cairo, during which their fingers were often so frozen they could scarcely manipulate the signalling key, once they had encoded the messages to be sent and deciphered those they had received, they had nothing to do for the rest of the day. Though they lived in reasonable security, then, they were almost anaesthetized by boredom, from which they were only occasionally roused by spasms of activity too violent to be really welcome.

Alec was hardened to this life from his previous mission in the summer, and was temperamentally suited to it; but for Joe, who was more accustomed to dealing with the enemy at a range of several thousand feet, these unwonted rigours must have seemed appalling, and though he never for a moment complained it was with great relief that he now left for Tom's area, from where he was to be evacuated a few weeks later.

Meanwhile, the rest of us went into hiding and waited for the hue and cry to subside. Until we learned more about the situation in Alones, we could not go and retrieve the wireless set and batteries that were hidden there; and until we set up the station again in some alternative position, we were forced to remain inactive in a reasonably inaccessible cave overlooking Asi Gonia.

Here we were joined by Father John Alevizakis, who since his son's arrest had wisely taken to the hills. Paddy and I could not help feeling overawed by the indestructible faith and goodness of this simple old village priest. "I'm a poor man," he had once told me, "so I can offer you little material assistance. But I have three sons, and all three will be sacrificed, if necessary, to the cause of Cretan liberty."

Spoken by him, these grandiloquent words had sounded completely sincere; they were now proved to be so. He knew as well as we did what Siphi's fate would be, for we had recently learnt how our operator, Manoli, and Andrea Polentas had been tortured before being executed a few days previously; but he brushed aside our expressions of sympathy with a phrase that came constantly to his lips: "God is great." Then, as he took out the bottle of raki he had brought with him, he asked us all to drink to the toast: "May the Almighty polish the rust off our rifles!"

Siphi's arrest must have confirmed the Germans' suspicions of our clandestine activity in this area, so that even when the enemy raid was at last called off, we felt it would not be advisable to continue our operations anywhere near Alones or Asi Gonia. We therefore decided to transfer the station to Arthur's beehive hut above Kyriakosellia.

Moving the heavy charging-engine and batteries that accompanied the set was no longer the simple matter it had been during the previous year, when the Germans still avoided the mountain paths and we had been able to use mules for transporting all our equipment in comparative safety even in broad daylight. Shifting our base had now become a feat of endurance involving the employment of at least half a dozen men, who had to carry the cumbersome gear piecemeal on their backs over trackless slopes at dead of night.

Aware of the horrid labour this entailed, I felt guilty at leaving Paddy to lead the expedition for retrieving the material from Alones while I remained impotent and ill in our hide-out; but I was suddenly laid low by a bout of influenza and felt too weak to accompany him. Not for the first time Paddy's stamina put me to shame; immediately on his return from the successful quest, during which he had spent twelve hours on the march laden, like each of his companions, with a pack made twice as heavy by the rain, he was ready to move on—much to my discomfort, for I still felt unnerved and devitalized.

By the end of our first day's march we had got as far as Vaphes, where we were met by Pericles and Vangeli Vandoulas. I was persuaded to rest here for a bit, for I had already retarded my companions' progress; so while Paddy and Alec Tarves pushed on to Kyriakosellia with George Psychoundakis, I took refuge in a stone hut outside the village—not my old hide-out in Uncle Antoni's vineyard, which was felt to be by now too insecure, but one lying in some open fields overlooking the main road, which, by virtue of its exposed position, would be less likely to cause suspicion than an obviously "safe" place of concealment.

Here I planned to spend one night only before moving on, but early in the morning I was woken with the news that a large enemy force had surrounded each of the neighbouring villages. As though they had got wind of our movements, the Germans had transferred their attention from Alones and Asi Gonia to the area between Vaphes and Kyriakosellia, through which they were now fanning out in strength.

I was therefore forced to remain in hiding, while messengers from the Vandoulas family crept down unobserved in the dark to bring

me food and the latest information. It was lucky my hide-out was
in the plains, for the Germans were reported to be concentrating in
the foothills above each village and searching the caves and valleys
of the higher slopes. One column had penetrated into the mountains from Kyriakosellia, and heavy firing had been heard from the
direction of Arthur's hut, but there was no news either of him or of
Paddy and Alec.

I was left in this state of apprehension for three days, until George
Psychoundakis turned up unexpectedly and told me his version of
the raid. The Germans had indeed reached the hide-out, climbing
up towards it in thick snow and through a sudden mist, but the
inmates of the hut had had sufficient warning to take cover and had
dispersed in time to hide the wireless equipment and themselves.
Paddy had spent a long Oak-apple Day in a tree; Arthur and Alec
had gone to ground in a nearby cave; Levteri Kourakis had been
fired on while leaving the village to give the alarm, but had fortunately escaped with a flesh wound in the ankle; and George himself, after being separated from the rest in the confusion, had been
lost for two days in the mountains on the fringe of the enemy cordon, until the mist lifted and he was able to make his way down
to Vaphes. He had no idea what had happened since to the companions with whom he had lost all contact, so as soon as we heard
the Germans had withdrawn from the area, I set out with him for
Kyriakosellia in order to find out.

We found them safely established in a cave above the village with
a new friend they had encountered during the raid: a fugitive from
justice called Stelio, who was said to have murdered his wife several
years before and had consequently been on the run ever since.

Now that Levteri was out of action, we badly needed someone
else to help us in this area, and Stelio proved a valuable contact even
though we did not officially recruit him into the organization at
once. Nor did he impose himself on us. He neither asked for help
nor offered it. Experience had taught him exactly how long it was
safe to remain in each successive hide-out, and his instinct told him
when and where to move; but not once did he suggest that we take
his advice and follow him. He would merely get up to leave without
previous warning, and we would move off with him. His habitual
silence and almost ludicrously modest manner were more impressive
than any loud-mouthed show of responsibility; and his lumbering

figure, thickened to twice its normal width by the number of sweaters he wore, engendered a comfortable feeling of security.

We gradually came to rely more and more on this mysterious Teddy Bear of a man. Although the crime he had committed had earned him a number of enemies locally, he still had countless friends in the surrounding villages through whom we were enabled to get enough food and wine to last us for days at a time; and with their help we managed to retrieve all our wireless equipment, which we finally set up in an underground cave naturally camouflaged by a wild fig-tree sprouting from its narrow entrance. It was a fairly safe hide-out, but so uncomfortable that we nick-named it the Chinese Torture Chamber. None of us could ever stand upright under its low roof, from which water dripped incessantly, forming stalactites that scraped our heads with every careless movement and stalagmites that pierced us from below; but somehow on this subterranean fakir's bed we contrived to find sufficient space for half a dozen people.

We did not remain there for long, however. A signal came in from Cairo informing us that Tom Dunbabin was shortly due to be evacuated and that Paddy was to take over his area. Paddy therefore set off at once for the east of the island, and soon afterwards Alec and I also left. From the isolated Torture Chamber it had been almost impossible to maintain regular contact with our agents in Canea and elsewhere, so that when Vangeli came and told me he had found a suitable alternative position in the mountains above Vaphes, I determined to move the station there, leaving Arthur in the care of Stelio who had meanwhile undertaken to help him accomplish his sabotage mission in Souda harbour.

For various reasons it was advisable for several members of our network to leave Crete at the first opportunity. Father John was of course high on the list for evacuation. Pericles, as Mayor of Vaphes, had been arrested at the same time as our operator, Manoli, and although he had managed to secure his release by brilliantly pretending to be almost half-witted, he was still suspect in German eyes and so would be better out of the way for a bit. George Psychoundakis, too, was by now "wanted" by the authorities, but even if he had not been he deserved a rest after the daily rigours and long

marches he had undertaken for over a year. These three, then, made
their way down to the eastern coast to be evacuated at the same
time as Tom; and to take George's place as messenger and guide,
Petro Petrakas recommended another lad from Asi Gonia: his own
nephew, George Phindrilakis.

Little George, as we called him to distinguish him from his predecessor, was a lightly-built young shepherd of seventeen, whose
youthful appearance was emphasized by the extraordinary shrillness
of his voice. Accustomed to shouting at his flocks at a distance on
the open mountain-side, he had not yet learnt to reduce his tone to
the level of normal conversation with human beings in an enclosed
space. But this habit, which might have been intolerably irritating
in anyone else, only added to the impression he gave of boisterous
strength—an impression that was confirmed by his conduct on the
first march we made together, when he helped us to shift the entire
station from Kyriakosellia to the hide-out above Vaphes.

It took five of us the whole of one night to transport the packs.
Alec Tarves, who was capable of carrying a tree-trunk as thick and
heavy as himself, found no difficulty in managing the transmitting set neatly packed in a suit-case. Two of the toughest Vandoulas
cousins undertook the equally heavy burden of a battery each. But
the most unwieldy load of all, the charging-engine, which brought
most men gasping to their knees after less than an hour's march,
was borne all the way by Little George, who not only made no complaint but showed no sign of weakness.

I could only judge the effort that march must have entailed for
him by doubling and redoubling in my imagination the effort it cost
me. Even under the more reasonable load of a rucksack crammed
with personal equipment, I soon felt bludgeoned by fatigue as in
pitch darkness we crossed the unbearable succession of lateral ravines which separated us from our ultimate goal. The irritation of
being tripped up by scrub-roots, impaled on needle-sharp rocks and
retarded by smooth cataracts of shale, which at first caused me to
swear out loud at these invisible and inanimate obstructions and
set about them with my stick, gradually gave way to sullen insen-
sibility—a more dangerous state for all of us, for in that frame of
mind our will-power, concentrated exclusively on the simple business of keeping our balance and our tempers, could not be instantly
diverted to deal with any emergency that might arise. Fortunately,
we encountered none. Dawn found us trudging through deep snow

along the windswept spine of the main range, and soon afterwards we reached the cave Vangeli had chosen as our hide-out.

From every point of view it was as perfect as he had promised. Perched under the very roof of the mountain-top, with a steep over-hang projecting like eaves above it, it could be approached—indeed it could only be seen—from one side alone. Looking out in that direction, as though from an attic window, we could view the stony slope stretching before us like a desolated back-garden walled in to right and left by subsidiary horse-shoe ranges, while the narrow scree on which we balanced, like seamen in a petrified boat about to plunge over a petrified waterfall, was dammed at its base by a third wall of hills which could only be scaled with ease at one point. Through this barely negotiable passage supplies could be brought up to us from Vaphes, less than four hours away, so that by means of messengers using that route news sent from Canea in the morning could reach me the same afternoon.

After the alarms and excursions of the past weeks, during which the station had had to be shifted from one place to another, I looked forward to a period of undisturbed activity in which we could settle down and deal with the back-log of incoming and outgoing signals. But we had not been there more than a week when this pleasant rou-tine was interrupted by the unexpected arrival one stormy night of a pair of unknown visitors.

They were as surprised by our unforeseen presence there as we by their sudden appearance. The cave, like every other hiding-place on these slopes, was well known to them; for they were fugitives from justice and had been on the run in this area for over a year. But they had not expected to find it already occupied when they came in to shelter from the rain. I was slightly irritated that the closely-guarded secret of our whereabouts should now be revealed to these two intruders simply by an accident of the weather; but remember-ing how useful our chance encounter with Stelio had proved, I was not at first seriously alarmed by this inevitable breach of security.

These two young men, however, did not give a favourable impres-sion. Unlike Stelio, they were talkative and boastful as well as sus-picious; and after questioning us, they ostentatiously fondled their rifles, vaingloriously declaring how many men they had killed or were planning to kill. I could have forgiven their air of bravado and furtive appearance. I could even have overlooked their reputation, which Vangeli told me was well deserved, for treachery and unreliability. But I could not easily dismiss their own admission that they were on their way to Canea to surrender their arms to the enemy so as to benefit by the latest amnesty.

For these amnesties which the Germans from time to time declared were organized less as a philanthropic gesture to patriots on the run than as a cunningly contrived recruitment drive for traitors. Outlaws were bound to know, from personal experience, every nook and cranny in the mountains that could conceivably be used as a base for our subversive activity. Outlaws were therefore essential to the German counter-espionage authorities. But they could not be approached until they were enticed into the open by a promise of official pardon. Many of them, understandably weary of a fugitive's life in the hills, had availed themselves of the German offer, had given up their rifles and returned unmolested to their villages with the freedom of full citizenship; and no one thought the worse of them for that. A few, however, no doubt beguiled by the promise of even greater benefits, had volunteered—as the Germans had hoped they all would—to act as enemy guides and informants.

These men hardly ever lasted long in their new careers. Traitors, even those who subsequently sought asylum behind German barbed wire, were hunted down by the relatives of their victims until a violent end was put to their activities. One of them, for instance, had recently met an unpleasant death in broad daylight, even though he had taken the precaution of moving into a house surrounded by German billets. His body was discovered still bleeding from seventeen knife-wounds, under a table-cloth on which the blood his assailants had wiped from their hands had not yet had time to congeal. I was not surprised to learn a little later that the successful "criminals" were related to Polentas; for their victim had been Comninas, a clever double agent who had ostensibly assisted our Canea network and thereby acquired the information leading to the capture of our operator in Vaphes and the simultaneous arrest in Vrysses of our chief agent, whose subsequent execution his cousins had thus avenged.

In a sense, then, the outlaws who turned traitors could describe themselves as brave, since in doing so they risked such an unpleasant fate. It took greater courage, however, to exploit the Germans as Stelio did, by accepting their offer of a pardon only so as to be able to work against them more effectively. He realized that so long as he was on the run he could be of little service to Arthur. He had therefore taken his oldest rifle into Canea, had handed it over to the authorities and been officially amnestied, and had then come back to Kyriakosellia, taken his best rifle out of its hiding-place and declared he was now ready to guide Arthur down to Souda Bay for a preliminary reconnaissance of the harbour.

They had set off together one morning, both dressed as labourers, carrying picks and shovels. They must have looked an odd couple, Stelio bouncing nimbly over the rocks like an india-rubber beach toy, with Arthur, towering two feet taller, stumbling along behind him. Their very incongruity was enough to attract attention, but Stelio, with his natural sense for cover and country, had managed to reach an observation post overlooking Souda harbour without either of them being noticed.

Their reconnaissance proved to be a negative success. But it confirmed what we already suspected, namely, that the system of sentries, searchlights, minefields and barbed-wire entanglements precluded the possibility of our sinking *H.M.S. York* by means of an individual sabotage operation. In a subsequent signal to Cairo, therefore, I had called for an air strike on the harbour at the earliest opportunity, suggested that Arthur devote himself to intelligence work, and commended Stelio for the part he had played in this extremely hazardous mission. His acceptance of the amnesty had indeed proved invaluable to us.

But I was not so sure that the two young visitors sheltering with us in the cave above Vaphes would prove equally loyal when confronted with German assurances of freedom. Nor was Vangeli, who sensibly pointed out that once they had left they might easily return to our hide-out within twenty-four hours—at the head of an enemy patrol. This was an ungenerous thought, perhaps, but in the circumstances we could not afford to give them the benefit of the doubt; so that as soon as they set off for Canea in the morning, we too prepared to leave. By nightfall we were once more on the march, cursing and staggering under our loads, bound for the mountains behind Asi Gonia.

CHAPTER TWELVE

1943

As usual when we were most hard pressed, we turned to Petro Petrakas for assistance. Levteri Kourakis and Stelio in Kyriakosellia had helped us as loyally and enthusiastically as the Vandoulas family in Vaphes, but the influence of both these groups was limited, and the recent German activity had made their areas insecure as a base for us. Asi Gonia was equally suspect and open to enemy raids, but Petro had the whole village to call on in an emergency so that, if unable to take flight during an attack, we could at least retaliate. We therefore chose as a site for our station a strategically placed hut from which an orderly withdrawal could be made, if necessary, under the covering fire of a support group commanded by Petro.

With the formation of this small armed force, our activity in western Crete assumed a completely different character. Until then safety had lain in lack of numbers and subterfuge. But now that the German counter-espionage service was active even in the more inaccessible areas, we were forced to expand our system of armed guards and sentries, thereby sacrificing a measure of the secrecy on which we had hitherto relied.

Guerrilla warfare would have been dangerously premature at this stage of the occupation. What I had heard of the terrible reprisals caused by the ill-timed activity of the two gangs in the east of the island, where countless hostages had been shot and several villages burnt to the ground with little purpose being achieved, discouraged me from risking a similar scourge in my area. I was therefore strongly opposed to any open show of local revolt, since it could not yet be supported by a general uprising or synchronized with an Allied landing; but arms and equipment for our small defence force were now an urgent requirement, and I reluctantly agreed to Petro's suggestion that these be dropped by parachute at the earliest opportunity.

A parachute drop in these mountains was always a chancy proposition, even in midsummer when weather conditions were more or less reliable. Winter was not yet over when we organized the one above Asi Gonia, on the only acre of flat ground within miles, about three hours away from our station. The snow lay thick on the adjacent peaks, and after collecting the brushwood for the signal fires, we huddled together for warmth in chattering heaps, for there was no natural cover on the bare surrounding slopes. The icy wind that blew over us must have impeded the aircraft we expected, for it failed to appear that night, and we had to wait for another twenty-four hours before we heard the noise of an approaching engine high above us.

We at once lit the bonfires, but in the moonless dark the reflection from the snow prevented us from seeing anything directly overhead, and although we heard the roar of engines close above us, the sky, as far as we could make out, remained an empty blank. It was not until first light, after we had trudged for hours over the area, hoping our feet would stumble up against a steel container or suddenly be immersed in soft folds of silk, that one of the look-outs sighted a parachute at the bottom of an adjacent ravine, its green-and-brown camouflage pattern easily distinguishable against the light grey of the rocks.

It took us the rest of the morning to collect seven more containers dispersed in gulleys and above precipices over a radius of many miles, and while we were organizing the transport and distribution of these stores, Little George arrived with the news that an eighth container had been found by some Kallikrati shepherds who had refused to give it up. Petro and I therefore set out at once for their cheese-hut—a long hour's climb away—to persuade them to hand it over. But they would not be moved by our pleas or threats. "Findings are keepings," they insisted.

"Well, at least show us what you've got hold of," I said. "Is it arms or ammunition?"

"Neither. Just foodstuffs. And we're as hungry as you are. Look, you can see for yourself . . ."

And they took out the container they had hidden away, which proved to be packed with small cylindrical tins, each containing, I knew, a ready-primed anti-personnel grenade.

I carefully opened one of these with my knife and showed the shepherds the contents. Whereupon they started crossing themselves and blessing our arrival.

"We thought it was bully-beef," they explained, "and we were just going to smash one open with a stone as none of us had got a tin-opener. God must have sent you in time. Please take these things away, and go in peace."

The drop had not been a complete success At least half the containers remained unaccounted for, but the material we recovered was sufficient to keep our small guard in clothing, equipment and ammunition for many months, which raised their morale and increased their efficiency. Our sentry system became so effective that an immediate alarm was sounded at the approach not only of a German patrol but even of a stranger in the neighbourhood, and it was by this means I learned a little later of the arrival in Asi Gonia of Niko Lambathakis and Pavlo Bernardakis, two of the men who had been evacuated with me the previous summer and who, after training in Haifa, had been sent in again on the boat by which Tom had recently left.

I was delighted to welcome them back. Niko, I hoped, would once more resume his activity in Canea, and I looked forward to Pavlo becoming my personal henchman, a position which had remained vacant since Pericles's necessary but much-regretted departure. They had been settled in with me less than a week before their qualities were put to the test by an experience which, for me at least, still remains as haunting as a nightmare.

Little George came in one morning with the news that a German had deserted from the nearby garrison of Kournas and was now in hiding in his cousin's cheese-hut just outside that village. No one in the neighbourhood knew what to make of him since he spoke no Greek and could not make himself understood. Manoli, George's cousin, wanted me to come and question him—and, if possible, take him off his hands. So I set off at once for the cheese-hut, taking Pavlo and Niko with me.

We waited till it was almost dark on the outskirts of the village, listening to the alien sounds emanating from it: guttural words of command, incongruous in that pastoral landscape, and occasional snatches of a tune I had never heard before, a typically Teuton melody dripping with *Brüderschaftsehre* and *Heimweh*—yet so compelling that in spite of myself I felt a lump in my throat. I was listening for the first time to *Lili Marlene*.

It was in this mood of fervent homesickness for Western Europe that I entered Manoli's hut that evening, which perhaps was responsible for the sympathy I felt at once with the fair-haired young soldier inside. The atmosphere was rancid with the smell of yesterday's boiled milk and half-matured cheese.

The only light came from the flame of a wick dipped in a tin of olive oil. And these overpoweringly primitive surroundings, compared to the picture of their cosy European equivalent that had been evoked by the song I had just heard, induced in me an upsurge of disloyal fellow-feeling for this enemy, beside whom the swarthy bearded figures of my companions seemed for a moment so intolerably uncouth that I almost turned in anger on Manoli when he said:

"When are we going to deal with him?"

"Deal with him?" I asked. "What do you mean?"

Manoli answered my question with a significant gesture, drawing an imaginary knife across his throat. Disregarding it, I started to question the boy in German.

His replies were spontaneous but worthless, not because he was withholding information but simply because he had none to give. I had the impression he realized this himself and was inventing details in the hope of pleasing me, for he was manifestly frightened. But all I gathered was that he came from Magdeburg, where he had worked in a factory before being drafted into the army, and that he hated military life so intensely that he had deserted, hoping to contact a British agent who would evacuate him to a prisoner-of-war camp in the Middle East.

Whether this was true or not, I could not tell. For all I knew, his desertion might have been part of a cunningly devised German trap—that, at least, was what I tried to persuade myself to believe. And when Manoli told me the lad had already made one attempt to regain his unit, I succeeded in doing so. For Manoli was unwilling to jeopardize himself and his family by letting him stay indefinitely in this cheese-hut, and I could not be expected to endanger the whole of our organization by keeping him, even under guard, at the wireless station, with no prospect of getting him off on a boat reasonably soon. There was therefore only one solution. Turning to Manoli, I said:

"We'll deal with him tomorrow."

Now that the decision was taken, I tried to compensate for the momentary weakness I had felt for the prisoner by an elaborate display of ruthless efficiency, by which I hoped to retrieve the respect of my companions; so after discussing in detail the operation we planned, we agreed to Pavlo's suggestion for the disposal of the body. He knew of a deep hole in the rocks high above the saddle we should have to cross on our way back to Asi Gonia; he would lead us to it in the morning.

"That's settled, then," I said, and turned to the German: "Tomorrow we leave for the south coast, where I'm expecting a submarine at one of our secret beaches. I'll put you on her when she leaves."

The lie was prompted by my own fear and disgust. I knew I was incapable of having him ceremoniously executed and had already made up my mind how to avoid doing so. I therefore made my proposal clear to the others:

"When we get to the place tomorrow, please leave everything to me. I'll deal with him in my own way. I don't want him to know in advance that he's going to die."

As we settled down for the night on our beds of twigs, I felt half-ashamed and half-elated.

At dawn I was more than ever disinclined to carry out the business. "Let's get it over at once," I said, speaking briskly to conceal my feelings. "No halting till we reach the hole. You lead the way, Pavlo."

As we silently ascended in single file, a sudden mist circling the White Mountains blew up behind and below us faster than we could walk and had enveloped us completely by the time we reached the saddle two hours later. Here Pavlo struck off the path to the right, straight up the nearest slope, so steep and stony that not even arbutus or scrub could lodge their roots in it. On all fours we clambered up the bare boulders, which formed a jagged cataract on the slope where they had slid and stuck, their surface now slippery with the fresh dampness of the mist.

Presently Pavlo looked round and sat down. I nodded. I had noticed the hole near him: a circular rift in the limestone about three feet wide. We drew our pistols and slipped forward the safety-catches. The German still showed no sign of alarm, but I felt so cowardly I could not refrain from telling yet another lie to justify our actions. "Just a precaution," I explained, "in case we run into a patrol . . ."

He smiled confidently back at me. He was sitting on a large square rock almost within arm's reach, and my pistol was pointing straight at him. I noticed, as though for the first time, the slim, almost skinny young body in patched field-grey, the camouflaged ground-sheet slung poncho-fashion over one shoulder and swelling like bellows over the heaving chest. He was breathing deeply, taking advantage of the mountain air, obviously enjoying the exercise after his dull days of confinement in the stuffy rancid hut. His smile unnerved me even more than the gladness in his eyes. I looked into them and saw their expression change a split-second before I pressed the trigger. He toppled backwards off the rock and disappeared.

My shot was still echoing over the saddle, when I heard a frightened shout—"Virgin Mary, you've missed!"—followed by two further shots fired downhill, and looking in that direction, I saw the German swiftly tumbling and bouncing on hands and knees from rock to rock till he somersaulted over a chasm and was out of sight again.

We found him a minute later in the crevice below. Both legs were bent and broken under him; his arms and chest were torn by his flight and fall; and I noticed the neat hole where my bullet had pierced his neck. He was still conscious, his gaze shifting interrogatively from one of us to another. He tried to speak, but his gasps were too rending for the words to form.

"Finish him off," I said to Manoli.

The German showed no surprise or fear as Manoli approached him, but stared into the barrel of the pistol, squinting upwards as it almost touched his forehead. Then a last shot rang out.

We put our pistols away. "We'd better tidy him up," Pavlo suggested, and began to wrap the body in the groundsheet, taking hold of the feet while Manoli and Niko attended to the other end. Then, leaving what remained of the top of the head behind, they scrambled uphill with the load until they reached the hole and bundled the body over the edge.

We sat down to rest, for we were all four trembling: my companions, with reason, from their exertions; myself probably less from nausea than from shame. But Pavlo was the only one to realize the true reason for my sense of guilt. "Cheer up," he consoled me, "you didn't miss him, after all."

Yet I knew only too well that I had bungled the killing. Had I made a clean job of it I might soon have forgotten the expression in that German's eyes and the sight of his scalp on the rocks.

For over a month we operated from the Asi Gonia base with scarcely a rumour to disturb our established routine; and when finally there was an alarm, we were warned of it in good time by means of our look-out system.

We had already received several reports of the German attempts to locate our station by means of direction-finding vans—a cumbersome and ineffective method in these mountains, since to achieve the required triangulation at least two of these machines were needed, and the main roads to which they were necessarily restricted were limited in number. No doubt the enemy were well aware of our presence in the neighbourhood of Asi Gonia, but they obviously could not pin-point our position. We were therefore surprised one morning when a small German section, equipped with what the messenger called "a machine with ear-phones," was reported approaching the saddle and heading straight in our direction.

Alec was in the middle of his routine schedule to Cairo at the time, but at once gave his emergency calling-off signal, dismantled the aerial and packed up the set so that we could all be ready to move off at a moment's notice. Whereupon the Germans, who were being kept under observation from the surrounding peaks, were seen to come to a sudden halt.

We could easily have encircled them and killed or captured them all, since we outnumbered them by at least two to one, but mindful of the reprisals that would have followed, we decided instead to remain on guard and wait for them to make the first move. But all they did was to set up camp in an abandoned shepherd's hut nearby and establish what looked like a wireless station of their own.

Alec, who knew more about these matters than the rest of us, assumed their machine was a device for detecting the clicks of his own signalling-key, which he therefore wisely refrained from using so long as they remained in the vicinity. But we were almost tempted, in spite of their proximity, to resume contact with Cairo at once; for there was something infinitely comic in the idea of these two rival camps busily engaged on their work of mutual destruction within a few hundred yards of each other. We resisted the urge, however, and for three days kept off the air, until the Germans, no doubt despairing of ever picking us up again, provided an inevitable anticlimax by packing up and leaving as swiftly and unexpectedly as they had arrived.

The relatively peaceful period that followed gave me an opportunity to collate the information streaming regularly in from Canea and the other sources, and to make plans for future activities, which included a conference with Paddy and the leaders of the Retimo network in Prines. But before setting off for that meeting, we had another unexpected visitor, this time a welcome one: a New Zealander belonging to the escape organization known as M.I.9, who had recently landed in Tom's area with orders to round up the remaining stragglers in the western half of the island, from where they were eventually to be evacuated.

The newcomer was a staff-sergeant, a dark silent man, so unassuming that to my shame I have even forgotten his name. But I do remember that he had once been a straggler here himself, one of the few who had successfully escaped to Africa during the first weeks of the occupation by the simple but hazardous expedient of stealing a small dinghy and sailing it due south. He stayed with us only two days before leaving for Kyriakosellia to make plans for transporting the crippled Australian there to the coast near Koustoyerako where a boat would later be coming in to collect the fifty or so other stragglers he hoped to round up in the course of the next few weeks.

Meanwhile I left with Pavlo for Prines, where I found Paddy waiting for me in the Rombolas house. As usual, we made our conference an excuse for the sort of civilized pleasure that we were denied for weeks on end in our mountain hide-outs. To sit in comfortable chairs in a properly-furnished home was an even more delightful experience than eating good food from a well-laid table; but more delightful still than the relief from the perpetual picnic conditions in which we had been living was being able to talk to people whose conversation was not limited to discussing the merits of one make of pistol compared to another or the advantages of rubber boot-soles over soles made of leather and other similar concerns that seemed to be uppermost in the average peasant mind. But there was one familiar feature of the household that Paddy and I both missed that evening: there were no Germans sitting in the room with us.

"Our friends seem to be avoiding us tonight," old George Rombo-las observed as he calmly puffed his narghile, filled with his favou-rite Persian tobacco which we had specially asked to be included in the most recent consignment of stores landed from the Middle East. It was almost a point of honour with him to have at least a couple of the enemy for us to meet whenever we called at his house. But one of his sons, Christo, a young man whose charm was matched by his foolhardy courage, quickly suggested a remedy for this deficiency.

"Well, if they won't come to us," he said, "we'll have to go to them. I know there's a party in the mayor's house tonight; let's go and see what it's like."

That our minds were by now affected by the abnormal life we had been leading, was clearly proved by our ready agreement to this absolutely pointless scheme, in which neither Paddy nor I had anything to gain and the Rombolas family had everything to lose. Cheerfully, we followed Christo out of the house and down the main street where countless figures, distinguished in the moonlight by the peaked Afrika Korps cap which each of them wore, were re-flected in silhouette on the white walls flanking our advance.

The Mayor's party consisted only of a couple of German ser-geants, one slightly less drunk than the other, who broke off in the middle of a song and greeted us effusively as we entered. Our host, who was entertaining them alone with his pretty daughter of nine-teen, introduced us as his cousins—"poor relatives of mine from a mountain village," he hastened to add in explanation of the shabby shepherd's cloaks we were wearing: incongruous garments in a main-road village.

But I doubt if the Germans even heard him; they had started singing again, and only stopped to clamour for more wine and three more glasses so that we might all drink a *Brüderschaft* together.

As always in such circumstances, it was impossible to feel any-thing but affectionate pity for the unsuspecting enemy; and as we went through the tedious Germanic ritual, linking our arms with each of them in turn as we tossed back our wine, I was not even faintly alarmed when my cloak slipped from my shoulders and revealed the bulge of the heavy Colt '45 under my jacket. And as they once more started to sing, embracing us and shuffling their feet in a mock dance, I was so confident that they were literally "blind" that later, when we got up to leave, I almost betrayed my surprise when one of them rested his hand for a second on the tell-tale bulge at my waist and, after a painful effort to focus his eyes on mine, gazed into them with drunken intensity. But his voice sounded full of sober disbelief as he smilingly stressed the last word of his fare-well: "Good-bye, *cousin*."

I should have liked to know exactly what his thoughts were at that moment.

There was bad news waiting for me when I got back to Asi Gonia. A messenger had arrived the day before from Koustoyerako with the report that the New Zealand staff-sergeant, who had already rounded up about forty stragglers and established them in a hide-out above the village, had himself been arrested by a German patrol while trying to contact another group of his compatriots in the foot-hills further north. Fortunately, he had been able to claim—and with some truth—that he was one of the many hundred Allied sol-diers left behind after our evacuation in 1941 and had been roam-ing the mountains ever since; so that although captured in civilian clothes, he was being treated as an ordinary prisoner-of-war—a fact confirmed a little later by a message from Canea, saying he had been flown out to a P.O.W. camp on the mainland.

To my signal to Cairo containing this information, I received orders to complete the arrangements for evacuating the stragglers myself. I was therefore to move to Koustoyerako at once, select a suitable beach and notify its position to Headquarters through the I.S.L.D. station which was still operating in that area. Any Cre-tan candidates for evacuation would be taken off at the same time, and Alec Tarves was to accompany me to the coast to take over a new transmitting set and wireless crystals which were due to be brought in.

All these orders were reasonable. There was one more, however, which I found hard to justify—a personal message from the Briga-dier, demanding that at all costs Arthur be sent out when the boat came in. I had already suggested, as soon as his reconnaissance of Souda had proved the futility of the sabotage mission for which he had first been proposed, that he remain in Crete and help me, as he had indeed been doing, with collecting and collating information. He was perfectly suited to this task, being a trained intelligence offi-cer, speaking Greek and—what was most important of all—really anxious to stay on, being fond of the Cretans who in return regarded him with deep affection and respect.

Not until I returned to Cairo nearly a year later did I learn for certain what I now only suspected: that the order for Arthur's evacuation was prompted solely by the animosity which the Brigadier still felt for him. Jack Smith-Hughes had put my suggestion for Arthur's employment in Crete to the Brigadier, whose only retort had been:

"What! Hasn't that fellow Reade been bumped off yet?"

Loyally Jack had forthwith sent in his resignation, whereupon the Brigadier had apologized for the remark, accompanying his apology, however, with the order for Arthur's immediate withdrawal from the field. There was nothing more Jack could do about it.

There was nothing more I could do either, except leave for Kyriakosellia and break the news as gently as possible.

CHAPTER THIRTEEN

1943

I FOUND ARTHUR comfortably installed in a new hide-out. Now that the month of May had opened with a sudden burst of midsummer weather, it was warm enough to sleep out of doors, and Stelio had discovered the perfect site for a temporary encampment: at the foot of a single carob tree sprouting from the bare slope of an otherwise denuded valley. Its branches formed an arbour large enough to accommodate not only Arthur's lanky frame but two or three normal-sized men as well, and the incline was so steep that we could effortlessly crawl into this nest from a ledge of projecting rock directly behind it.

It was so exposed as to be above suspicion, and as long as we limited our movements round it and obliterated our tracks leading to it, a whole battalion of Germans might have passed though the valley below without giving it more than a cursory glance. Its only disadvantage was that we, naturally, could not light a fire there to cook our meals, so that our diet was restricted to dry food supplemented by an occasional saucepan of luke-warm beans in oil which Stelio brought to us ready-cooked from the village.

But Arthur managed to lend an air of luxury to these primitive banquets. He insisted they end conventionally with coffee, and since we had no Thermos flask for a proper hot brew he had devised a unique method of his own for making it, using his mouth as a makeshift percolator. He introduced us to this system as soon as we arrived, and after every meal we would follow his example, taking a spoonful of ground coffee in our mouths, followed by another of castor sugar, then mixing the two together with a swig from the water-bottle and crunching the resultant paste between our teeth. It was better than nothing.

Arthur was understandably angry and saddened by the news I brought him, but once he had resigned himself to being evacuated he did his best to overlook the Brigadier's monstrous edict and concentrated instead on helping me with the plans for our march across the mountains to the south coast. The task of rounding up the stragglers had already been completed. The last one on our list had reached Koustoyerako a few days before and had joined the others in a hide-out in the foothills above, so that they were all assembled and ready to move down to the coast—all, that is, except the paralysed Australian. We had made arrangements for him to be transported, disguised as a sick old woman, on the back of a donkey; but at the last moment he refused to be lifted out of his cave. So reluctantly we were forced to leave him behind.

Apart from the stragglers and Arthur, I decided to evacuate Niko Lambathakis as well. He had been suffering from an old war-wound ever since his return and had therefore been unable to resume his work in Canea. Accustomed to the pavements of the capital, he would have found life in the mountains a hardship even without the pains and cramps he complained of every day; so there was no point in keeping him on in the hope of a rapid recovery. Besides, his perpetual sick-monkey expression, which had prompted Alec to refer to him as "Chimp"—a description which suited him so perfectly that I adopted it as his official code-name in my signals—was a constant irritation to all of us who had to live in close confinement with him, and he had not sufficient charm in other respects to overcome this serious personal defect which in the circumstances endangered the morale of the entire station.

Another Cretan due for evacuation at the same time was Katina Beirakis, the younger daughter of a rich Canea merchant. By ostensibly fraternizing with the Germans (all of whom were anxious to be on good terms with the well-to-do and therefore influential families in the capital) she had been one of our most valuable sources of information, but had since been compromised and forced to go into hiding on her father's farm in the plains below Kyriakosellia where she was now waiting for me to come and escort her to the coast.

I had not met her before and was delighted with the prospect of doing so. For months the only women I had seen, with the exception of Elpida Vandoulas, the two school teachers of Vaphes, and George Rombolas's pretty daughter, were either buxom peasant girls, simperingly shy and by local custom unapproachable, or else their mothers, black-hooded, simple and prematurely aged. I therefore looked forward to seeing an educated "modern" woman of the world again, even if she looked like a blue stocking and dressed like a shopgirl.

But Katina did neither. When Stelio and I reached the farmhouse early in the morning after an easy descent from the hills, I felt almost embarrassingly excited and horribly conscious of my filthy unshaven appearance and outlandish louse-ridden clothes while she welcomed us on the balcony of her lovely country home, once the property of a sybaritic Turkish pasha and now surrounded by lemon and orange-groves watered by an ingenious irrigation system which transformed the whole estate into a lush oasis in the middle of the barren rocky plain. This was the only house of its kind I had seen in Crete: a property designed for holiday pleasure instead of the usual rude shelter erected for the use of the poultry and beasts of burden with which their owners seemed to live almost like interlopers in their own roughly furnished rooms. And Katina fitted naturally into these surroundings, dressed in the leisurely manner of an English woman in the country and not, as any other town-dwelling Cretan girl of her age and class would be in similar circumstances, in high heels and black satin.

My one concern was how she would put up with the rigours of a long march over the mountains, but this was dispelled as soon as we started back for Kyriakosellia. Effortlessly, she kept up with us all the way, even at the breakneck pace which Stelio habitually set, and without a murmur settled into our nest in the carob tree; sleeping, as we did, fully-dressed, making a pillow of her small knapsack whose meagre contents differed from those of our own only in one item—a modest object, unknown to the peasants on whom we modelled our disguise, and one which we had therefore learnt to do without—a toothbrush.

_____

We must have presented an unusual sight as we started off early next morning, with Stelio's eye-catching figure leading the way, followed by Arthur whose height and flaming red hair were only accentuated by the Cretan waistcoat he had donned in a vain attempt at additional disguise, and by Katina who looked like a young memsahib on safari. Behind them Niko, who might have been taken for a shepherd provided he stood still, stumbled so clumsily up the rough path that he appeared to be more of a stranger to the country than either Alec Tarves or myself, while Pavlo who brought up the rear was the only member of the group who fitted unobtrusively into the landscape, although even his features—the lank fair hair, green eyes and Slavonic slant of cheek—were by no means typically Cretan.

There was no hope of such an outlandish procession passing unnoticed through these mountains, and so, since we should in any case have attracted the attention of any German patrol at a distance of over a mile, there was accordingly no point in travelling unarmed. We therefore each carried a sten-gun with four full magazines of ammunition, which, with the food we had to take with us to last at least three days, reduced our inevitably slow progress to a crawl.

The burst of good weather had prompted the highlanders to move their flocks to their summer pastures in the topmost folds much earlier than usual, so that although Stelio avoided the main mountain tracks and led us over summits and through valleys more suitable for goats to tread than human beings, we were nevertheless observed from time to time by solitary shepherds who hailed us at a distance and, when we did not stop, came scampering over to have a closer look at us.

We left Pavlo to do all the talking at these encounters, for he had a successful manner of dealing with impertinent enquiries without giving offence. To the inevitable questions as to our purpose, destination and provenance, he gaily replied that we were outlaws on our way to surrender our weapons so as to benefit by the terms of an amnesty.

"But Canea's in the opposite direction!" our interrogator would protest. "And the young lady with you? What's she doing?"

"Oh, we've just abducted her," Pavlo would explain. "You see that tall gentleman there with the red hair? Well, he wants to marry her, only her parents object—so it's got to be a marriage by theft!"

Rather than risk being made a fool of any further, the shepherd would generally curb his curiosity and ask us to have a drink of milk or spend the night in his hut. These invitations, prompted by a natural instinct for hospitality, were all the more pressing for being reinforced, as they were now, by an almost uncontrollable curiosity, and it required all Pavlo's tact and ingenuity to refuse them with grace. But he succeeded, and at the end of the first day's march we

Kiwi Perkins (right) at Selino gang headquarters,
summer 1943

*The author (shirtless in the centre)
in a hide-out above Asi Gonia*

Villagers of Asi Gonia in a mountain hide-out

settled down to sleep undisturbed in an isolated cave that Stelio had remembered from the time, not so long before, when he was a professional fugitive.

By noon next day we had climbed so high that, although from the foothills the snow on the main range had appeared to have melted all away, we came across large drifts in the more sheltered areas and were thus enabled to replenish our water-bottles—a heaven-sent opportunity since the nearest water-supply from the point we had then reached was the Omalo Plain, which the Germans were reported to be using as an auxiliary landing-field for light aircraft. That evening, when we came in sight of the plateau, we could see their makeshift runway—a strip of earth flattened by a steam-roller which had been transported here at the cost of many torn muscles and broken limbs, by a forced-labour gang of over a hundred men and mules—and beside it, the small Luftwaffe detachment encamped in a couple of commandeered cheese-huts.

At dusk we dropped down into the plain and skirted it at its opposite circumference until we reached the southern exit; a saddle leading to the foothills above Koustoyerako, where we arrived the following morning after another night spent out of doors in the shelter of a small cypress forest. The wooded slopes in this area would have provided ample cover for a whole division, and we should probably never have unearthed the stragglers had not a guide from Koustoyerako, who had been on the look-out for us for the last twenty-four hours, shown us the way to their camp.

The little dell in which they were assembled looked like a brigands' lair. The sight of it and the sounds from it reminded me of a similar scene I had witnessed just after my first landing in Crete: the coffee-ship of Akendria, which had likewise been thronged by a crowd of potential evacuees. But these men, though more desperate and destitute after a year and a half longer in the hills, did not fill me with the same apprehension as their former counterparts, not only because I was now perhaps more inured to the violence and lawlessness which I felt they represented, but also because they themselves were in a more co-operative frame of mind.

Their high morale was naturally due to the prospect of freedom. For their unusual discipline, however, I had to thank the trio of Australians who had first helped us by recovering the kit we had lost in our shipwreck the previous winter. As soon as the New Zealander responsible for organizing the evacuation had been captured, these three had spontaneously taken over his duties. Not only had they helped to assemble their comrades from other areas; having done so, they had themselves reconnoitred a suitable landing-beach, notified its position to Headquarters through the I.S.L.D. station and arranged for the boat to come in and fetch them that very night. All we had to do now was to wait till it was dark before moving down to the coast.

———

The beach they had chosen was all but inaccessible except from the sea: a mere opening at one end of a narrow fissure in the littoral cliffs. The ravine behind it led only to the base of a sheer precipice, and this cul-de-sac was flanked on either side by natural ramparts which could be scaled at one point alone; so that unless the operation was already betrayed and the Germans from the nearest coastguard detachment just under a mile away were in position there before us, we had no fear of being spotted by a chance mountain patrol.

My only anxiety, then, was whether the boat would turn up on time. If it failed to arrive that night we should have to take to the hills again at dawn and come down once more the following evening, for in spite of the relative security of the beach we could not allow such a large assembly of people to be concentrated in broad daylight at a point on the coast from which it would be impossible to withdraw in a sudden emergency. But I need not have worried. We had been signalling for less than an hour, when we heard the sound of an engine out to sea—a deep purr, much louder than I expected, which quickly increased to a full-throated roar utterly unlike the noise made by a submarine or John Campbell's *Hedgehog*.

I could not believe that such a deafening vessel had been chosen for a clandestine operation, and my fears that it might be a German E-boat seemed to be confirmed when a silhouette closely resembling one came into view round the nearest promontory. Unless a searchlight was turned on us, however, we were still safe; so while the boat drifted in towards us with engines barely ticking over, we stood where we were, each of us prepared to take individual flight since the circumstance demanded a policy of every man for himself.

Alec had instinctively stopped signalling as soon as the boat appeared, and the ensuing darkness and silence increased our tension to such an extent that for several seconds we remained as though dazed before breaking into nervous laughter and cheers at the sound of unmistakably English invective directed at us across the water:

"Put that bloody light on; we can't see where we're going!"

With delighted surprise I recognized the voice as John's, and a minute later the dinghy in which he was being rowed ashore grounded and he was pressing a bottle of gin and several tins of cigarettes into my hands.

He seemed surprised when I told him how alarmed we had been by the boat which had brought him in. "It's a perfectly ordinary naval M.L.," he explained.

But Cairo had never warned me to expect a naval motor-launch. I had been waiting either for one of the S.O.E. craft or a submarine, and it was only now that I learnt for the first time that the former had been diverted for operations elsewhere in the Mediterranean, while the latter had not been used since the previous year for clandestine missions of this kind.

Meanwhile, embarkation had started, Katina and Niko going off in the dinghy while most of the Australians saved time and trouble by swimming out to the boat. Arthur was the last to leave shore, hoping against hope that something would crop up to prevent his departure. He was genuinely grieved by the prospect of his return to Cairo, and so was I, not only because his deep emotion was infectious but also because his absence, besides creating a void in our organization, would also deprive me of a companionship which was all the more precious to me in Crete, and already I was beginning to feel a sense of loss.

We said good-bye in Cretan fashion, embracing each other on both cheeks and five minutes later his tall silhouette, sitting upright in the dinghy, had merged into the long, dark profile of the motor-launch.

His troubles, however, were not yet over. Among the passengers on the M.L. was the S.O.E. psychiatrist, who had come in ostensibly to sound the reactions of the evacuees. It was he who on landing in Africa reported that Arthur had been dead drunk during the operation, and as a result of this report Arthur was dismissed the service and sent back in ignominy to England.*

---

*Publisher's note: Major A. E. E. Reade was not "dismissed the service." He was ordered to resign his commission but was later re-instated and continued as a serving officer until 1948.

Whether the psychiatrist was a creature of the Brigadier's or not, I still do not know. All I do know is that Arthur was victimized in the most ruthless and cowardly manner, for the only person who could have spoken in his defence was myself. Arthur realized this and sent me several letters entreating me to state what was only the truth: that for two days prior to the evacuation the only liquid that had passed our lips was, when we were lucky enough to get it, either goat's milk or water.

But I never received these letters until I was myself evacuated almost a year later. They were held up, in the same way that evidence in favour of Dreyfus was withheld—"whenever a staff officer takes off his cap a secret document pops out"—for although my mail was regularly delivered either by parachute or small boat during the subsequent six months, all the letters Arthur wrote me were retained in our Cairo office on the usual pretext which covered the Lord knows what multitude of sins—"for security reasons" it was, they told me.

CHAPTER FOURTEEN

1943

A T T H A T S T A G E of the occupation the foothills above Koustoyerako were probably the only habitable area in the whole of Crete which could have sheltered in safety such a vast clandestine concourse as ours had been. Unlike the northern slopes of the White Mountain range, which swept down to the plains in a single more or less unbroken sweep, the ground here was criss-crossed by a network of intersecting valleys and deep ravines which restricted movement in all four directions. The Germans scarcely ever penetrated into this highland labyrinth, where they would have been hopelessly lost without a local guide; and no guide from this intensely patriotic and warlike area ever offered his services to the enemy.

Rather than take the transmitting-set and batteries that had just been landed all the way over the mountains back to our old hideouts, I decided to set up a new station in this remote district which, although more inaccessible from Canea and from our sources of information in the north, was for that very reason more likely to offer us the opportunity of working undisturbed.

We therefore established camp by the side of a mountain spring on a thickly wooded slope about five miles inland: an idyllic spot, to which there was only one disadvantage—the water there was renowned for its health-giving and appetite-provoking properties, so that however much we ate we remained constantly hungry. Our concern over supplies was aggravated by the large number of villagers who attached themselves to the station; for although they all arrived with sackfuls of beans or rice and cheeses the size of cart-

wheels, which they offered as presents, none of them could carry
sufficient quantities up the rough track from the village, so that
we were perpetually short of food until we managed to organize a
weekly supply service direct from Canea where we replenished our
stocks from the German-promoted black market.

Meanwhile we supplemented our diet by the feasts to which we
were regularly invited by the inhabitants of Koustoyerako, Moni and
Livadas, the three nearest villages. For this area was still as unaffected by enemy activity as the Amari Valley had been in the early
stages of the occupation. We could wander quite openly in broad
daylight from house to house as though we were ourselves natives of
the place; but being in fact strangers, we were entertained still more
lavishly than if we had in reality formed part of the local population.

The hospitality and fearlessness of these three closely interrelated
communities were such that I was even invited to act as godfather
at a christening, a service which was as freely attended as though no
German had ever been heard of in Crete. According to the rites of
the Orthodox Church, the child's name is chosen not by his parents
but by the person who stands as sponsor at the baptism—which on
the few occasions that I acted in this capacity gave me the opportunity of commemorating the occupation by calling my godchildren
"Freedom," "Victory" and even "England": appellations resound-
ing with topical patriotism, which in spite of their inherent danger
delighted these infants' parents whenever they had occasion to refer
to their children by name.

At Koustoyerako the ceremony was followed by an all-night feast
culminating in a *feu de joie* from twenty or thirty massed rifles, for
even the proximity of the German coastguard detachment was not
enough to prevent these revelers from letting off steam in their own
traditional manner, by a show of fire-arms, even though shotguns had
been declared illegal and carrying one incurred the death penalty.

In this splendidly uninhibited atmosphere our clandestine station
assumed the carefree character of a peacetime holiday camp, and
I should no doubt have grown fat and lazy during the summer we
were based there, had it not been for the regular tours of inspection I
undertook with Pavlo in other parts of my area as far afield as Prines
and the Amari, both of which Paddy and I continued to use as convenient half-way meeting-places for our monthly conferences.

For Alec Tarves this period of undisturbed activity must have
been a godsend after the excursions and alarms he had been through

in the eight months since our arrival. He was now able to leave his aerial up for weeks on end instead of having to pack away all his equipment after each schedule in case of a sudden German raid. He put the consequent leisure he enjoyed to good use by learning Greek, and his fluent command of local invective, understandable even when emitted in the accents of the Scottish Highlands, became a byword in the villages. So did his appearance. Anxious to resemble the Cretans as closely as possible in every respect, he washed even less than they did, and was soon so indescribably filthy and vermin-ridden that everyone referred to him in tones of admiration and affection as "The Tinker."

About the middle of August we received a signal to say that a boat would shortly be coming in to the beach from which Arthur and the stragglers had been evacuated, in order to land a consignment of food and clothing I had ordered and also an assistant who was to relieve me of some of my duties so that I should not have to be constantly on the march. The area for which I was then responsible consisted of well over a thousand square miles of mountainous country with a population of nearly a quarter of a million, and since the station was situated in its furthest corner I needed almost a week on the road each time I wanted to hold a conference with the resistance leaders at Prines.

I felt sure the German coastguards must have heard the noise the boat made the last time it came in, and so, since they probably already suspected the area was being used for clandestine landings, they were now more likely to be on the alert. In themselves they represented little danger to us, for they were unable to move about in the dark, and by dawn, if all went well, the landing would already have taken place and we should have left the beach and been safely under cover of the inland hills. But a report had recently come in of a caique which had started to patrol this particular stretch of coast every night, and if this vessel was in wireless contact with the coast-guard station we risked being attacked from the direction in which we were most vulnerable—the sea.

I therefore took steps, which were more in the nature of a joke than a genuine precaution, to drown the noise of our boat's approach. Serving with the Germans on the coast was a detachment of Cretan gendarmerie, one of whom was an expert lyre-player. On the night the boat was expected I accordingly arranged for him to entertain the enemy to an impromptu recital, in the hope that the strident notes of his instrument would muffle the deeper roar of the engines out to sea.

Whether his attempt was successful or not, I never found out. After the long climb down to the beach we started signalling as soon as darkness fell. All night long we kept flashing the prearranged message in Morse at the required intervals until, shortly before dawn, just as we had given up all hope, we heard the throb of an engine approaching through the gradually receding gloom. Then, with a suddenly increased burst of sound that seemed to drive straight up the ravine in which we stood, the shape of a vessel appeared round the promontory on our left and started crossing the narrow channel which represented our restricted field of view as far as the cape directly opposite. It was still far out to sea, but close enough for us to tell that it was not the boat we expected.

It was obviously the caique the Germans had commandeered for their coastal patrol; and even as we watched, it turned towards the shore and came chugging straight towards us. The men on board must have seen our signals, although Alec had automatically stopped flashing as soon as the boat came into view.

What the enemy hoped to achieve by this manoeuvre, it was difficult to say. They must have been incurably optimistic if they expected to find us waiting for them on their arrival. For long before they approached the beach we had climbed out of the gorge—unmolested, for in the half-light we still offered no target for their guns—and it was from the safe vantage-point of the surrounding heights that we watched them make a tactical disembarkation as though they were the forward troops of a full-scale seaborne invasion.

They scrambled up the beach in open formation with shouts of "Komm! Komm!"—an invitation which was scarcely encouraging since they accompanied it by a volley of shots into every bush and cave they could see. From where we were we could have retaliated with great advantage, but this would only have provoked reprisals later. Besides, their obvious nervousness made us feel nothing but pity. Action against what they called "terrorists" was never popular among the occupation forces, who usually assigned to this task men who had been court-martialled, promising them a remission of sentence if they succeeded in killing or capturing a British agent or a native in British employment. But this, I felt, was hardly the way to set about it. We were barely able to refrain from jeering as we slowly withdrew back to our station in the hills.

Had I taken proper precautions, I should have postponed the operation until the following month or at least chosen an alternative beach for it some distance away. But I had been lulled into a false sense of security by the happy-go-lucky inhabitants of this area. I had also, I suppose, grown lazy. Although the climb down from the station was difficult, it only took three or four hours, and I dreaded having to make a far longer march in order to meet the boat. Two days later, then, when we were notified that a landing would once again be attempted, we set off in the direction of the same beach.

We had now become so accustomed to the inland cliffs and the hazards we had to negotiate on our way down that we accomplished the journey more quickly than we thought we should. It was still light when we reached the heights directly above the ravine—which was fortunate, for otherwise we should not have known for certain that the spot was under enemy observation. There were no troops in position there, of course—nothing short of a brigade would have sufficed for patrolling every nook and cranny in this labyrinthine coastal section—instead, a single seaplane kept flying overhead, hedge-hopping over the surrounding cliffs and dipping down into the ravine itself, so low that from where we were it frequently disappeared out of sight beneath our feet. These manoeuvres it continued until the late evening, when it finally flew off on the direction of the setting sun.

And still I hesitated to call off the operation. In any case, it was now far too late to notify Headquarters, for the boat would already have left in the morning and so, whether we were there to meet it or not, would be running an almost equal risk. I did, however, take the precaution of avoiding the ravine itself, which was clearly suspect, and decided to signal instead from a group of rocks a few hundred yards to the west where I was told there was a suitable cave right on the shore.

I wished we had known about it before. For an operation involving a small number of personnel, it was the ideal spot: to all intents and purposes inaccessible from the sea, and invisible from the land at a distance of a few feet. The water here had tunnelled an underground corridor into the cliffs, at an oblique angle so that the entrance to the cavity would scarcely show even to a rowing boat close inshore; and this subterranean passage led for a dozen yards or so inland straight from deep water to an aperture in the ground barely large enough for a man to slip through. Once we had entered one by one through this hole and had pulled a rock or bush over it as camouflage, a division of Germans could have tramped along the path a yard or two away without suspecting we were inside.

So we settled in there until it was time to start signalling out to sea. If the worse came to the worst, we thought, all we should have to do was put the torch away and keep quiet. It was only then we discovered that we had not brought a torch with us.

It was one of those silly minor mistakes that often had major consequences, and no one was to blame for it but myself. I thought Alec had brought his torch with him; he thought I had brought mine. None of the Cretans with us had one of his own, but with typical ingenuity they soon rigged up a signalling fire, building a chimney of stones with a hole in front and using the furze that grew nearby as fuel.

It worked, and that was its only recommendation. Poor Alec was half-suffocated by the smoke as he stood over it, masking the light of the flame with his jacket which he lifted in a series of jerks so as to spell out the letters of our Morse message; and while he was occupied on this task, which must have been more tiring than conducting a symphony orchestra or fighting a bull—both of which he seemed at times to be doing—the rest of us were kept busy collecting more furze to feed the flames.

But even though this Heath-Robinson contraption was perfectly efficient, I hardly expected the boat to turn up that night, partly because its failure to arrive forty-eight hours before made me illogically doubtful of its ever arriving, but mostly because I felt we should somehow be made to pay for our negligence in forgetting the torch. I was therefore neither surprised nor disappointed when, after six hours' arduous activity, dawn put an end to our vigil and we once more retraced our steps to the station without having heard or seen anything out to sea.

———

I had now decided definitely to postpone the operation until the following moonless period, but, encouraged by a message from Cairo saying that the boat was to make a third attempt to come in, we again climbed down to the beach two days later.

This time everything went off without a hitch. Alec and I both brought torches, just to make sure of one of us doing so. There was no seaplane patrolling the coast, no caique off-shore. We signalled less than two hours before hearing the sound of an engine out to sea, and a quarter of an hour later the boat glided in, so close in the deep water that the dinghy lowered from it needed to be rowed ashore on its first trip only; for the remainder it was pulled in and out on a line.

The first person to land was an army officer who introduced himself as Sandy Rendel.[1] By the light of the flickering fire I could hardly see his face, but even had he been wearing a mask the pleasure I felt at meeting him would not have been less. It was the sound of his voice that delighted me—the first educated English voice I had heard, except during my rare meetings with Paddy, for over two months.

He told me he was soon going to be infiltrated into the far east of Crete, so as to relieve the officer in charge of that area of half his commitments. This present trip he was making only in the capacity of "conducting officer"; he would be returning on the boat as soon as all the stores and personnel were safely ashore. Part of the stores he handed me in person—a haversack containing a thousand sovereigns. As for the personnel, besides my future assistant—a New Zealand N.C.O. called Kiwi Perkins[2]—there was only one other person coming in. Before I could ask who it was, my unvoiced question was answered by the sound of singing and laughter from the incoming dinghy. The words came clear across the intervening stretch of water:

Hitler has only got one ball . . .

and, presently, George Psychoundakis was standing beside us, being embraced in turn by everyone in the cave.

Behind him another figure stepped ashore, a slim long-headed silhouette against the golden firelit sea, which in the firelight itself assumed the three-dimensional contours of a young man in breeches and tattered jacket. I could barely make out his features but was

1. Capt. (later Major) A. M. Rendel; author of *Appointment in Crete*; at present diplomatic correspondent of *The Times*.

2. Sergeant Dudley Perkins of Christchurch; killed in action in Crete a few months later.

impressed by the sound of his quiet voice though he uttered only the three words:

"I'm Perkins, sir."

With the tow-rope shuttle-service in operation, all the stores were landed in under an hour. Sandy returned to the boat on the dinghy's last outward trip, the roar of the boat's engines echoed for a moment round the cave, and long before it had died into the distance we were preparing to move off. On the long climb back to the station there was only one thing that disturbed my feeling of comfort and content—the terrible weight of the haversack containing the sovereigns. This was the first and only time in my life that I have ever been conscious of riches being a burden.

CHAPTER FIFTEEN

1943

FOR SOME TIME I had no opportunity of testing Kiwi Perkins's qualities, though I felt sure he would be more than useful in any emergency. In appearance he was much as I imagined Lawrence of Arabia must have looked—blue eyes in a long lean face with a high straight forehead, the two parallel lines which ran from each cheekbone to the corners of the square jaw-line forming three sides of an almost-perfect rectangle—and in character too he closely resembled what I had read about the famous Arab leader. He gave the impression of being a man with a vocation, and beneath his habitual silence I could discern a terrier-like restlessness.

He had been one of the first stragglers to escape from Crete after the battle, and had put those weeks of wandering in the hills to good purpose by acquiring a working knowledge of Greek. He therefore had an additional asset. He had since applied for a commission, and had been incomprehensibly turned down even though, more than any other N.C.O. I had met, he had the makings of a brilliant officer. But I was grateful that in his case the authorities had shown their usual blindness, for otherwise he might have been posted elsewhere and I should have been deprived of his assistance in Crete.

Now that he was back here, however, I could not immediately find him a suitable position of responsibility. The intelligence and organization networks were both working so efficiently by now that I scarcely ever needed to be absent from the station. When I did have to leave it for a conference in another part of the island, it was

Kiwi who took my place; but the duties that then devolved on him were more or less limited to being a companion for Alec Tarves.

For the handful of men who acted as our sentries and guards were quite capable of looking after themselves. The nucleus of the small body was formed by the Paterakis, a family of six brothers whose ages ranged from sixteen to thirty. One of them, Manoli, had been in the east end of the island for almost a year, serving as Paddy's right-hand man; the remainder, with various uncles and cousins, were welded into a homogeneous potential fighting force under the leadership of the eldest brother, Vasili, and it would have been unwise to disrupt this natural hierarchy by appointing a foreigner to command in his place.

For the time being, then, Kiwi was at a loose end, though he did not allow this to disturb his almost yogi-like equanimity. He voluntarily appointed himself camp cook, and out of old biscuit tins constructed what we had never before had in the mountains; an efficient oven. Thanks to him and to the supplies of food which had come in with him, we lived luxuriously for the rest of the summer.

Those months would have been idyllic, but for the internal political situation. General Mandakas, realizing as well as I did how much easier it was to work in a relatively secure area like the mountains above Koustoyerako, had also transferred his headquarters to this neighbourhood; and his supporters were now busy disseminating the Communist-inspired doctrines of E.A.M. throughout the surrounding villages.

At first I was not alarmed by the reports I received of this insidious local propaganda. At that time the National Liberation Front was still masquerading as a patriotic movement, and although it was in opposition to our officially recognized National Organization of Crete I was naive enough to imagine that the two parties could cooperate in perfect amity. I therefore went out of my way to meet and hold discussions with the rival leaders whenever I could. But every conference ended in the same way, with the E.A.M. supporters demanding that I arrange for arms to be dropped to them while at the same time refusing to accept my suggestions as to how those arms should be distributed and used. Naturally, I could not acquiesce to their wishes.

The situation was aggravated when G.H.Q. Middle East was forced, after many months of indecision and prevarication, to recognize E.A.M. on the Greek mainland. Colonel Kondekakis, General

Mandakas's nearest representative, at once approached me with the ultimatum that if I did not recognize the General as the official Cretan resistance leader, E.A.M. would in their turn refuse to acknowledge me as the local Allied representative. He would not listen to my explanation—and to do him justice, it was hard to understand such an anomaly—that in S.O.E. the Greek office and the Cretan office were completely independent of one another; the directive for the mainland therefore did not apply to me. In the heated argument that followed we both lost our tempers and I made the fatal mistake of saying:

"You'll have to recognize whomever I appoint as a leader—even if it's only a donkey."

It was a purely figurative phrase, of course—for the Mayor of Canea had already been appointed—and Kondekakis knew it was. But that did not prevent him from spreading the news throughout the area that, thanks to me, a donkey was going to be appointed as the leader of the Cretan resistance movement. Among ignorant peasants this puerile propaganda might have been fatally successful, and it said a great deal for the natural intelligence of the Cretan villagers that, in spite of it, all but a few remained loyal to the official National Organization. The E.A.M. supporters became in consequence progressively more hostile, and for a short time I feared this hostility might break out into open conflict as it had already done on the mainland of Greece.

It was largely due to Mr. Skoulas himself that this disaster was averted. As Mayor, he not only wielded considerable influence among the local inhabitants but had also won the respect of the German authorities, so that the value of his work was beyond praise or measure. It was therefore a particularly hard blow when, in September that year, he came under suspicion of the Gestapo, had his home raided and barely escaped with his life. He had been forced to go into hiding in the hills to the north of the Omalo, where I went to see him as soon as I heard the news.

Nicholas Skoulas, then over sixty years old, had spent most of his life at a civil servant's desk and so, though younger than many other fugitives from justice I had met, was unaccustomed to the rigours of an outlaw's existence. He was already suffering from the diet-deficiency and exposure to which he was condemned, and the summer was not yet over. When winter came his hardships would be increased tenfold. Another man in his position would have been

justified in asking to be evacuated immediately, as Colonel Papadakis had been, but Mr. Skoulas insisted on sharing the discomforts
of the rank and file. It was the example he set as much as the actual
work he continued to accomplish from his mountain lair that held
the organization together through the critical period provoked by
Mandakas's activity.

But the good that was done through his agency was in danger of
being undone by another source—one that I was least likely to suspect—none other than the British-sponsored I.S.L.D. party which
was still operating in the hills near my own station. Until then I
did not realize why the leader of the team, Stelio Papaderos, had
been evacuated so soon after his arrival—he had left Crete at the
same time as Arthur and the large group of stragglers—though I
had heard he had been on bad terms with his two colleagues. I now
concluded that the differences of opinion among this team must
have been on political grounds and that pressure had been put to
bear on Stelio; for as soon as he left, the remaining members of his
station had recruited into their service every E.A.M. supporter in
the neighbourhood. They had since put their transmitting set at the
disposal of General Mandakas, who was thereby enabled to boast
to his followers that he was in regular and official communication
with Allied Headquarters, an assertion which in their eyes lent cre-
dence to the report which Colonel Kondekakis had threatened to
spread and was in fact spreading, that I was not the acknowledged
Allied representative.

My position was inadvertently rendered still more insecure by an
order from Cairo. According to the signal I received, the Government in exile in Egypt wished it to be known that all members of
recognized resistance groups on the mainland and in the islands
were to be regarded, for purposes of pay and promotion, on the
same basis as the troops of the regular Greek army. I was to transmit
this message throughout my area.

Very reluctantly—for I did not see how this undertaking could
ever be implemented, since we naturally kept no nominal roll of our
personnel—I obeyed the order and notified every local leader of this
deceptively encouraging statement made by their own Prime Minister. Mandakas and his E.A.M. henchmen were not slow in turning
this news to their own profit. Perhaps they genuinely and sincerely
believed the message was a fake, for like me, they must have found
difficulty in understanding how a responsible head of a state could

make such a rash promise. Anyway they said it was; adding that it was simply a personal invention of mine, designed to attract recruits into the National Organization.

I was still not seriously alarmed by these Communist attempts to denigrate the movement I had sponsored and thereby to belittle my own position in the island. For the propaganda was successful only among the people who least needed it—Mandakas's personal supporters. Nevertheless, I thought it advisable to institute a counter-propaganda drive—if only to show the local patriots that the National Organization was well aware of its rival's activities—and as a first step in this direction, I decided to canvass some of the villages in the immediate vicinity that I had not yet visited.

This mountainous area contained very few large German garrisons but was constantly patrolled by small enemy sections specially selected from the Alpine troops which formed part of the occupation force. Their daily movements, however, were plotted and reported to me, so that there was little risk of running into any of them. Yet for all these precautions I did run into one on the very first day I set out.

On trips of this kind I usually travelled alone with Pavlo Bernardakis, but he was absent in his village two days' march away, so this time I was accompanied instead by Vasili Paterakis and two other young men from the station called Stelio and Noumphri. We started the long climb down into the valley early in the morning, before the clandestine situation report could reach us, but we were confident of being warned about any German activity in the first village on our route.

But we never reached that village. A mile or so short of it, the path we had to take ran along the bottom of a deep indentation and parallel to a dried-up river bed which it crossed before leading over the opposite slope behind which the village lay. Pools of stagnant water and patches of damp mud, sole remnants of what a few months before had been an icy torrent, imbued the landscape with an atmosphere of almost Himalayan remoteness which was intensified by the giant oleander bushes sprouting from soil that seemed to be a mixture of desert and jungle. These grew so thick at the base of either bank that to cross the gulley we had to force our way through them by parting the tangled branches with our hands.

At this point Stelio was leading the way, walking a few feet ahead of me. As he drew back one of the successive curtains of leaf and twig, he came to a sudden halt and turned round so abruptly that our heads knocked together. I was conscious simultaneously of his eyes, grotesquely magnified by proximity and alarm, staring for a fleeting second into mine; of his mouth opening, so close to me that in my confusion I could not tell whether it was in a whisper or a yelp that he uttered the single word "Germans!"; and beyond, before the branches he had parted had time to snap back into position, of a number of figures in Afrika Korps uniform.

This glimpse could not have lasted much longer than the click of a camera shutter, for in that time I too had turned and followed Stelio's panic-stricken flight. But although my eye, like an immediately sensitized plate, had faithfully and automatically recorded the scene, it was unable to transmit it at once to my brain; so that only after running more than twenty yards did I clearly see, not the boulders and roots over which I was stumbling at that moment, but the Germans as they had appeared to me several moments before—one of them stripped to the waist, with a skin-coloured scar running down the side of his lathered cheek as he dipped a shaving-brush into a mess-tin full of soapy water; and his companions lying or sitting in the shade in which he stood, their rifles and machine-pistols hanging like primitive ornaments from the wall of oleander behind them.

As this image developed in my mind, two thoughts impressed themselves on me: first, that the Germans were most certainly no longer in the relaxed attitudes in which they had posed for my present mental snapshot; and, secondly, that I had no business to be floundering up the river-bed, which I seemed to be negotiating as though in a slow-motion film, when there was a perfectly good path to use as a line of retreat. Yet though I was conscious of the panic that had put me in this position, I could not control it, but blindly followed Stelio, deriving meanwhile an inexplicable satisfaction and consolation from the sound of the footsteps of my other two companions stampeding close behind.

It was the inevitable cry of "Komm! Komm!" that brought us all to our senses. Though our escape was bound to be cut off by the Germans rushing unimpeded up the path while we clumsily struggled and splashed through bushes, mud and water, we now at last had sufficient presence of mind to draw our pistols and take up a defensive position.

But there was not enough cover to enable us to carry out a tactical withdrawal. Before I could aim at what I imagined to be the leading German, another had appeared a few yards further on, his head and shoulders barely visible above the leafy wall between us. But there was enough of him showing for me to see that in his hands was a machine-pistol and that it was pointed straight at me. I did not wait to find out if his finger was on the trigger, but plunged flat into the boulder-strewn undergrowth, conscious, above the rattle of his weapon, of the twigs and leaves all round me being slashed and snapped by bullets, and of Stelio's body flying through the air by my side.

With the firing increasing in intensity, we crawled together through the mud, hoping to outflank the enemy whose numbers we could only roughly estimate by the sound of the various weapons in action; but reaching the opposite bank, we found that side of the gulley already occupied by two more Germans whom we had not accounted for, and as we began to retrace our steps the noise of their automatic weapons added to the din above and around us.

Suddenly the firing stopped, brought to an end not by a Cease Fire order, but by a sound far more blood-curdling. With the effect of a referee's whistle, though louder and more strident, a man's shriek of agony proclaimed, as though by mutual agreement, a ten-second silence.

During the whole of that time I was kept guessing as to the source of that ghastly signal. Since our dive into the undergrowth Stelio and I had lost contact with our two companions, who, with only a pistol each, could have been no match for an enemy force at least ten strong; I was therefore fearful that it was either Vasili or Noumphri who had uttered that agonizing yell. But just as I was wondering how I could go to their rescue and so abandon the rather ignominious part I had so far played in the engagement, I heard both their voices raised in the ensuing conversation, carried out in that garbled mixture of Greek, German, French and onomatopoeia which served as a common language in the villages between the local inhabitants and their foreign oppressors:

"Nix-boum-boum! Parti, parti!"

"You nix boum-boum! German soldier kaput!"

"Nix boum-boum. We parti."

"Nix, nix! Parti, you parti!"

During the course of this conversation the voices of our companions grew fainter, and I realized they were retreating up the hill.

From what had been said I gathered with amazement that one of the Germans had been shot and that his comrades, although heavily outnumbering us, were reluctant to continue the action and were allowing Vasili and Noumphri to get away before any further damage was done on either side.

This might have been the opportune moment for Stelio and me to break cover and take to our heels as well. On the other hand, any attempt to escape on our part might have led to a renewed exchange of shots before the other two could get clean away, while we should clearly have been at a disadvantage. We could not decide at once which course to adopt, and therefore missed our opportunity, paying dearly for our indecision. For as soon as our companions were out of range, the Germans concentrated on unearthing Stelio and myself. For an hour or more, over a distance of fifty yards on either side of us, they sprayed both banks of the river bed with an almost continuous stream from their machine-pistols and rifles, punctuating this fire with an occasional hand-grenade and the repeated exhortation of "Komm! Komm!"

But we realized it was now too late to come to terms, even had we been able to emerge without being hit by one of the unaimed though far from "stray" bullets. All we could do was cower still more closely to the ground under the meagre protection of the bushes and boulders. Finally, either because they had exhausted their ammunition or considered we must by now both have been killed, the Germans stopped firing, leaving us in the sudden silence with our senses still reeling at our miraculous escape from the whirlpool of noise which might for us have proved lethal.

Our troubles, however, were not yet over. Although they had ceased fire, the enemy did not abandon their attempt to winkle us out of our hiding-place—whether because they supposed we were still alive or in order to recover our bodies if we happened to be dead, it was impossible to tell. Sentries were posted all round us— one of them, only a few feet away, I kept aligned in the sights of my pistol for more than a quarter of an hour until he shifted his position further up the path—and these were presently reinforced by a body of civilians from the nearest village, who as soon as they arrived began to comb the bed of the river itself. From their murmured remarks I was able to learn what had happened and was happening outside our own small world encompassed by the rocks among which we had taken refuge.

During the recent hour-long hail of bullets and grenades the wounded German—he had been shot in the stomach, hence his scream of agony—had been carried into the village by two of his comrades, who had then rounded up a score of the inhabitants and brought them here to search for us while they themselves stood guard on either bank. They naturally wished to avoid further casualties in their own ranks and were reluctant to risk their skins in case Stelio and I were still alive—a possibility which, to judge from the orders of their sergeant, must have seemed remote; for I clearly heard him tell the villagers to look for "two Cretans kaput."

It was, at least ostensibly, an intensive search. One of the men taking part came across my walking-stick, the handle of which protruded from the undergrowth while the tip remained resting on my own foot; and I had no means of knowing whether he had seen me or not as he triumphantly seized this trophy, brandishing it in the air and calling excitedly to the Germans:

"Bastouni here, but no one kaput! No one here at all!"

Even though the Germans might by now have concluded we had managed to get away in the flurry of the initial encounter, they still did not call off the attempt to find us; and the river-bed continued to be trampled over by so many people that for a moment I was almost tempted to creep out and join them myself, hoping to be taken by the Germans for one of the search-party. They were unlikely to have counted the men they had drafted and would probably not recognize each of them individually, so the subterfuge might have been successful. I was deterred from attempting it, however, by the thought that if Stelio and I were not discovered, the men who had failed to find us might themselves have to pay the penalty and be arrested as hostages. By posing as one of them I should therefore only put myself in a still more unenviable position.

Meanwhile, though hunger and thirst were my least concern since fear had made me indifferent to the absence of food and water all day, a physical torment intruded nevertheless on my mental discomfort: a longing which, however ludicrous, was a source of consternation as well—a simple irresistible urge to cough. I was inhaling dust from the shattered leaves and twigs with every breath I took, and I had no means of relieving my desiccated throat. I tried sucking the ends of my trousers, still damp from the pools I had plunged through during my flight several hours before, but the fluff from the cloth only made matters worse.

Stelio was in the same plight, but even in the present circumstances his Cretan talent for improvisation did not desert him. Since there was no water available, he promptly and silently made some; and though most of it immediately drained through the pebbles underfoot, a little settled on a small patch of earth, turning it into a liquid muddy paste. This he scooped up and slowly swallowed, deriving, apparently, as much relief from it as if it had been a particularly delicious cough mixture. I regret to say I had not the stomach to follow his example.

During the morning and afterwards, while the search was still in progress, I had felt almost certain that we should never get out of the hole we were in—the metaphorical hole, that is, not the hole in which we were hiding, for clearly we could not stay there for ever— and I had tried in my imagination to plan the course we should have to adopt on being discovered. But as the afternoon advanced into evening and we still remained unrevealed, I began to cherish the opposite conviction that whatever steps the Germans now took, we were bound to get away unscathed. Curiously enough, this thought gave me no pleasure. I had envisaged so clearly the running fight in daylight for which I had unconsciously prepared myself that the vision of crawling to safety in the dark, which I now knew for certain would be our method of escape, was a disappointing and somehow shaming anti-climax.

And so it turned out. When night fell the search was called off and the villagers returned to their homes. Stelio and I could not tell if the Germans, however, had remained or not; for in the gathering darkness every natural sound seemed to our overwrought senses to be man-made, every bush in our distorted imagination appeared as an ambush. Besides, it was not unreasonable to assume that the enemy were camping out and that sentries had been posted. In any case, we worked on that assumption and took the necessary precautions.

About midnight, then, in darkness so thick that we could only try to pierce it with our ears since we were virtually sightless, we began edging forward inch by inch through the bushes towards the nearest bank. The path there was only a few feet off—we took over a quarter of an hour to reach it, testing every twig we had to brush against, waiting, if it snapped, for at least a minute before taking another step. Once clear of the bushes, we had to contend with the pebbles on the slope behind the path, which we avoided except to cross it. Testing these with our feet, as we had the twigs with our hands, we slowly wormed our way uphill, unaware if our silhouettes would be visible or not to an observer below us.

At this point, perhaps even in broad daylight, we could have taken to our heels with every expectation of getting away without being hit if fired on; but exaggerated caution had by now become a habit. It was only after advancing a further fifty yards, which in this manner took almost two hours, that we finally got up and ran for it, heedless of the noise we made and expecting at any moment to hear a shout or a shot.

We heard neither. The Germans, then, must have packed up and left hours before; so that to the feeling of anti-climax engendered by our escape, our method of escaping only added a sense of ridicule and shame.

This rather lamentable check to my activities was, fortunately for my self-respect, no more than momentary. In the course of the following weeks I managed to complete the tour on which I had originally embarked. I also tried to persuade myself that our encounter with the Germans had not been altogether unprofitable. It had taught me at least that even in this relatively secure area of Koustoyerako the enemy still represented a very real danger—a fact which I had almost overlooked after being left so long in peace—and that the danger was likely to spread as our activity progressed. I therefore decided to increase the personnel of the station.

There was no shortage of volunteers. My only problem was how to feed and equip the number of men who joined us. Supplying them by air was the best solution, so I organized in quick succession two parachute drops which, despite the worst possible terrain for such an operation, were both a hundred percent successful. In the pure mountain night it was a joy to watch the containers come drifting down, all within the dropping-zone and some launched with such accuracy that they landed right on top of our signal fires. Fortunately, these did not happen to be the ones containing the ammunition I had ordered.

For, in spite of my aversion to armed activity at this stage, I had ordered ammunition—as well as rifles, machine-guns and hand-grenades. I realized that, whether I wanted it or not, a potential guerrilla gang was imperceptibly growing round the nucleus of our station guards; so rather than discourage its formation, I had decided to put it on a proper fighting basis; and in the hope that some sort of uniform would help to instill a sense of pride and discipline, I even included, as an additional refinement to the arms and equipment I gave each man, an Australian-pattern khaki hat.

I felt fairly confident that under Vasili's orders the gang would not betray my trust by going into action prematurely. Creating an armed body of this kind was naturally a risk, but I consoled myself that it was a risk worth taking in view of the general war situation, which might, I hoped, at any moment demand an armed uprising in Crete. I had just received news of the Italian capitulation, and since there were several thousands of Italian troops in the east end of the island, perhaps there would be some interesting developments locally.

But in my area the effect of the Axis rift was not immediately noticeable. The Italians were simply disarmed by their former allies and left more or less to fend for themselves or else were drafted into sections of the Feldgendarmerie, which was always short of German recruits since this department of the Wehrmacht was usually employed on the unpopular task of hunting down Cretan "terrorists."

Paddy, however, was instantly involved. He sent me a letter saying he was just off to contact the Italian G.O.C., General Carta—an extremely risky mission which necessitated wearing enemy uniform as a disguise—in the hope of persuading him to be evacuated to Cairo with all his staff and archives. A few weeks later I received another note, this time from Tom, telling me that the operation had been successfully completed, that Paddy had left Crete in order to escort his important prisoner to G.H.Q., that he, Tom, had meanwhile returned to resume his duties in the east of the island and wanted to meet me somewhere near Asi Gonia in three days' time.

I accordingly set off at once with Kiwi and Pavlo.

CHAPTER SIXTEEN

1943

Not until I reached Asi Gonia did I learn the purpose of Tom's visit. A runner came in with the news that he was approaching with a vast horde of men, including the whole of one of the two guerrilla gangs that had been operating in the east of the island, all of whom were due to be evacuated in two days' time from the beach Papadakis and I had used just over a year before. Due to the gang's unwise activity which had already caused several villages to be burnt to the ground in reprisal, not to mention the arrest and execution of countless hostages, the beaches in Tom's area were no longer safe. Hoping the presence of these hotheads here would not prejudice the security of those in my area as well, I started at once for the spot where they were reported to have halted—a saddle in the mountains above Alones, not far from the hideout I had shared with Papadakis before our evacuation.

My worst fears were confirmed as soon as I saw them. I could not tell if it was their usual practice to camp by the side of a main path without attempting to keep under cover or whether, now that they were out of their own area, they simply felt they could afford to be careless—whatever the reason, the exposed slope on which they had halted seemed to be pullulating with armed men whose weapons in the setting sun cast flashes of light which must have been visible for miles, and the noise they made could have been heard at an almost equal distance away.

I was not particularly impressed by this show of bravado. Nor, I imagined, were the inhabitants of the nearby villages; for even if they had not helped the gang—and with typical Cretan generosity they naturally had, depleting their flocks to provide the food that was needed—they knew they might have to pay, if not with their lives, then at least with the loss of their homes, for their unfortunate proximity to such an enemy-provoking target.

But my annoyance was slightly mitigated by the pleasure of seeing Tom again and hearing all the latest news from Cairo. With him was another I.S.L.D. team which had recently been infiltrated, consisting of Ralph Stockbridge, who had now returned to Crete as an officer, and a young captain called John Stanley who was likewise a wireless operator. Their only camp-follower was a German deserter, for whom Ralph had thoughtfully made himself personally responsible—a necessary precaution, for otherwise this youthful representative of the enemy forces would not have lasted long among the bearded desperadoes surrounding him.

Niko Souris was also there, and as we moved off in the evening to the shelter of Papadakis's old hide-out I noted with alarm that he was singing—singing beautifully as he only did when he felt worried or apprehensive.

In the well-remembered shelving cleft, where Paddy and I had once spent the night following the moon from rock to rock as we drank our raki, we settled down in the gathering darkness. One of the sheep which the gang had acquired on the march was slaughtered, a fire was lit on which to roast it, and in the light of the flames, while Niko continued his serenade with scarcely a pause, Tom and I divided our share of the burnt, but uncooked meat with the leader of the gang, Manoli Bandouvas, a dark burly man with sad ox-eyes and a correspondingly deep-throated voice in which he was fond of uttering cataclysmic aphorisms such as "The struggle needs blood, my lads."

When at last I curled up in my cloak to go to sleep he was still talking, as indeed were most of his followers, for even the fatigue of several consecutive days on the march did nothing to curb their innate love of chatter. I woke up in the middle of the night to find them even more vociferous than before, for now, instead of conversing in separate groups, they were all concentrated in a body round the fire, apparently intent on a single communal topic. It was only when I got up to listen more closely that I saw the object of their new attention.

There was a stranger in their midst—a stranger, that is, to me; for he was clearly known to the rest of the company, who addressed him by name each time they fired a question at him. At first I thought he must be a member of the gang who had turned up in the night with a vital report on which he was now being interrogated; but by the light of the flames I noticed he was kneeling uncomfortably on a jagged stone, with his hands tied behind his back and his arms likewise pinioned to his sides. He looked so much like a suppliant or the victim of a sacrificial rite that in my semi-comatose condition I was scarcely at all surprised to hear him address his main inquisitor, Bandouvas himself, with the words:

"You wouldn't kill me, now, Captain Manoli? You wouldn't kill me, would you?"

In answer to my sleepy enquiry as to what was going on, I was told the man was a suspected traitor. He originally lived in the area where the gang had been operating, but since his alleged treachery he had fled to a village near Alones and, by passing as a refugee from the German reprisals in the east, had found employment with a wealthy farmer. After almost a year fate had overtaken him: Bandouvas had heard of his presence in this neighbourhood and had despatched two of his henchmen to arrest him and bring him to book. Hence this impromptu court martial.

Considering he was probably responsible for the death of the relatives of several members of the gang, his trial was extremely fair. There was no attempt to force a confession from him: no taunt, no threat; only question after question. I realized now with a mixture of pride and relief that the bark of the Cretans was worse than their bite. I had often heard them outline in blood-thirsty detail how they would deal with a traitor if ever they caught one; but now that one was in their hands, there was no question of summary justice. They were taking time and trouble to establish or disprove the degree of their victim's guilt; indeed the only torture involved in the process was due, unintentionally, to the very duration of the trial, which was necessarily and inevitably prolonged by the intervention of the large number of prosecuting counsels present.

Since it looked like lasting all night, I prepared to go to sleep again. In any case I wanted to get out of range of that firelit circle which seemed to throw off alternate tangents of fear and revenge. For even though the trial was a fair one, I could not overlook the expressions of hatred and contempt on the faces of the men conducting it; and more disquieting even than these was the look of expectant horror on the face of their victim. With his shaven pate and thick coarse features, he was an ugly man by nature; and his ugliness was now intensified by circumstance. To avoid the irrational pity which I knew would overwhelm me if I stayed, I turned away from the group and lay down with the hood of my cloak pulled over my head. Even so my sleep was disturbed, punctuated by the barely-muffled reiteration:

"You're not going to kill me, Captain Manoli? You're not going to kill me, now, are you?"

He was still alive in the morning. How much longer he was likely to go on living, I could not tell; since the trial was not yet over. His life indeed might have been spared—for clearly his guilt was not yet established—had it not been for an unforeseen occurrence which sealed his fate as decisively as a death sentence.

As the sun flooded into the cleft from the east, a look-out posted on a peak overlooking the west gave a shout of "Germans!" And as the members of the gang seized their arms and rushed into position along the natural castellation of the ridge on that side, the first bullet to be fired was fired into the base of the suspect's skull. With the enemy in unknown strength so close to us, it would have been unwise to keep a man of unproven loyalty alive in our midst; and the German deserter, for the same reason, would have suffered a similar fate had he not been under the personal protection of Ralph Stockbridge.

To judge by the firing that immediately followed—for already sten-guns and even revolvers were in action—we might have been about to be overwhelmed by a superior force at a distance of a few yards. Tom and I and the rest of us who were armed only with pistols therefore rushed forward, expecting at any moment to come to grips with the first wave of attackers, but when we reached the ridge all we could see were half a dozen figures dispersed in flight over the exposed rocky slopes almost a mile away.

Confident of their excellent marksmanship, the Cretans had as usual opened fire too early. Had they waited they might have surrounded and captured this small enemy section without wasting a shot. Now that they had broken it up in panic, however, they were

forced instead to follow up with an arduous counter-attack, dividing
into small groups, each concentrated on chasing and bringing down
a single individual. For the next half-hour the landscape before us
was filled with a mob of shouting, gesticulating puppets.

It was hard for us, looking on as we were, to regard them as living participants in a genuine battle. As on so many previous occasions when I had stopped to think objectively of our activity in
Crete, I could not help viewing this particular engagement as
though through the eyes of a disinterested spectator. There was no
excitement in the sight, which I was unable to associate in any way
with the cause to which we were supposed to be dedicated. The
thrill of the manhunt, of which I had been vaguely aware whenever
I happened to have been the quarry, seemed less palpable now that
I was on the hunter's side, and it was only the final kill that affected
me at all.

Even then the effect was reduced by the number of the victims.
The sudden death of a single person can be a shattering event, but
mass murder becomes inevitably ridiculous—and in the short space
of half an hour we had killed the whole of this Italo-German section except for one Italian, who was mortally wounded, and the
local civilian guide who had at once surrendered. Niko Souris, being
the only Italian speaker among us, was detailed to question the
wounded man before giving him the *coup de grâce*. But he was too
gentle a person to undertake a task of this nature. After a few minutes he came back and reported to Tom:

"I couldn't finish him off, I'm afraid. As I took out my pistol he
looked at me and said '*Mama mia*'—I remembered my own mother,
and my finger refused to press the trigger . . ."

So leaving the man to die by himself on the mountain, we left
the battlefield as quickly as possible and concentrated in a body on
the summit of a hill two miles further on: a strategic point which
we hoped we should be able to hold against further enemy attack
before moving down to the evacuation beach in the evening. Here
we started to question the civilian guide who had made himself
our prisoner.

He was a young student from the county of Retimo, who claimed
he had been forcibly recruited because of his knowledge of German.
We could not tell whether he was speaking the truth or not; but
what told against him, as far as we were concerned, was the rifle
he had been carrying when captured—bearing arms for the enemy

was naturally an unlawful act in the eyes of us outlaws. Yet it would have been ungenerous to judge him paradoxically by the letter of an unwritten law; so we gave him the benefit of the doubt, taking the precaution, however, of introducing our deserter to him as another fellow-prisoner.

He fell into the trap almost at once. Assuming the German had been captured in a previous skirmish and was only waiting, like himself, for the opportunity to escape, he reassured him in a whisper that they were both certain to be liberated soon since the authorities had been notified of the presence of the gang in these mountains and were even at that moment preparing a full-scale raid against us—the Feldgendarmerie section we had encountered that morning was merely the forerunner of the vast patrol to come.

Loyally or disloyally—though I doubt if the moral aspect of the problem ever entered his head—the German repeated to us this valuable piece of information which his companion had treacherously withheld. On hearing it, Bandouvas characteristically gave no immediate thought to the implications of the German plans, but concentrated instead on dealing with the traitor. After questioning him more thoroughly for a few minutes, he ordered two of his men to take him off to a nearby cave and there put an end to him. As the trio disappeared round a rock on their way to this hastily selected execution ground, Tom had the presence of mind to call after them:

"For God's sake use a knife!"

But it was too late. A split-second later three shots rang out—an unnecessary thrice-repeated warning of our presence here to any Germans who might have been in the neighbourhood—and immediately afterwards the escort reappeared, their guns still smoking.

Perhaps, after all, Bandouvas had been right not to treat the impending raid as a priority consideration. For we could avoid it only by dispersing at once and abandoning the evacuation. Having come so far, and being now so close to their departure, his followers would scarcely have welcomed such a decision; so we prepared instead to take up a defensive position on the summit of the hill where we had all assembled, hoping to remain there undisturbed till it was time to move down to the coast.

Meanwhile we amused ourselves by studying the Feldgendarmerie list of "wanted" men, which we had collected together with the rest of the contents of the dead men's pockets. Almost every one of the company present was included in it; and I noted with regrettable but only human pride that the entry under my local pseudonym, which outlined in detail my physical characteristics, aliases and activities for a period of eighteen months, took no less than three-quarters of an octavo page in closely-set small-point type.

———————

We reached the beach without mishap in the dark, the prospect of an early departure raising the spirits of everyone but the handful of men, myself included, who were not due to leave. For if the evacuation were successful, we who remained behind would be left without the support of the guerrilla gang to deal with the large German patrols which would soon be combing the area as a result of the gang's activity.

Selfishly, then, I sighed with relief when, after signalling for several hours, there was still no sign of the boat we were expecting. Its failure to arrive even seemed to indicate that a form of natural justice was at work.

In the circumstances, we felt it would be inadvisable to stay on the beach, as we usually did, till dawn. With the trail of corpses in the hills above us betraying our position on the coast, and with the Germans likely to surround us at first light, we could scarcely risk being cut off in this unhealthy spot on the off chance of the boat arriving in the early hours of the morning. Shortly after midnight, then, we abandoned the operation and started making our way uphill and inland, instinctively moving westwards, away from the scene of the morning's battle.

The path we took led through Rodakino, a village that had recently been burnt down in reprisal for a German killed in the neigbourhood some time before. We smelled it when still half a mile off, the bitter smell of desolation being wafted out to us on the late night breeze, and as we passed along its single shattered street the houses on either side, uncannily humanized by death, seemed blindly to return our glances of awe and pity. Some stood scalped and scarred, stiff skeletons on a gigantic funeral pyre; others, charred and swollen like drowned corpses, were smoking still, the embers in their grotesquely distended bellies the only live thing in sight. I could not help wondering if Alones was not even at that very moment being reduced to the same condition.

For I was certain the Germans would by now have raided that village and possibly put it to the sword and firebrand; and in the morn-

ing my fears appeared to be justified by the arrival of Little George
and several other refugees from Asi Gonia, who joined us at our first
resting place at the bottom of one of the many gullies that patterned
this stretch of hinterland like the whorls of a human brain. They
reported that the Germans had indeed invaded Alones in strength
and were preparing to surround all the adjacent villages as well.

Strangely enough, however, none of these communities suffered
for their proximity to the scene of our battle. The Germans were
likewise out in strength throughout the area which we were now
crossing—during the whole of that day and for most of the following night we kept dodging them, playing hide-and-seek through the
numerous ravines and round the intervening peaks—and at dawn
we learnt it was the village of Kallikrati that had been chosen as a
victim for the enemy reprisals.

We had camped for the night just outside it, each one of us awake
and alert in anticipation of a German patrol. At first light, though
we had heard no untoward movement during the hours of darkness, we were alarmed by the sound of machine-gun and rifle fire
a few hundred yards away; and presently we noticed several separate pillars of black smoke rising from the plateau below. This sight
was explained to us a little later a couple of shepherds we chanced
to meet.

The Germans had apparently surrounded Kallikrati during the
night, and at dawn small raiding-groups had broken into the scattered houses, driving the inmates into the open, while machine-guns
posted round the circumference of the plateau had discouraged any
attempt to escape by directing a heavy cross-fire just above head-
level. Most of the male population slept out of doors, so apart from
the women and children who were at once herded into the village
church, the total German bag was five old men. These greybeards
were forthwith lined up for execution against a wall in the church-
yard so that their relatives and fellow-citizens might see and hear
them being shot; and when they had been disposed of, the houses
were systematically set on fire. Then, while the survivors were
marched off under escort to the garrison town of Sphakia, the raid-
ers had dispersed with the threat that every village in the surrounding countryside would be similarly destroyed unless the whereabouts
of the Bandouvas gang were disclosed.

The gang could not, of course, surrender on terms such as these,
but having already caused so much damage by its presence here, it

was at least prepared to quit the district. Much to my relief, then, we decided to divide our force into small groups and try to break through the enemy cordon that night. So when darkness fell, while Bandouvas and his followers moved off with Tom in the direction of their lairs in the east—where I sincerely hoped they would in future remain—I started out for the main mountain range in the west, accompanied by the I.S.L.D. team with their deserter, Kiwi Perkins, Little George and a homeless guide from Kallikrati.

To reach our haven we had to cross the Sphakia motor road near the village of Askyphou, which was then being used as the field headquarters of the German raiding forces, whose voices and footsteps sounded uncomfortably close in the windless night. If we crossed all together in a single furtive group, we should inevitably draw their attention. On the other hand, we did not wish to risk losing contact with each other by slipping over individually one by one. We therefore formed up in single file, and tramping noisily on the unmetalled surface in the hope of creating the impression of an enemy section moving up the line, we marched along the road until we were out of ear-shot, then struck off to the left straight uphill the other side.

By dawn we had reached the spine of the main White Mountain range and were well out of immediate danger. We had had no food or sleep for over seventy-two hours, during which we had probably marched as many miles, but I consoled myself with the thought that in a further forty-eight hours we should have reached our station in the far west, where I looked forward to a peaceful rest of several days.

This, however, was denied us. No sooner had we started out again after a few hours' sleep than we were met by Alec and a guide coming from the opposite direction. They told us Koustoyerako had been raided two days before and was now, like Kallikrati, a heap of blackened stone and smouldering ash.

CHAPTER SEVENTEEN

1943–44

LIKE KALLIKRATI, Koustoyerako had been destroyed in reprisal—perhaps on account of the German soldier shot during our recent skirmish in the river-bed, but more likely because the enemy must by now have learnt that this area had served as our base throughout the summer. The only wonder was that they had not been aware of this before. Perhaps it was for that very reason—because they had been hoodwinked so long—that the steps they took were even more severe than usual.

They had followed their normal practice of first surrounding the village by night, then invading at dawn and rounding up the few inhabitants who still slept indoors. In Koustoyerako they found not a single man, for the whole of the male population had long since learnt to prefer the security of the mountain to the comfort of home; the women and children were therefore lined up for execution instead.

This scene was meanwhile being witnessed by some members of the Paterakis gang who, warned in advance of the Germans' nocturnal approach, had descended during the night to a convenient observation post on a crag overlooking the village square. Sensibly assessing the enemy strength and mindful, too, of our policy not to provoke a clash of arms, they had withheld their fire while the cordon tightened round their homes, withheld it even while it developed into a stranglehold, squeezing the inmates out of every house. It was only when they realized that the hostages were being assembled, not, as they had at first thought, in order to be marched away under escort, but in order to be mowed down by a machine-gun, that they restrained themselves no longer. Costi Paterakis, one of the finest marksmen in the gang, neatly killed the German officer in charge of the raid with his first shot, while his companions simultaneously opened fire on the execution-squad; and in the subsequent confusion, before the enemy forces could regain their composure, the women and children scattered in all directions out of the village, some taking to the hills behind, others rushing for cover down the valleys below, every one of them escaping miraculously unscathed.

The Germans did not retaliate at once. But during the course of that day further reinforcements were called up to Koustoyerako; and the village was set on fire and then systematically bombed from the air, while raiding-parties began to fan out in strength through the surrounding countryside in search of its scattered inhabitants. Alec had managed to hide all his wireless equipment before taking flight with the others, but we could not tell how long we should have to wait before being able to retrieve it; for that area was now as overrun and unhealthy as the enemy-held district behind us.

Caught on the top of the mountains between these two forces which threatened at any moment to come together and engulf us, we had no choice of action. So late in the year, and at such a height, we could not survive indefinitely without food or shelter; there was therefore no alternative but to creep down to some friendly village on the lower slopes in the hope of finding temporary refuge and sustenance.

Vaphes was our nearest goal, but, in the circumstances, our presence there would have imposed too great a strain on old Uncle Niko, since most of the Vandoulas family were either in hiding or else had been evacuated for their own safety to the Middle East. Our numbers indeed would have imposed a strain on any single household. We therefore decided to divide our little force; so that while Ralph and his I.S.L.D. party set off in the evening in the direction of their old lairs further east, we started to make our way down to Kyriakosellia where we were sure of obtaining the help of Levteri Kourakis.

Levteri had recovered from the wound he had received during the raid on the beehive hut earlier in the year, but he already showed signs of the consumption of which he was shortly to die. His black-bearded ascetic's cheeks were wasted as much by the arduous service he had rendered us as by the disease from which he was suffering; yet he spared himself no more than did his wife, Kyria Phrosso, who, though in constant pain from stomach ulcers which gave her face in its black hood the expression and contours of that of a miraculously preserved and shrouded saint, had nevertheless steadfastly fed and succoured our messengers and runners who used her house as a regular port of call.

This extremely valiant couple were visibly working themselves to death on our account, and as though they were more conscious than the unafflicted of the short span of human life, they seemed prepared to shorten their own still further by sacrificing themselves for our protection and comfort. When we reached their home in the early hours of the morning, they immediately and drastically reduced their own small stock of food to provide us with enough to eat for over a week; and it was only with difficulty that we dissuaded them from giving up their beds to us as well. Tired though we were, we could not accept this intrepid gesture of hospitality which, with the Germans likely to descend on the village at any moment, would have jeopardized their own security as well as ours.

We therefore prepared to spend the night out of doors, and laden with the stores they had so generously provided, we climbed up to a certain cave, which we were told, Stelio was then using as his latest hide-out—for he was once more on the run, having forfeited the benefits he might have retained from his amnesty as a result of his continued assistance to us.

The weeks that followed were the most frustrating period I ever spent in Crete. Out of contact with Cairo, and surrounded daily by enemy patrols, we were forced to remain in hiding without appearing above ground-level for days on end, growing progressively colder and more irritable as the autumn advanced into winter and the first snow began to fall. None of us had yet developed to a sufficient degree the virtue of patience, which is the fugitive's first weapon of defence, and we kept cursing this situation which inflicted on us all the practical disadvantages of danger without offering by way of mitigation any of its emotional zest. Through sheer boredom we might have prematurely emerged from our hateful retirement, had the Germans not withdrawn their raiding-forces in time to save us from such thoughtless action.

Our first task, once we could move about again more freely, was to discover how the refugees from Koustoyerako were faring. At the same time I was anxious to resume wireless contact with Headquarters as soon as possible. But since we could not yet tell what had happened to the set that Alec had hidden, I decided to use the one we had been operating during the spring and early summer, which we were certain of finding intact at Asi Gonia. Kiwi therefore volunteered to go off on his own to organize the Paterakis guerrilla gang, which by now must have inevitably doubled in strength with recruits from the homeless local population, while Alec and I set off in the opposite direction to set up our new station.

Petro Petrakas, invaluable as ever in an emergency, helped us to move into our old base above his village; and with his efficient sentry system established as before, I hoped we should be left undisturbed to deal with our back-log of signals. But our first incoming message upset the placid routine I had planned.

Headquarters had apparently decided to enlarge the scope of our activities in Crete. Until then the internal organization of the island had been in the hands of Tom Dunbabin, Paddy Leigh Fermor and myself, two of us operating simultaneously in our respective areas while the third was away on leave. This rather informal and amateur system was now about to be put on a more professional footing: Tom—very properly, since he was the eldest and most experienced of the three—was to be recognized as Field Commander with the rank of lieutenant-colonel, while Paddy and myself, as majors, were to command East and West Crete respectively. To assist us a number of captains and lieutenants had been recruited, some of whom had already been infiltrated into the island, each with his own wireless set and operator. Sandy Rendel, for instance, whom I had last met as Kiwi's conducting officer, was now established in the far end of Tom's old area. Another officer had been landed more recently on the same beach and was at this moment on his way to report to me. Yet a third was shortly coming in direct to my area as soon as the Koustoyerako beach could be safely used—he was to relieve me since I was well overdue for leave, having been in the field almost exactly a year. And, finally, Alec, whose leave was likewise overdue, had instructions to make his way at once to a beach in the east of the island, from where a boat was due to evacuate him in a week's time.

So I was left provisionally without an operator, and was once again temporarily out of contact with Cairo. But this inconvenience was the least regret caused by Alec's departure. I missed him professionally, of course; but even more so for personal reasons. He had been a perfect companion, humorous, even-tempered and hard-working; and if it was only the unnatural conditions of war that had cemented the close friendship between us, then I was grateful to the war for providing those conditions without which we two might never have met. Now that I no longer heard the fearful oaths and cheerful obscenities that constituted the greater part of his daily conversation, I felt extraordinarily lonely and bereft.

But my mountain solitude did not last long. A few days later the officer whom Cairo had warned me to expect arrived, having meanwhile visited the local leaders in Prines which was to be his base of operations. Already known throughout that area as Pavlo, he introduced himself to me as Dick.[1]

At first glance he looked so unmistakably English that I felt he would never be able to pass for a local, however well he spoke the language. He was a few years older than myself but appeared to be much younger, the fair hair flopping over his forehead intensifying his youthful expression in spite of the aggressively adult moustache half concealing his upper lip. Then, however, I imagined how these features would be transformed by a few weeks of dirt and neglect; I envisaged him a little more unkempt and slightly less pink than he was at present, and realized at once that with his blue eyes and rather stocky build he might eventually come to be regarded as a perfect example of the modern Sphakian shepherd.

He told me that a suitable base had been found for him among the rocky hillocks north of the Retimo road—an unusual departure from our normal practice of establishing our stations in the less comfortable but more secure folds of the main mountain ranges; but for that very reason the terrain he had chosen might be less suspect, and in any case the enemy forces were less numerous in the area he was about to take over than anywhere else in Crete. I commended him on his choice, and envied and admired the intrepidity which had prompted him to make it. He was clearly a man of resource and courage: two qualities which would be indispensable to him in his future activities.

He also showed a third quality, no doubt common to us all: impatience. He was so anxious to start work that he stayed with me only one night before returning in the direction of Prines, taking with

1. Capt. Dick Barnes; now in the Foreign Office.

him as his station staff George Psychoundakis and another boy from Asi Gonia called Alexander Barbounis.

—————

Meanwhile, Kiwi's news was reassuring. He had successfully rounded up all the male refugees from Koustoyerako—the women and children having taken refuge with friends and relations in neighbouring villages—and they now swelled the ranks of the Paterakis guerrilla gang, which was a potential fighting force no longer, having twice been in action against the enemy.

Realizing that such a large number of men could not remain indefinitely scattered and in hiding, Kiwi on his own initiative had assumed the offensive by martialling them into some semblance of a military formation. He had established a properly appointed camp for them on the highest slopes near our previous station. This he had organized and equipped by means of three successful parachute drops ordered over the I.S.L.D. wireless, so that his group was now completely self-supporting. Almost overnight, in fact, he had revolutionized the character of the resistance movement in that area.

The conditions he had involuntarily created might have been extremely dangerous elsewhere in the island, where the Germans would only have had to burn down a few more villages to terrorize the inhabitants into submission. But in those uninhabited and trackless wastes the opportunity for repeated reprisals was well-nigh non-existent, and the destruction of Koustoyerako had only strengthened the villagers' determination to strike back at the enemy now that they had nothing further to lose.

The Germans themselves must have been aware of this, for they seemed far from anxious to risk another full-scale raid in that area. Unwilling, however, to neglect the situation altogether, they had foolishly compromised with their conscience by sending out small patrols, which had twice stumbled into the ambush that Vasili Paterakis had laid for them. On both occasions they had been wiped out to a man, the only casualty on our side being Kiwi who received a flesh wound in his shoulder. But this had, if anything, raised his morale and in his last report to me he announced that, provided air supplies could be continued, he was confident of being able to hold out, if necessary, until the end of the war.

Trusting in his confidence, I was therefore able to carry on undisturbed with our routine work in the rest of Canea County.

To our duties of organization and espionage there was now added a third: propaganda. For some weeks thousands of pamphlets had been landed or dropped in by parachute. One batch of these, which had been designed to discourage potential treachery, represented a man hanging from the branch of a tree, with a knife driven up to the hilt into his stomach from which the blood coursed down in a melodramatic crimson streak. Underneath was the terse admonition in Greek: "Traitors, beware!"

Obeying the instructions from Cairo, I had had these posters distributed throughout my area. But since there were not enough suitable recipients for them—for the known and suspected traitors could be numbered in dozens rather than hundreds—they were mostly used either as practical jokes or for reasons of personal enmity. Perfectly good patriots all over the island would wake up to find one of these offensive placards stuck to their front door— placed there either by a local wag or rival—so that they had little effect on the few guilty men for whom they had been intended to act as a serious deterrent.

The rest of the propaganda material, however, effectively served the purpose of undermining the morale of the German troops at whom it was directed. Some of it consisted of indecent and highly-coloured postcards depicting an obviously Latin lover lying on a bed, stark naked and in a state of advanced eroticism, next to an equally obvious German lady, likewise naked and sexually excited. The caption, in the form of a bawdy and provocative verse, was aimed to leave no doubt in the mind of the front-line German soldier as to how his wife was enjoying herself in his absence with the gallants of the Italian Labour Corps safe at home in the Fatherland.

There were other leaflets, still more insidious. These were messages of alarm and despondency—ostensibly the work of a clandestine press—printed in German on the back of Wehrmacht maps so as to give the impression that they emanated from a dissident group among the enemy forces of occupation. Whether the text was believed or not was less important than the immediate attraction that these "secret" documents and pornographic postcards had for the bored and homesick German troops' abroad. The authorities decreed that any soldier discovered in possession of any of this material would forthwith be put under close arrest; with the result that the number of men in detention became almost unmanageable.

The distribution of these pamphlets was a fairly tricky business since, in order to maintain the illusion that Germans themselves were responsible for them, they had to be carefully infiltrated into enemy billets, offices, canteens and barracks. I put hundreds of men to work on this task alone, and Pavlo Bernardakis and I usually had our pockets stuffed with them whenever we set out on a journey so as to miss no opportunity of leaving a handful or two in any suitable enemy installation we happened to pass.

Returning one day from a hilarious march during which we had successfully left these visiting-cards of ours at several temporarily evacuated gun-positions on the main road, we decided to celebrate the occasion at Pavlo's home in Kastello, a village in the plains next to the large enemy garrison of Kournas. We both knew this decision was inexcusable, for Pavlo was high on the German "wanted" list and his house had already been searched several times. But we were so tired that we had reached that state of light-headed apathy which made the long climb up to the hide-out above Asi Gonia seem far more frightening than the prospect of arrest. As a precaution, however, we agreed not to sleep indoors but to leave the house immediately after dinner.

Dinner lasted longer than we thought it would. It was almost dawn when we crept out, fuddled but still elated after singing and drinking all night with Pavlo's friends and family. In the early-morning half-light the natural acropolis on which the village stood appeared to be pulsating noiselessly in an alien element, like a faintly stirring growth at the bottom of the ocean bed. Day broke without a sound—neither cock-crow nor dog-bark initiated the usual clamour of rustic awakening—and in this abnormal silence, which only intensified our state of euphoria, we settled down to sleep in a thick patch of undergrowth a hundred yards away from the nearest house.

After what seemed a few seconds we were woken by a voice shouting words of command, followed by the uniform beat of a company on the march. The sound came directly from under us, as though legions of heavy-footed insects were tunnelling into the cliff on which we were perched; and looking over the edge, we saw the troops from the garrison next door performing the evolutions of an early-morning drill parade. We turned over and went to sleep again.

Shortly afterwards we were roused once more, this time by a noise perceptible only because it was close—the twigs in the bushes straight ahead of us were snapping under the pressure of a moving body. We were both abruptly wide awake, our sudden transition from sleep to vigilance prompted more by habit than apprehension, for we had nothing to fear—no doubt this was Pavlo's younger brother bringing us breakfast. From where I lay I could still see no movement in the audible undergrowth. Pavlo apparently could, but his voice sounded so unperturbed that I did not at once grasp the meaning of the words as he blandly turned to me and said:

"Get your pistol out, it's a German."

Even then I would have thought that he was joking had I not seen him take out his own pistol, seen his finger curl round the trigger, and heard, as he squeezed it, not the shot I expected but a light metallic click. Almost simultaneously, however, a shot did ring out—from the tangle a few yards in front of us—followed by a succession of blasts on a police whistle, not quite piercing enough to drown the sound of Pavlo's voice yelling:

"Fire! For God's sake, fire!"

I could still see no target, but Pavlo's wild expression as he struggled to clear the blocked weapon in his hand incited me to action. Without taking aim, I fired twice in the direction of the sound of the whistle. For some reason I felt my shots should have silenced it; but the shrill blasts continued, indeed grew louder; and almost at once I saw the source of the noise—a figure in Afrika Korps uniform bleached white by sun and scrubbing—stampeding straight at me through the intervening bushes.

I fired again, unconsciously resting the barrel of my pistol on a convenient ledge of rock, which my bullet, I thought, must have grazed; for in spite of the confused visual and aural effects of that instant—the sound of my own shot and a second simultaneous detonation, and the sight of a flame spurting from the flash of white as it abruptly altered course, streaking diagonally across my field of vision—I was conscious of a blow on the forehead, painless but stunning, and of the automatic reflex of my left eye which felt as though a speck of dust had just been blown into it.

Blinking and still fuddled, I found myself racing downhill at Pavlo's heels, cursing myself for my clumsy marksmanship. In my confusion my only clear sensation was of shame; I felt no wonder at our headlong pursuit of the German fifty yards ahead of us; nor was I

surprised that he still blew his whistle as he ran, the sound seem-
ing merely to stress the effort of his breathing. It was only when
machine-guns opened fire all round us that I came with a start to
my senses.

The abrupt din brought me to a slithering stop, as though the
rattle beating on my ear-drums had been a stream of bullets piercing my body. It was less than a second, however, before I was once
more trying to keep up with Pavlo, but in that time my brain had
gone through a miraculous procession of deductions and I knew
with absolute clarity what was happening.

The German was indeed in full flight. But so were we. The illusion of being in pursuit was created simply by an accident of terrain: down this steep slope there was only one path to follow, and
what I had imagined to be our quarry was in fact nothing more
than a fellow-fugitive with a fifty yards' lead. Only the cause of
our flight differed. His main concern was to get out of range of
two men armed with pistols; ours—a rather more difficult proposition—was to break through a full-strength enemy cordon, whose
presence was being made clear to us by the continued bursts of
machine-gun fire.

What I did not understand, however, was why a single German
had attempted to unearth us on his own. Obviously, the troops that
had surrounded the village in the night had seen us creeping out at
dawn and had marked down our position in the bushes. But even
had we both been unarmed, one man by himself could not have
been sure of arresting us. Whether our would-be captor was also a
would-be hero aflame with dreams of military glory or simply one
of the many Germans in detention who were regarded as expendable, I could not tell. Whatever the motives behind his action, I was
grateful to him; for without his intervention we should have had no
warning until the cordon round us had been drawn into an inescap-
able noose. As it was, the encirclement was not yet complete. The
two main entrances to this rustic citadel were blocked; but Pavlo,
being a native of the village, knew of an unsuspected escape route
straight down the cliff-face. This we took, reaching level ground
unobserved as the raiding forces closed in on the houses above us.

It was only then I realized that I was soaked through with fear
and exertion. Anxious to wipe the tell-tale streams from my face,
I put my hand to my forehead. When I withdrew it I saw it was
drenched not with sweat but blood. So the enemy had proved him-

self a better shot than I had during our recent skirmish—his bullet
had at least grazed my head.

The wound, completely painless, might have been taken for little
more than the deeper prolongation of a wrinkle just below my hair-
line had it not been bleeding so profusely. But the red streaks down
my face would have betrayed our participation in a recent clash of
arms, so it was essential to go into hiding as quickly as possible. The
nearest suitable refuge I could think of was Dick's station almost
fifteen miles away. Asi Gonia was closer, but to reach it we should
have had to scale several bare slopes up which any German reinforcements were likely to advance. So instead of climbing for cover
into the mountains, we set off at a jog-trot straight across the coastal
plain where the thick olive groves and succession of high stone walls
concealed our line of flight.

Dick's station had another advantage over Asi Gonia—through
his wireless I was able to contact Headquarters once again. My first
task on arrival, then, was to encode all the undispatched information I had accumulated since Alec's departure. Cairo's signal in reply
contained the news for which I was by now secretly longing: the
officer who was to relieve me when I went on leave had landed safely
on the Koustoyerako beach the week before; and so all that was
required of me now was to join him in Kiwi's guerrilla camp and,
after handing over to him, arrange for my own evacuation.

Fortified by this prospect of safety and comfort in a future which
no longer seemed tantalizingly distant, I set off after a few days'
rest on my last long march through the Cretan mountains. Not
even the atrocious weather could prevent my spirits from soaring as
Pavlo and I trudged westwards through continuous rain and snow-
storms. Our Christmas dinner on the way—rock-hard rusks with a
piece of cheese and a raw onion each, which we washed down with
melted icicles before going to sleep on the sodden floor of a cave—
appeared to me only as an advance penance for the subsequent orgy
of food and drink I was planning for myself in Egypt. And when we
reached our destination—most appropriately, I felt, on the evening
of December 31st—the New Year seemed to stretch before me as
long and lovely as a new existence.

It was not until a month later, however, that I finally reached
Cairo. Two days after my arrival at the guerrilla camp an unusu-

ally heavy snowfall cut us off from the rest of the world. Had it not been for the arrangements Kiwi had made, we should never have been able to survive in those conditions. But he had wisely built up a sufficient stock of food for just such a contingency, and the tents he had ordered in a recent parachute drop not only gave us protection from the cold but also instilled in their inhabitants, unaccustomed to such luxurious efficiency, a sense of martial pride and confidence. Our thin canvas walls might have been made of reinforced concrete, so impregnable did our position appear to us.

In this grave-like isolation, which in my imagination turned our snow-covered bivouacs into tombstones, I had ample opportunity of studying my successor, a young major called Dennis Ciclitiras, who for some time had assisted Jack with the staff work in our Cairo office before being sent into the field. He was therefore well acquainted with Cretan affairs and I could add little to the directive he had been given: yet I was not altogether happy about handing over to him. For, through no fault of his own, he had already proved himself unpopular. His Greek surname and Levantine features made him suspect in the eyes of the local peasants, who preferred to regard every Englishman as a direct descendant of Lord Byron; and Dennis's manner and appearance did not quite fulfill their expectations.

It was Kiwi whom they still regarded as their leader. He had endeared himself to them forever by the behaviour he had shown when wounded in the last skirmish a few weeks before. The bullet which had struck him during a dashing counterattack had lodged in his shoulder, but he had continued to fight with one arm disabled, and it was only when the enemy had been finally routed that he sat down and asked someone to deal with his wound. There were no medical supplies, and none of the gang had any knowledge of surgery; but Kiwi had simply demanded:

"Come on now, haven't any of you killed a sheep before?"

And so it was with a butcher's knife that the bullet was extracted, without an anaesthetic beforehand and with no disinfectant afterwards. Fortunately, in the pure air of those mountains sepsis was unknown.

But it was not only his valour but also his administrative ability that they admired; and when at last the snow melted sufficiently to enable us to plough a path through the drifts down to the beach in preparation for my evacuation, it was he, and not Dennis, who took

charge. After completing the descent, which gave me the same satisfaction as a flight from fog-bound London to the South of France,
and which took almost as long, I felt confident that so long as Kiwi
was present Dennis's mission in Crete would succeed.

That was still my feeling when, after an uneventful departure and
calm crossing, I reported to Cairo at the beginning of February.

CHAPTER EIGHTEEN

1944

ONCE AGAIN Headquarters had undergone a metamorphosis
during my fifteen months' absence. Not only were few of the officers
I had once known still on the staff, but much of the staff itself had
been transferred to Bari, the new base for most of the S.O.E. operations in the Mediterranean. With the capitulation of Italy and the
liberation of the North African coast, Cairo had become a strategic
backwater. The change, however, was for the better if only because
the brigadier who was responsible for Arthur's downfall had now
been removed.

Even so there was little encouragement for me to remain there
longer than was absolutely necessary; so after writing my report I
went to Syria for a month's leave, which was extended to six weeks
so as to enable me to go on a fortnight's parachute course in our
school at Haifa. When I got back it was almost time to start making
plans for my return to Crete.

But there was an important question I was anxious to settle before
committing myself to a further mission in the island. By now it had
become quite clear that the Greek Government's promise to recognize all resistance groups as members of the regular armed forces
would never be implemented. Since, in spite of my better judgment,
I had been ordered to transmit this false message throughout my
area, I wanted to know what possible explanation I could give on my
return to the thousands of men I had thereby involuntarily duped.

I therefore applied for an interview with Mr. Tsouderos, who was
then Prime Minister. Nothing came of it. I was simply referred to
the Minister of War, who promised to look into the matter. But

163

since he resigned a couple of days later, that quest too was unsuccessful, the file that I was after being lost in the rapid succession of ministerial changes, while each new Minister disclaimed all responsibility for the policy of his predecessor.

I found this mixture of inefficiency and prevarication most disturbing; and I was still further discouraged by the policy of our own Government, from which I deduced that a major Allied landing was no longer contemplated in the Balkans and that the Second Front would be opened in Western Europe. Crete was therefore doomed to remain in enemy hands until the end of the war, when the Germans stationed there would simply lay down their arms. This was a bitter disappointment after the dreams I had cherished of a glorious internal uprising supported by a British invasion, for which every patriot in the island was still preparing; and though I never for a moment questioned the wisdom of this official decision, I could not help feeling that because of it our efforts in Crete, humble though they were, had all been in vain.

In a fit of depression, then, and also with a sense of guilt and ingratitude—for I recognized my debt to the Cretan Office, thanks to which I had enjoyed a more rewarding war than I could ever have imagined—I applied for a transfer to the French Section of S.O.E. Since I had been brought up in the South of France and knew the language and the country from childhood, I had little hope of being accepted. To my surprise, however, I was.

To assist me in my future operations I chose as my second-in-command a South African friend called "Lizzy" Lezzard.[1] Lizzy seemed to be almost as well known in the Middle East as General Montgomery, but fame was the only thing he had in common with the Commander of the Eighth Army; for he was large-bodied and liberal-minded, and he had a sense of humour.

I had originally caught sight of his mobile, rather fleshy face across a baccarat-table in Alexandria, and had seen it several times since wherever any form of gambling was in progress. Later, I learned he had been transferred from one unit to another probably more often than anyone else in the whole of the British armed forces; so that although still a captain at the age of forty, he had seen more varied service than most colonels. Obviously unsuitable as a regular officer—which made him automatically more sympathetic to me—he

---

1. Capt. Julian Lezzard; now an impresario in London.

had volunteered for a number of paramilitary missions in almost every "private army" then operating in the Middle East; and each of his commanding officers, who had taken him on simply as a court jester, soon discovered that his irreverent wit and unpractical jokes merely served to conceal a quality of which he seemed to be positively ashamed—namely, courage.

So I was delighted when he agreed to join me, even though he immediately committed a burlesque breach of security by telling everyone he met:

"I'm just off to be dropped into enemy-occupied France in a mission commanded by my son!"

Fortunately no one believed him, since weeks went by and still we remained in Cairo. The authorities responsible for our transfer required almost three months to disentangle themselves from the red tape in which they floundered even at the height of the war; and it was not until after the Normandy landings that Lizzy and I were at last flown to Algiers, our base for operations into Southern France.

Soon after landing in Algiers we began to regret leaving Cairo. I suppose we had been spoilt by living so long in a neutral capital, with a comfortable flat to return to after coming out of the field. At any rate we were not prepared for the austerity of the seaside camp twenty miles outside the town to which we were posted, where we had to sleep, two to a room, in half a dozen ugly little concrete villas reserved for the operational personnel, and where we were forced to feed no longer on reasonable meals in more or less civilized surroundings but on army rations in a dreary Mess. Worse still, there were no transport facilities, so that it was only when an official car was returning to the staff offices situated on a hill above Algiers that we managed to get a lift into the casino.

There we stayed for a fortnight before anyone was able to decide what to do with us. Finally, we were told that we would shortly be dropped into Région Deux, a prospect which particularly delighted Lizzy since that area included Monte Carlo, its boundaries being the southern coast, the Rhône valley, the Italian frontier and a line stretching eastwards from Grenoble. Our briefing was even scantier than the directive I had received on my first mission to Crete. "You'll find out when you get there," seemed to be the gist of our instructions.

Our practical preparations, on the other hand, were exaggeratedly thorough. For ten days we were put through a cyphering course, which neither of us could take really seriously since it was more than certain we should never have an opportunity of putting this freshly-acquired knowledge of ours to the test. We were then instructed in the use of an individual code by means of which we were supposed, if captured, to pass on messages to Headquarters concealed in ostensibly innocuous letters written from our prison camp; but since there was little likelihood of our being regarded as ordinary prisoners-of-war if we fell into enemy hands, we could not treat this instruction either with the gravity that was demanded of us. Finally, we were each given a code name under which we would be known to our comrades in the field. I was to masquerade as "Cathédrale," and Lizzy, being one rank lower, as "Eglise"; being also a Jew, he was disappointed that those responsible for our ecclesiastical nomenclature had not had the good taste to call him "Synagogue."

Since I was to operate in civilian clothes, I was also furnished with a particularly hasty narrow-waisted French suit of indigo-coloured serge, into the lapel of which was conveniently sewn a poison tablet which I was meant to bite out and swallow in the event of being captured so as to avoid betraying any secrets under possible torture. My shirt, tie, socks and shoes, all in keeping with the suit, were chosen for the genteel-shabby type of flashiness which would appeal to the sort of man whom I was to impersonate—a young clerk in the Electric Company of Nîmes. My name, according to the personal documents I was to carry when wearing this hideous disguise, was Armand Pont-Levé.

For a further ten days I rehearsed my "cover story," learning by heart the life history of this mythical character; and it was only when I could instinctively identify myself with him that Lizzy and I were considered ready for the field.

One evening in early August, then, my clothes and other equipment packed into the containers that were to be dropped with us, we took off from a dusty airfield outside Algiers. Our destination was Seyne, a little village in the Basses Alpes, which was at that time the main base of Roger,[2] the English colonel in charge of our area. His code name, together with that of Christine Granville, his female

---

2. It was not until the end of the war that I learnt his real name—Francis Cammaerts, D.S.O.; at present Headmaster of Alleyn's School.

assistant, was the only information we were officially given about the mission on which we were about to embark. Unofficially, however, we learned before leaving that the Allied landing in the South of France—which for some weeks had been an open secret all over North Africa—was due to take place on August 15th. So our participation in the French resistance movement looked like lasting no longer than a fortnight.

With such a short time ahead of us, we were therefore all the more disappointed and impatient—though to some extent illogically relieved as well—when the crew of our American Liberator failed to pick out the ground-to-air signals of our intended dropping-zone and we were forced to return to base after an uncomfortable eight-hour flight which we spent lying uneasily half-asleep in the belly of the machine, trussed up in our parachute harnesses as if in strait jackets.

A second attempt was made to drop us two days later—with the same result. And when, for the second time in a single week, we unexpectedly turned up to breakfast in the Mess next morning, we were too weary and shaken to answer the ribald comments of our fellow-officers, which made us feel almost as though we were ourselves personally to blame for the failure.

The following evening we took off yet again, this time with a different crew. I wished it had been a British aircraft, for I was beginning to lose confidence in American knowledge of world geography. If the navigator knew as little about Europe as I, for instance, knew of the United States, it was scarcely surprising that he was unable to find his way about in the dark. After our two previous unsuccessful attempts to locate the dropping-zone I could not help revealing my fears to the plane's despatcher—the sergeant responsible for launching the personnel and containers out of the body of the machine.

"Quit worrying, buddy," he replied, "whatever happens, this crew always dumps its load."

It was scarcely a reassuring boast; for the rest of the flight I kept picturing Lizzy and myself floating through the night over an enemy-held continent without even knowing in which country we were likely to land.

But the despatcher was as good as his word. Shortly after crossing the French coast he roused me from the comatose state to which I am always reduced by air travel, cupped his hand to my ear and shouted:

"We've picked up the lights. Let's go."

Ungainly as a pair of hobbled bears, Lizzy and I stumbled in our heavy packs towards the circular hole in the bottom of the aircraft. Its cover was removed, and at once I was wide awake, ripped by the sudden incursion of cold and noise from the uterine warmth and peace of the metal belly in which we had been lying; and as we circled our target, the whine of the slipstream issuing from the aperture at our feet sounded like a taunt or a threat delivered through a megaphone from the invisible ground below.

These few minutes before the actual jump were what I hated most about parachuting. The unnatural act of launching oneself voluntarily into space had become progressively more frightening each time I had been through it during training, the memory of the previous jump intensifying the dread of the next; for each time my perception had been sharpened and I was able to analyse with greater clarity every fearful motion to which my falling body was subjected as it was snatched up in the tornado raging beneath the aircraft's hull. My expression must have betrayed my feelings, for as he motioned us into a sitting position on the edge of the hole, our sympathetic despatcher gave us each a reassuring pat on the shoulder, followed by a thumbs-up sign, before cupping his hand and yelling:

"Running in right now. Get ready."

Lizzy and I sat facing each other across the black circle of space into which our legs uncomfortably dangled, as though we were two small children perched on an adult's chair; and as the engines throttled back and the aircraft lost height, I was seized by an additional misgiving.

Hitherto the only jumps we had done had been either through a door in the side of the fuselage or, when making a floor exit, through a smaller unobstructed aperture into which each man swung his legs only after the man before him had launched himself through. Now, apparently, I was expected to slip past Lizzy's feet on my way down, and I felt certain my nose would catch on his toe-caps. It required all my willpower to take my eyes off his boots, which in my imagination had grown grotesquely giant-sized, almost blocking the diameter between us, and to concentrate instead on the warning light which had just flashed on in the panel above his head. Then, before I had time for another thought, the green bulb of the "Go" signal lit up and I instinctively jerked into the required position of attention which lifted me off the edge where I sat and sent me plummeting like a hangman's victim into the turbulent darkness outside.

During the split-second that followed, I had the impression not of falling but of being lifted up in the air; for though I had left the aircraft feet first, my head now pointed to the ground which, discernible only by a deeper black than that of the sky, seemed to be receding rather than approaching. In fact I was merely describing the uncontrollable somersault to which anyone of my weight was invariably forced to submit when jumping with his face to the slipstream. Like the female performer in a music-hall exhibition of adagio dancing being propelled across the stage from the shoulders of a muscular partner, I completed this involuntary acrobatic convolution with as much grace as I could muster—not, needless to say, for the benefit of an unseen aerial audience, but simply to avoid getting caught up in the rigging lines of my parachute. Then a tug at the straps of the harness round my groin jerked me upright once more, and I found myself floating gently earthwards, oscillating through a series of progressively diminishing arcs against a sky that was suddenly and mystifyingly silent.

The relief and release I always felt immediately after leaving the aircraft was this time accompanied by the pleasant realization that despite my turbulent exit past Lizzy's boots my nose was undamaged; and as I glided effortlessly downwards, as though suspended in a breeches-buoy or comfortably cradled on an all but motionless ocean wave, I looked up with delight at the canopy swaying above me, dilating delicately like a monster jellyfish, its dark circumference blotting out the stars.

Far below me I could see the signal lights of the dropping-zone shining like planets in an incomprehensibly inverted heaven, so distant that I seemed to be hovering in outer space, delivered from the normal laws of gravity. I kept my eyes fixed on them—the only landmarks visible in any direction or dimension—and as I tried to judge how long it would take to reach them, I noticed with alarm that instead of growing larger and drawing nearer they were decreasing in size and retreating diagonally across my field of vision—until they finally and abruptly vanished, leaving me alone in the dark uncharted sky.

I realized then that I was drifting in a strong wind which had carried me over a ridge of hills standing between me and my objective; but I still could not tell how far off course I was or how far away I was likely to land. For without the lights to guide me I had no idea of my altitude. I had asked to be launched at eight hundred feet, but I felt my descent had already been twice as long; and since the ground remained invisible, there was no means of judging how much longer it was going to last. I wondered if Lizzy was in a similar plight and tried to picture at what point in the surrounding darkness he would be at this very moment. His position in relation to mine and our respective height above the ground appeared at me as matters of immediate concern, the two questions assuming a disproportionate importance in my mind. But before my apprehension had time to turn into torment, I was given a rough answer to both. There was a crash like the sound of a nearby house collapsing, followed at once by a loud cry less than a hundred yards away—Lizzy had landed.

A second later so had I, although "landing" would be too mild a word to describe the impact. I had braced my legs to receive the shock, but my first point of contact with the ground was my cheekbone—still oscillating violently at the end of descent, I had come face to face with an outcrop of rock at the top of a steep slope. Lizzy must have fallen in equally rough country, but far more heavily, for though he had jumped after I had, he had come to earth just before me in a swifter, more vertical drop, and his cries continued as I struggled out of my harness. Guided by them, I made towards him over the boulder-studded hillocks.

I found him lying motionless on his back, incapable even of releasing himself from his parachute, so that the rigging lines entwined round his body made him look like a helpless parcel. That he was in great pain was obvious—for the first time since I had known him he was treating a crisis without his usual levity, and groans instead of the customary quips were all he could utter as he tried to explain what had happened.

"Oh, my back! My back!" he kept repeating.

I was frightened he might have broken it, and so did not dare to move him without help. Luckily we each of us carried a couple of morphine syrettes—an ingenious gadget, like a small tube of toothpaste with a hypodermic needle attached—so that I was able to give him an emergency injection. But even this failed to relieve the pain, and although I had wrapped him up for warmth in the thick silk folds of his canopy, his teeth continued to chatter. Disregarding the single dosage officially prescribed, which I hoped erred on the side of caution, I injected him again. Yet he still felt no relief. Guiltily I then took his own syrettes from his pocket and, feeling almost like a murderer, was preparing in despair to apply them both one after the other, when I was hailed by some of the maquis reception party who had managed at last to locate us from the dropping-zone by following the line of our flight.

Among them was a young medical student, to whom I gratefully entrusted my patient. He took one look at Lizzy and, more confident or rash than myself, emptied the rest of the morphine into his thigh. This quadruple dose had the desired effect. Lizzy stopped groaning, and though still fully conscious, made no complaint as he was lifted on to a sort of sledge and dragged over the smooth grass downs to an isolated farmhouse where we were to spend the night.

CHAPTER NINETEEN

1944

EARLY NEXT MORNING, leaving Lizzy still asleep, I went off to contact Roger and Christine in the village of Seyne a mile further down the valley. I found them both in the "safe house" which had been described to me during my briefing in Algiers as belonging to the local grocer, Monsieur Turre. Since his name was in fact Turrel, I was glad I had with me a member of the maquis band who was known to him; for without this personal introduction I should never had been admitted into that valiant but cautious household, even though Headquarters had obligingly given me at least the correct password.

The Turrels were typical of the hundreds of thousands of "small" people all over France, whose role in the resistance was unspectacular but beyond measure valuable. Without any of the vainglorious conceit that characterized some of the self-styled *chefs*, and with no thought of ultimate reward or glory, they had placed their home at our disposal since the beginning of the occupation, thereby endangering their lives far more than any member of an armed maquis band. Yet neither their expression nor manner betrayed the slightest sign of the precarious existence they were leading. Monsieur Turrel, fat and jovial in a waistcoat three sizes too small for him, looked as carefree and contented as an actor in a documentary film. He offered me a glass of wine while his wife, with peasant impassivity, went upstairs to wake up Roger and Christine.

Headquarters had given me no description of Roger, so I was not prepared for his great height and apparent youth. I had pictured him as a swarthy middle-aged man, sufficiently nondescript to be able to pass unnoticed in a crowd; instead I was faced with a smiling young giant whose coltish appearance was exaggerated by sloping shoulders and an easy resilient poise. These features, to begin with, obscured the contradictory qualities of leadership and modesty with which he subsequently impressed me. It was only later I realized that for him resistance was tantamount to a new religion, which he had been preaching and practising with remarkable success for over three years.

Christine was similarly dedicated, and appeared to be more obviously so only, perhaps, because I already knew something of her exploits in the past. Ever since the military collapse of her own country, Poland, she had been employed on the most hazardous missions in other parts of occupied Europe; and this reputation of hers had led me to expect in her the heroic attributes which I fancied I immediately divined beneath her nervous gestures and breathless manner of speech. Not that she in any way resembled the classical conception of a female spy, even though she had the glamorous figure that is conventionally associated with one; but this she preferred to camouflage in an austere blouse and skirt which, with her short, carelessly-combed dark hair and the complete absence of makeup on her delicately-featured face, gave her the appearance of an athletic art student.

She and Roger were an imposing pair; and since I was still in uniform, which in the circumstances I despised as lay clothing, I felt rather like a novice in the presence of a prior and prioress as we climbed up to the dropping-zone together after breakfast.

I felt not only strange to the job but also strange to the country; for I had been out of Europe for six years, and the overnight transition from Asiatic and African landscapes to Alpine scenery left me momentarily stunned with delight. These mountains, though higher, were tamer than the crags of Crete; motor roads ran through them; and instead of the gaunt stony slopes over which I had grown accustomed to stumble, which barely offered pasture for goats, we walked now through meadows which in peace time must have been rich grazing ground for cows—animals which for so long I had not even visualized that to me the species almost seemed to have become extinct.

Our conditions of work, too, were so manifestly different that I could scarcely believe I was on a clandestine mission. The only occu-

pied territory that I had so far known was a dangerous and uncomfortable Tom Tiddler's Ground, where we led a hole-in-corner
existence, surrounded by an ever-present and ubiquitous enemy. But
here, where whole areas the size of counties were to all intents and
purposes free, we could sleep secure indoors and walk, and even
drive, for miles with no fear of an ambush round the corner.

Collecting the material that had been dropped with us during the
night therefore presented no problem. We took the whole leisurely
day over it, while Roger told me something about the development
and present state of the resistance movement in Région Deux. His
clear, concise summary confirmed what I had already begun to suspect: that the arrival of Lizzy and myself at this late stage of the war
was an embarrassment rather than a help—there was no specific
task for either of us. As far as Lizzy was concerned, this was just as
well; for a doctor had examined him, diagnosed two cracked vertebrae and arranged for him to be admitted into the nearest Maquis
hospital. But I could not be so conveniently disposed of. Rather
than abandon me to boredom and inactivity, however, Roger generously suggested that I accompany him next day on a tour of his area.

"At least it'll give you some idea of what's going on," he concluded.

And so, while Christine was despatched to the Italian frontier
where she was organizing the mass defection of a Polish unit that
had been pressed into Wehrmacht service, Roger and I drove off to
his wireless station which was installed in a house a few kilometres
outside the village. There, after an excellent dinner with the two
French operators, we spent a comfortable night before setting out
next morning in a private car with a driver and another colleague, a
French major, who was introduced to me as "Chasuble."

The car, I believe, was ostensibly a Red Cross vehicle and the driver
had a special licence, so that there was little danger of our being
stopped or questioned in any of the enemy garrisons on our route.
And even if we were checked, we only had to show our identity-
cards and other personal documents. While I was examining mine
so as to make sure they were all there, I counted out the money I
had brought in with me. Such a large sum might have looked suspicious if discovered in the pockets of one man, so Roger and Chasuble between them relieved me of over half of it; and as an additional
precaution we agreed that, if stopped, we would disclaim any knowl-

edge of each other and say that we were hitch-hikers who had been individually given a lift.

It was full of confidence, then, that I started out on my first journey through enemy-occupied France, my only worry being the baggy Charlie Chaplin trousers I was wearing without braces—for since the container with my clothes and personal equipment had not been found, I had had to borrow a suit from one of the operators. In these flapping garments, I felt almost like a freak beside Roger and the dapper Chasuble, a suave, silent man with greying hair, neat dark features and a tired, urbane manner.

Our drive was so uneventful and enjoyable that I had to keep reminding myself that I was not on holiday but on active service—a fact which escaped me at each of the delightful villages where, while Roger conferred with the local leaders, I drank a glass of wine outside the café under the plane trees. It was only on the way back, as we were approaching the large garrison town of Digne, about noon the following day that, the wail of an air-raid siren put me in mind once more of the war.

Since the enemy were in the habit of manning additional road blocks during a raid, we got out of the car and asked the driver to pick us up again at the opposite end of the town; meanwhile we took cover with the rest of the civilian population. As soon as the All Clear sounded we mingled with the crowds emerging from the shelters, made our way along the busy streets, and found the car waiting where we had arranged to meet it. We got in and started off on the last lap of our journey back to Seyne.

We had not gone more than a few hundred yards, however, when we noticed straight ahead of us a barricade across the road, and beside it some figures in Feldgrau uniform with a machine-gun trained on the bridge over the river which we were due to cross. "I wonder what they're up to," muttered our driver. None of us, in fact, had accounted for this unexpected obstacle; but since our car must have already been observed, we could not turn back. We therefore drove on without altering our speed, until we were brought to a halt by one of the enemy section standing in the middle of the road with his rifle at the port.

Our feigned expressions of innocent surprise were wasted on the soldiers who immediately surrounded us and motioned us out of the car. Nor could we make ourselves understood to them since they spoke no French, no German, no European language at all. For they were Caucasian troops whom the enemy, short of man-power, were now employing on garrison duties. Their sub-human Mongolian features remained inscrutable while they searched our vehicle and prodded us to see if we were armed; and their expressions did not alter when we showed them one by one our identity cards, labour permits and ration coupons. They clearly could not make head or tail of these documents; but impressed, no doubt, by their number and the official stamps on them, they indicated with noncommittal grunts that we would be allowed to continue on our way.

We were on the point of driving off, when a second car drew up behind us and I heard Roger mutter out of the corner of his mouth. It was not his tone of voice that set me tingling with alarm—for he had purposely kept it under control—but his single word of warning:

"Gestapo!"

The newcomers had apparently turned up with orders for the road block section to withdraw now that the air-raid was over; but seeing our car halted there as well, they at once turned their attention to us, and the young civilian who was evidently in charge started questioning us—to my secret horror, in perfect French.

Though that language had once been my mother tongue, after so many years' absence from France I could no longer converse in it with practised ease. My vocabulary and accent were still sufficiently convincing for me to be taken for a native by any German I might have accidentally met, and even, in a short conversation, by a Frenchman; but I was not confident of my ability to delude for any length of time a trained local interrogator, which this young *milicien* clearly was. It was therefore with considerable trepidation—which manifested itself physically, I regret to say, by an uncontrollable tremor in my right leg—that I answered the questions he started firing at me:

"Where do you come from?"

"Forcalquier."

"Where are you going?"

"To Gap."

"What for?"

In spite of the care I had devoted to my "cover story" in Algiers, I had never imagined I would really have to use it, and so had not prepared myself in advance for the contingency I now had to meet. I hesitated for the fraction of a second before giving the reply that came into my head:

"To see about a house for my parents. They're old and sick, and want to get away from the bombing at home."

"Where's your home?"

"Nîmes."

"What's your job?"

"I'm a clerk in the Electricity Works."

"Let's have a look at your papers."

I handed over my wallet, which contained all my money as well, and as he examined the documents he asked:

"What about these two fellows with you? Who are they?"

"I don't know," I answered—readily enough this time, for I had expected the question—"they were already in the car when I stopped it and asked for a lift."

Still with his eyes on my papers, he murmured:

"So you're a clerk in the Electricity Works at Nîmes, are you?"

"That's right."

"Then can you explain why this"—and he waved one of the papers in my face—"is out of date? There's no stamp on it for this month."

Naturally, I had no explanation to give.

"I'll deal with you later," he said, pocketing my wallet; "go on, get in." And as he motioned one of the soldiers to escort me to the Gestapo car, he switched his attention to Roger and Chasuble.

I was bundled into the empty back seat; and as I sat down, the soldier next to the civilian driver in front turned round and—rather unnecessarily, for I was far too bewildered to move—covered me with his machine-pistol.

I suppose I should have forthwith cudgelled my brains for some plausible excuse for being in possession of papers which, thanks to an oversight on the part of our Algiers staff, were invalid; but my mind was a blank, and I found myself instinctively trying to divert my attention from the man with the gun by staring with invol- untary intensity at the back of the driver's neck—or rather at the place where his neck should have been, for he appeared to be one of those monstrous men described by Othello, "whose heads do grow beneath their shoulders." He sat there motionless, his ears barely vis- ible above the black hump of his back, so that I was unable to tell what he looked like until, glancing accidentally at the driving-mir- ror, I saw reflected there a single eye of hideous malevolence which gazed without blinking straight into mine.

I knew it was only half his face I saw, but this optical illusion
which had transformed him into an apparent Cyclops unnerved me
so much that the tremor in my leg, which had stopped as soon as I
sat down, immediately started again. Fear took the form of a sense
of abject loneliness, and I realized to my shame that I was almost
consciously longing for my two companions to be arrested with
me so that I should not have to face whatever was to come entirely
by myself.

There seemed little likelihood of my cowardly prayer being answered, however. Both Roger and Chasuble appeared utterly unconcerned as they showed their documents and emptied their pockets,
the former with an expression of surprised amusement on his face,
the latter with a look of contempt. As I watched them with admiration, I could not help wondering if they were genuinely less frightened than I was, and if not, how they were able to conceal their
feelings with such a brilliant display of self-assurance. But just as
I was beginning to derive a little courage from their example, I
sensed—not from their attitude, which remained unchanged, but
from a sudden sparkle of triumph in the eyes of their interrogator—
that something had gone wrong. Exactly what, I could not say—
until, unexpectedly, I was myself summoned from the car to be
questioned again.

"You say you don't know these two men?"

"No, I don't," I answered; "I'd never seen them before in my life."

The next question was addressed to all three of us:

"Then can you explain how these banknotes, which each of you
was carrying individually, happen to be all in the same series—no,
don't answer; I won't have any more lies. Into the car, the whole lot
of you."

———

I was horrified by this abrupt development, partly because I felt I
was actively to blame for my companions' arrest, but mostly because
I had consciously wished for it and the wish had come true; nevertheless I could not help deriving a certain comfort from their presence as we were driven off together to the central prison.

Here, as soon as we arrived, we were made to stand for several
minutes facing a wall of the courtyard with our hands held above

our heads. If this was a psychological move intended to intimidate us, it had on me the opposite effect; for it served only to increase my sense of apathy and irresponsibility now that I realized that not one of my actions depended any longer on my own free will. It was therefore with a feeling of complete indifference that I followed the armed guard who finally pushed all three of us into a basement cell.

Even here I remained unaffected by the surroundings and devoted no more than a cursory glance to the four dirty bunks in two tiers ranged along one of the bare stone walls, to the small barred window above the level of my head, and to the half-filled bucket of excrement and urine standing in the corner underneath. In this squalid isolation we could have destroyed any incriminating object we might have been carrying, for surprisingly no attempt had been made to search us thoroughly; but no doubt we should then have been reported by the cell's fourth occupant, a stranger who might or might not have been a *mouchard*, or stool-pigeon. Working on the assumption that he was, I discouraged his attempts to draw me into conversation, for fear that my accent might betray me as a foreigner; and leaving my two companions to answer his questions, I lay down on one of the bunks and pretended to go to sleep.

Little pretence was needed. I was soon actually sleeping, regaining consciousness from time to time only when I felt the recurrent and alternate need for a cigarette and some food. But there was nothing to smoke, and we were given nothing to eat. After twenty-four hours in this comatose condition I was woken by the clatter of the door being unlocked. I was hoping this heralded the arrival of our first meal; instead it was a summons for us to move. We were herded out of the prison and into a waiting car, and after a short drive were deposited outside a house called the Villa Rose, which I knew was the local Gestapo headquarters.

Here we were locked up in a room on the first floor which, like our previous cell, already contained another occupant. I followed what was now becoming my normal practice and lay down at once on one of the four bare mattresses—the only furniture I could see—and, closing my eyes, listened to the conversation that followed. Our new room-mate seemed to be a more obvious "plant" than the one we had suspected in prison; for after a few minutes I heard him demonstrating how to undo the handcuffs which fastened together the shutters of the two windows.

"That's all that separates us from freedom," he explained; "unfortunately it's a seven-metre drop, and they've got trained police-dogs outside."

I went to sleep with surprising ease, considering I had already spent almost a whole day and right sleeping, and did not wake up till the late afternoon, when the door was opened with, I suppose, intentional violence to reveal a young man standing on the threshold in a theatrically menacing attitude. He was a perfect young Nazi—blue eyes, fair hair, fresh skin, breeches and jackboots: not a single essential feature was missing from this typical example of the Stormtrooper—and he waited in purposeful but senseless silence, darting glances at each of us in turn, before he finally fixed his eyes on Roger and barked out:

"Du! Komm!"

So we were to be interrogated at last, one by one.

Roger came back within half an hour, when the young Nazi again enacted the same comedy before picking on Chasuble. Then it was my turn. I was encouraged by the length of time each of my friends had been absent, and also by the fact that in that short period neither of them apparently had been maltreated. Even so I could not help thinking of what I had heard about Gestapo methods of extracting information, as I was marched off along the corridor, down the stairs and into a room leading off the hall.

The first person I saw there was the *milicien* who had arrested us at the road block; then I noticed, silhouetted against the window, the figure of another man seated at a desk, in front of which I was brought to an abrupt halt by the Nazi jerking my collar from behind. Coming straight from the shuttered room upstairs, I was dazzled at first by the sunlight in my eyes, so that the features of my interrogator shifted into focus only gradually; but as soon as my vision was adjusted I found to my amazement that his appearance was, if anything, reassuring. With his grey hair, dark suit and almost benign expression, he looked rather like a provincial bank-manager. But I detected in his voice the cold precise tones of the professional over-draft-refuser, as he put his first question:

"What exactly were you doing, where were you making for, at the time of your arrest?"

It was no use pretending I was legally employed. A man with an out-of-date permit like mine could only be engaged on one of two sorts of criminal activity: either as a *refractaire*, in other words an outlaw; or as a black-marketeer. I chose to associate myself with what I thought to be the lesser offence and, since I had been caught with hundreds of cigarettes on me, confessed that I was selling smuggled tobacco.

This statement provoked no comment from my questioner, who at once changed the subject by asking me to give him a short account of my previous career. I knew that my "cover story" was pitifully transparent; to explode it completely all he needed to do—and had probably already done—was to ring up the Electric Company at Nîmes where he would at once learn that Armand Pont-Levé was a myth. Yet I had to say something. In despair, then, I embarked on my palpably false autobiography, expecting at the end of each unplausible chapter to be interrupted by an angry refutation. Instead, I was listened to in silence, prompted only at each hesitation by a thump in the kidneys and once by a blow in the face delivered by the man standing behind me.

I came to the end of my story, and still the interrogator said nothing. He gave no indication that he disbelieved me, no sign that he suspected me of anything at all; and I found this silence more unnerving than any threat, as I was quietly dismissed and escorted back to the room upstairs. Yet as soon as I lay down again I fell into a deep untroubled sleep, from which I woke only when the door was flung open in the early morning to reveal once more the young Nazi of the evening before. I thought we were in for another interrogation; but this time, instead of one of us, it was our suspected stool-pigeon who was summoned—no doubt to report to his superiors on our demeanour during the night.

His short absence from the room gave the three of us an opportunity—the first we had had since our arrest—of discussing the situation together. A comparison of our individual interrogations, all of which seemed to have followed an identical pattern, made it quite clear that the enemy suspected us of clandestine activity and that the only way of saving our lives was to attempt a mass escape. We therefore hurriedly drew up a plan of action and agreed that as soon as night fell we would throttle our room-mate, break open the shutters and jump out of the house; even with the sentries outside and the police-dogs prowling round the garden, there was a reasonable chance of at least one of us getting away safely.

But we had no chance of putting this plan to the test. For early that morning we were taken back to the central prison, not to our

old cell but a larger one in a different part of the building; and we
knew without being told that it was the death cell.

We knew, too, that since our arrest the Allied landing had taken
place on the Riviera and that Digne, being so near the coast, might
be liberated within the next few days. I was therefore frightened
that in the heat of the moment we might be shot out of hand; but
that fate, on further reflection, seemed preferable to the torture,
both physical and mental, that might be inflicted in the process
of a "legal" trial and official execution. I kept thinking of the poison tablet sewn into the lapel of the suit I should have been wearing, and wondering at what stage of the proceedings I would have
nerved myself to swallow it. The problem was purely academic, but
it had the practical result of diverting my mind from thoughts even
more unpleasant.

Now that there was apparently no possibility of escape, the idea
of the firing-squad held no terror—provided there was no pain beforehand. Incongruously, what I resented most was the prospect of
dying under a false identity—for presumably my true one would
never be established—and I envied the three American prisoners
whom I could see across the courtyard in a cell directly opposite
ours. Members of the crew of a damaged bomber, they had baled
out over France, and after being picked up by a local maquis band,
had fought in its ranks and been captured in a recent engagement
with the enemy. They had subsequently been brought here for interrogation, and though their own position was scarcely less lamentable than ours—for they, too, were likely to be shot—I should have
given a great deal to be in their shoes; for at least they could converse together without pretence in their own language, and each of
them wore, strung round his neck, a little piece of stamped plastic
or embossed metal which, though worth nothing, I now prized as
highly as an amulet—a soldier's identity disk.

I gradually worked myself up into such a morbid frame of mind
that when, about midday, the first meal we had been given since our
imprisonment was brought in—an ominously good meal of vegeta-
ble soup and brown bread—I could not help regarding it as the last
we were ever likely to have. And when, later that afternoon, the *milicien* who had arrested us called to summon us outside, I felt sure
it was for execution, especially since he now wore, over his civilian

trousers, a Wehrmacht tunic which invested him with the same air of formality and ceremonial gravity as the black cap on the head of judge delivering the death sentence.

But once outside the prison gates, instead of turning left towards the football ground which the firing-squad normally used, he led us in the opposite direction, walking with Roger by his side while Chasuble and I followed a few paces behind.

A thin drizzle was falling, and the darkening sky seemed to have caused the sun to set earlier than usual. Soon it would be night. Now, if ever, was our chance to escape. Escorted by a single semi-civilian whom we did not even know to be armed, we could have made a sudden dash up one of the cobbled side-streets and dispersed through the town in the dark with every prospect of being safely away in the hills by the morning. But my mind, at least, had become so dull after three days of apathy and irresponsibility that I lacked the necessary resolution.

In any case the situation was beyond my personal control. Even the events of which I knew myself to be an integral part—like walking down this street in this rain—seemed to be happening outside myself, as though I was a disinterested spectator; so that when, after a few hundred yards, we drew level with a waiting car, I reacted without hesitation and without surprise to the *milicien*'s order:

"Quick! Get in, all three of you!"

Slamming the door on us, he got in himself beside the driver, and at once we were skidding round the nearest corner and heading straight for a road block on the outskirts of the town. The sentries there, seeing an official car approaching at high speed with a uniformed man leaning out of the front window, automatically drew back; and we flashed past them into the open country—only to stop a moment later at an isolated building round the first bend in the road. A solitary figure was standing there, outlined against the white wall, and I recognized—with bewilderment, but still without surprise—Christine.

After so much had already occurred that I could not explain, her presence there did not seem altogether incomprehensible. From her harassed expression as she squeezed into the front seat I simply assumed that she, too, had been caught; for, as the car started off once more, she seemed determined not to risk betraying by the slightest word or gesture the fact that she knew us, but stared straight ahead, like ourselves, in silence.

Presently, on the edge of a steep embankment, the car stopped again. The *milicien* jumped out and, since I was the one nearest the door on his side, he motioned me to follow him down the bank to the river-bed beyond. Incapable by now of keeping pace with this dream-like sequence of events, I slithered through the mud behind him and incuriously watched him as he took off his uniform jacket.

"Here, help me with this," he said, as he began to scoop a hole among the pebbles and boulders at the water edge.

Indifferently, I helped him to bury his discarded garment; then together we climbed back and got into the car again. As we drove off in the direction of the mountains, Christine for the first time turned round and smiled.

It was only then that I realized we were free.

Characteristically, Christine never told us exactly what methods she had used to secure our release. But from what I heard on the spot immediately afterwards, together with the little I learnt from her years later, I managed eventually to form a rough idea of the events leading up to our unexpected reunion at the isolated roadside house.

The news of our capture had reached her on the Italian border. She had acted at once with outstanding speed and self-sacrifice. Within twenty-four hours she had established contact, through a series of intermediaries, with the prison authorities and the Gestapo; and by the end of the following day she had come down to Digne in person for a meeting with the *milicien* who had arrested us. In other words, she had voluntarily risked her life in the hope of saving ours.

Fortunately, her courage was matched by her wits. The Allied landing which had taken place that very day was a happy coincidence, and she was quick to exploit it. To the *milicien* she openly confessed who she was and who Roger and I were—exaggerating, however, our importance and stressing the fate in store for our captors if we were to be found dead when the liberating armies entered the town.

She pointed out that he, the *milicien*, being not only the man who was primarily responsible for our imprisonment but being also a Frenchman, would be the first to suffer; there was no escape for him even though he was for the time being under enemy protection. The German garrison, as he had no doubt seen for himself, was unable to withdraw in the face of the Allied advance since every line of retreat was blocked by the local resistance forces; it would therefore have to surrender. For the Wehrmacht troops this would not be catastrophic; they would simply be sent to a prisoner-of-war camp, and since the war was now nearly over they would soon be free again. For him, however, the liberation of Digne would have more serious consequences. As a civilian, he would not be allowed to give himself up to the Allies, but would be handed over as a traitor to the maquis authorities—who had a peculiar way of dealing with those found guilty of treachery.

On the other hand, if he engineered our release he would be guaranteed a safe conduct to our nearest G.H.Q. outside France.

Sensibly, he had agreed.

The plan he subsequently made for our joint escape had worked so perfectly that in retrospect the whole operation seemed absurdly simple; and indeed for the three of us under sentence of death it was simple, since it involved no effort of will or action on our part. But for Christine, who had of her own volition risked the death penalty, the responsibility must have been almost beyond endurance. For apart from the considerations of personal courage, she had also had to decide whether from the S.O.E. point of view her action was ethically permissible. As an individual, she would not have hesitated to barter her own life for the lives of three others. As an agent, however, she was obliged to assess the value of those lives against hers; and if hers proved to be worth more, it was her duty to keep it.

In the assessment she made it was Roger's life that weighed the scales in favour of the decision she took; for in comparison Chasuble's and mine were of small account. Had Roger not been arrested with us, Christine would have been perfectly justified in taking no action if action meant jeopardizing herself. Indirectly, then, I owe my life to him as much as I do, directly, to her.

1944–45

A L T H O U G H T H E W A R in Europe had another ten months to run, my release from the death cell virtually ended the personal interest I felt in hostilities. For four years I had been actively engaged on resistance work, on helping to prepare for liberation; but when liberation came it brought with it disenchantment more than satisfaction. I had been proud of my own small contribution to liberty—until I saw the uses to which liberty was put; for nowhere did the result of victory appear to justify the effort involved in attaining it.

In Digne, which was liberated two days after our release, my *post coitum tristis* reaction was slightly relieved by the sight of Lizzy—a casualty still, but no longer a stretcher case—installed on a chair in the middle of the main street, with a queue of women lining up to kiss *ce héros blessé*, who kept apologizing for his inability to thank them adequately in their own language by explaining:

"Moi, je parle français—comme un anglais."

But a few streets further off another kind of procession had been organized, in which the main participants were made to parade up and down in front of a jeering crowd. Bedlam, I imagine, must have been much the same as this; for the object of the mob's derision—a handful of sullen creatures with shaven pates—looked like frightened lunatics. At first it was impossible to tell if they were male or female, for physical freakishness had deprived them of all apparent sex; but their state of semi-nudity revealed at a second glance that they were women, each of whom had been cropped for the crime of having spent a night or two in the arms of a German soldier.

This humiliating scene was enacted all over France, wherever a local girl had been pretty enough to attract the enemy and rash enough to succumb to him; and though it may not in itself have been an outstandingly significant factor, to my mind it symbolized the wave of vindictive brutality that invaded the whole country on the tide of liberation, when, in the name of patriotism, a convenient excuse could be found for almost any form of criminal activity and political intrigue.

In the South of France, where the resistance forces were mostly adherents of the Commmust-inspired "Franc-Tireurs et Partisans," the experience of my own brother-in-law provided me with a perfect example of the treatment meted out to any French patriot of opposing political views. Though he and my sister were both imprisoned by the Gestapo for over a year as a result of their activity during the occupation, on being released at the time of the Allied landing they were immediately sentenced to a further sentence by the left-wing maquis authorities who then took charge—because my brother-in-law was known to be that dangerously outdated type of French citizen, a Royalist.

But France was not the only country on which liberation poured its concomitant accessory of shame. A month later I landed in Greece, where my pleasure at being one of the first Englishmen to enter Athens since the occupation was marred by the sight of a man being lynched in Constitution Square on the day of my arrival and by the outbreak, a few weeks afterwards, of civil war.

This internecine strife, which inflicted on the mainland even more damage than the four years of Nazi occupation, was fortunately averted in Crete. But here, too, it seemed that injustice was triumphant. For when I returned to the island in December that year, I found on my arrival at Vaphes that the man who had been appointed local resistance leader since the German withdrawal from that area was not one of the Vandoulas family, nor any of my old comrades-in-arms, but, of all people, the retired army officer who had once considered me such an unwelcome neighbour when I was hiding out in Uncle Niko's vineyard that he had threatened to betray me to the Germans.

In the Far East, to which I was posted in the following spring, I was unable to judge the immediate effects of liberation; for by the time the S.O.E. staff in Calcutta had decided what to do with me the war with Japan was already over. But I did witness its eventual effects on one country at least, when I was flown into Saigon a few days before the Annamite revolution. Those effects are still evident in Indo-China today.

With all these examples in mind, I could not face the end of hostilities with anything but a sense of disillusionment and misgiving. It was some time before I was able to persuade myself of the inevitability of events and to view the post-war world in its true perspective. But I finally managed to do so; and I might even have adopted the present fashionable attitude of cynicism towards the tragedy both of nations and of individuals, had I not been so closely associated with one particular tragic case—Christine's.

After the physical hardship and mental strain she had suffered for six years in our service, she needed, probably more than any other agent we had employed, security for life. After her outstanding personal contribution to our victory, she deserved it. Yet a few weeks after the armistice she was dismissed with a month's salary and left in Cairo to fend for herself.

Her courage and natural resilience enabled her to deal with the situation, and though she was too proud to ask for any other assistance, she did apply for the protection of a British passport; for ever since the Anglo-American betrayal of her country at Yalta she had been virtually stateless. But the naturalization papers, which, from the moral point of view if for no other reason, should have been delivered to her immediately, on demand, were delayed in the normal bureaucratic manner.

Meanwhile, abandoning all hope of security, she deliberately embarked on a life of uncertain travel, as though anxious to reproduce in peace time the hazards she had known during the war; until, finally, in June 1952, in the lobby of a cheap London hotel, the menial existence to which she had been reduced by penury was ended by an assassin's knife.

If society's responsibility for individual crime is axiomatic, then we should all feel as guilty of Christine's murder as the man who was hanged for it. For it would never have occurred if we had protected her, as we could and should have done, from what she often used to refer to—and not entirely in jest—as "the horrors of peace."